Naked on the Page

Naked on the Page

THE MISADVENTURES OF MY UNMARRIED MIDLIFE

JANE GANAHL

VIKING

VIKING
Published by the Penguin Group
Penguin Group (USA) Inc., 375 Hudson Street, New York, New York 10014, U.S.A.
Penguin Group (Canada), 90 Eglinton Avenue East, Suite 700,
Toronto, Ontario, Canada M4P 2Y3 (a division of Pearson Penguin Canada Inc.)
Penguin Books Ltd, 80 Strand, London WC2R 0RL, England
Penguin Ireland, 25 St Stephen's Green, Dublin 2, Ireland
(a division of Penguin Books Ltd)
Penguin Books Australia Ltd, 250 Camberwell Road, Camberwell,
Victoria 3124, Australia (a division of Pearson Australia Group Pty Ltd)
Penguin Books India Pvt Ltd, 11 Community Centre, Panchsheel Park,
New Delhi – 110 017, India
Penguin Group (NZ), Cnr Airborne and Rosedale Roads, Albany, Auckland 1310, New Zealand (a division of Pearson New Zealand Ltd)
Penguin Books (South Africa) (Pty) Ltd, 24 Sturdee Avenue,
Rosebank, Johannesburg 2196, South Africa

Penguin Books Ltd, Registered Offices:
80 Strand, London WC2R 0RL, England

First published in 2007 by Viking Penguin,
a member of Penguin Group (USA) Inc.

10 9 8 7 6 5 4 3 2 1

LIBRARY OF CONGRESS CATALOGING-IN-PUBLICATION DATA
Ganahl, Jane.
Naked on the page : the misadventures of my unmarried midlife / Jane Ganahl.
p. cm.
ISBN: 978-0-670-03824-4
1. Ganahl, Jane. 2. Ganahl, Jane—Relations with men. 3. Journalists—United States—Biography. I. Title.
PN4874.G295A3 2007
070.92—dc22 2006042121
[B]

Printed in the United States of America
Set in Electra
Designed by Daniel Lagin

For Erin:
daughter, parent, friend

Contents

Naked on the Page

Leo Would Not Iron His Jeans

This man is wearing jeans with creases. Ironed-in creases. And tassels on his expensive loafers. Like my dad's.

He's smiling at me, laughing at our hosts' jokes, and he seems nice enough. (Just now he offered to help Rosalind bring out the brie and fruit.) He's not even bad-looking—despite the fact that his plus-size, ultra-round head makes him look a little like Elmer Fudd. But his style is just . . . so . . . corporate-goon. What was Rosalind thinking, thrusting his corduroy-jacketed bod in the direction of someone who once dated rock stars and who still waves the flag of Bohemia? Didn't I always tell her that my worst boyfriends—at least the worst in bed—were the yuppies?

Creased jeans. This is both tragic and funny—and sums up my luck of late.

I suspect he was thinking the following: *I only feel comfortable in the Italian suits I wear to the museum, but I think I need to look more "street" because I'm being set up with a music journalist. So I'll wear the jacket with the elbow patches and jeans. But I'll iron them first. No reason to take this Casual Friday thing too far.*

Creased jeans plus loafers plus patched blazer elbows equals too much of a compromise.

My darling friends were just trying to be nice in making this dinner happen. They know it's been months since I've had a positive romantic encounter—or even been laid. The last time was when Lenny was in town doing a show, but that ended inconsequentially, again, and I was bereft, again. Afterward, Rosalind scolded me for the umpteenth time. "He is *so not good for you*! I don't know why you keep expecting this to become a real relationship. If you want one, we'll have to find you someone else."

The events of 9/11 a few months ago shook Rosalind, a lifer newspaper reporter who has somehow never acquired the armor that goes with it, to the degree that she is now on a crusade to find mates for all her single friends. Terrified by the world since then, she finds solace in her French-born artist fiancé, Dieter, who is, despite numerous eccentricities and fears of commitment, deeply devoted to her. She is physical perfection—with Monroe-like curves and perfect eyebrows and nails—and Dieter (a decade older) is her Arthur Miller: not beautiful like she, but possessing prodigious intellect and wit, and a snappy collection of art. He has never been married or even engaged, and all their friends rejoiced when Dieter and Rosalind came back from a Wailea vacation a year ago with a giant rock on her finger.

Sometimes these things work out. It's sweet—and rare as a dodo—when they do.

I think Rosalind hit on the idea of Fudd as a romantic candidate for me after we met at a reception for one of Dieter's artists—despite an absolute dearth of chemistry.

"What do you think of this artist?" he had asked me pointedly, his mouth turned southward in a studious frown, as I studied the Austrian postmodernist's work on the wall in the too-hot Market Street gallery. I knew he was a museum curator so it would be transparent if I tried to fake it.

"Well, first of all, fine art is my shortest suit," I disclaimed, without taking my eyes off the painting in front of me—an oil-painted photograph of a little boy wearing what looked like an S&M ball gag. I turned to the interviewer coolly. "But I'd say this guy has some serious issues. He probably vacations in the back streets of Thailand."

He pulled away from me with a head jerk, as if I'd sprayed him with mace. "Uh-huh. I see," he stammered, and with a weak smile, disappeared into the crowd. I found Rosalind and told her what happened.

"Oh, you *didn't*!" she laughed. "He wrote the intro to the artist's book. He is a true believer in his genius. They are friends."

"Oh God," I groaned. Caught again in the act of being impolitic. "Well, even if I'd known, I'd have said the same thing. This art is some nasty shit."

Apparently undaunted, the moon-headed curator returned minutes later with what looked like a college report in his hand. "Here." He smiled, putting the plastic-encased folder in my hand. "Maybe this will help you understand. I wrote this last year. My thesis is that he should be credited with spearheading the confrontationalist movement."

"No kidding?" I said, way too gaily, trying to set the apple cart back on its wheels. "I'm also a card-carrying member!"

He does not smile. Realizing I had nothing to add to the conversation after that, I stopped yapping. What did I really know about modern art? Not much. But what I *do* know about is men, and this one, despite his condescending art-snob presentation, was kind of cute, in a bespectacled, moon-headed, I'm-too-brilliant-to-care-that-I-have-a-bad-haircut kind of way.

"Thanks! I'll give it a read!" I told him, realizing it was like promising to spend a Saturday interpreting the Koran. He beamed.

Rosalind said later, as we were leaving: "I think he likes you!"

I cackled. "Only because men seem to love women who disrespect them and treat them badly! Just like some women do."

Myself included.

"I don't know . . ." I told her, looking in his departing direction and noticing a distinct lack of ass. "He ain't no Leo."

(Where art thou, astrologically perfect, sexually compatible man of my future?)

Rosalind stopped putting her coat on and glared at me. "Is *anyone* Leo? Really, you need to quit with this fantasizing. In the meantime, this guy might grow on you!"

"You mean like a fungus?" I responded cheerfully. "Hmmm, maybe I'll invite him to a salon!" This has been my ruse of choice on several occasions—inviting someone I want to know better to one of my monthly dinners. I swathe myself in my cocoon of creative friends, and if he and I don't click, it won't give anyone indigestion.

"Come on, you know you're always pulled on by too many people at those dinners to have a real conversation with anyone," she protested. "Let me just have you both over. And be open-minded!"

So two weeks later, here I am, trying to be open-minded. It's not like, at this stage in my life, I have men standing in line and taking a number as if they were at Baskin-Robbins. It's not like before. Ten years earlier, in the ten minutes I had spent with Fudd, not only would he be wanting to have sex with me, he'd be writing me bad poetry. No, it's not like before at all.

I know I'm still a decent catch: I'm smart, I have decent table manners, I'm a fair-to-good writer, I'm connected in the world, I own my own home—a condo in Miramar also inhabited by three cats. But in fifteen months, I turn fifty. When the reality seizes my mind, it throws me down the rabbit hole of self-doubt. *You're getting old! You've had your last sex, your last boyfriend! You're fated to die alone and unloved, and your cats will gnaw on your corpse!* The good news is, if I keep padding the pounds, they will have plenty to nosh on. I don't know this body sometimes; it greets me in the morning mirror like a Creature Feature movie—a blob with a face that has taken over my wiry frame. I don't know this formerly fearless woman either, who now frets about aging and no longer flirts well.

And I should be grateful to Rosalind; so few of my friends try to set me up anymore. Partly because everyone is oh-so-busy and partly because these things rarely work out. And let's face it: I'm not an easy setup these days. As my friend Po said a few months ago over lunch: "It's kind of like you've priced yourself out of the market. You're too smart for lame guys, and men are easily intimidated. They can sense you wouldn't tolerate any bullshit. It's the reason men like younger women—they're easier to impress, and you can teach them things."

I remember feeling despair at this. Acting stupid, even as a teenager, in order to get guys was just out of the question. Still, perhaps a little more femininity would help make me seem, I don't know, more pliant? I thought this while getting dressed tonight in a short-ish skirt. If I can't act awed, perhaps my legs will still win me girl points. And Jesus, what would Betty Friedan say if she could hear my thoughts?

I, of course, had not read Fudd's book report on the Austrian artist—well, I had tried, but it was not unlike reading ancient Greek ("His portraiture is not the mere artistic replication of physiognomy . . . his art is the apotheosis of confrontationalist, blah . . . blah . . .") and I absorbed little. And of course he asked me about it as soon as I walked in the door, late as always. Did I have a better understanding of him now?

I decide to rely on the classic blind-date tactic: lie like a rug. "I think his art is the apotheosis of confrontationalist." I smile. Rosalind rolls her eyes. Fudd beams.

I stare at him while he helps Dieter open a French Bordeaux, which, since it's coming from Dieter's cellar, is bound to be *muy fino.* There is really nothing wrong with Fudd; he is just so . . . average. And I don't do average at all well. My love life has included some extraordinary men, men of brilliance and edge and notoriety, including Lenny, and it's hard to go from a past like that to a present where I feel so invisible that the pressure is to date anyone who looks at me twice. That opens the door to all kinds of ugliness, both physically and metaphorically.

Perhaps I should lighten up. Give up Pirates and go for a Nice Man. Consider a clean-cut insurance agent from Fremont, perhaps? An accountant from Vallejo who bowls every Thursday night with the church league? Someone with creased jeans and a moon head?

Maybe this is what midlife is about: lowered standards. Fuck me.

"Tell him about your new column!" Rosalind calls from the kitchen, sensing that since Fudd can't converse with me about alt-country music or emo-core, and I don't know my Chagalls from my Calders, we might be lacking in bonding material.

"Well, they want me to write about what it's like to be single and dating at midlife," I tell him, then chuckle. "Although I haven't had a lot of experience to draw on lately!"

Ha ha—very funny, Jane. Reel in the self-deprecation, you're sounding like a loser.

Dieter interjects, in a crisp French accent, over the top of the wine bottle, "Is this mostly for women? Instructions on how to get a man to marry you?"

Rosalind shoots her fiancé a hurt look; if anything could cause this love match to fail, it's his inability to set a date for the actual event.

"Heavens no! It's for any single person," I retort. "And anyway, I disagree that *all* women want to get married. That's truer of younger ones, but women my age who have been married once or twice aren't so keen. But I can't think of a single person of any age—male or female—who doesn't want to be *loved*. And to find love you have to go through one of Dante's inner circles of hell, called dating."

Rosalind and Dieter laugh, but Fudd just furrows his brow. "So you'll be writing about . . . yourself and your love life? I cannot even imagine wanting to give up my privacy like that. Letting a million people on Sundays in on your personal life?" He shudders. "That would be like going to the opera in your underwear!"

More laughter from the kitchen, and I join in halfheartedly. "You could be right." I shrug. "I could be letting myself in for some weirdness. But after twenty years of doing every other kind of newspaper writing there is, I'm ready for a change. And, you know, being a columnist is the top of the heap."

He's not ready to let me off the hook. "So right now you're doing rock 'n' roll reviews, and soon you're going to be writing about dating? Do you ever think about doing something more substantial, and less . . . fluffy? I thought the *Chronicle* was trying to emulate the *New York Times* these days."

I stare at him. *Look, Fudd, creased-jeans man, I realize I weigh more than I ever have in my life (it's hormones! I swear to God!) and my self-esteem is in the crapper, but calling me out on the discomforting truths of my life will not get you laid. Not that anything would at this point.*

I draw a breath. "I used to be what *you* would consider a stone-serious journalist—covered city hall, police investigations, and such. But it gets boring and disheartening dealing with the dregs of humanity. I'm more interested nowadays in humanity's mating dance and how it redeems itself. You know—through love?"

He is looking unconvinced.

"Besides, single life has become a huge pop cultural focus," I continue, aware that I'm sounding defensive. "Look at how many TV shows are devoted to the pursuit of romance!"

He grins, foxlike. "And you think you can give people advice in that regard? Give them a leg up in the pursuit?"

It *is* a rather dazzlingly good joke: Jane Ganahl being asked to play relationship guru. I, who have been married—twice—for only ten of my forty-eight years on the planet. A former serial seducer of younger men because they never demanded much, and a bailer on every relationship that got difficult. A woman whose recent losing record rivals that of the 1985 Giants.

Before I can conjure a humble response to his question, Rosalind shouts from the kitchen: "Jane gives the best advice of anyone I know! It's why her daughter turned out so great!"

I holler back: "Not true! Erin saved *me* from a life of sex, drugs, and rock 'n' roll, not the other way around!"

Fudd clears his throat in sudden mild discomfort. "How old is your daughter?"

"Three. She's at home, taking a hammer to my furniture and waiting for me to get home and change her diaper."

His face changes. In a second I'd gone from prospect to non.

I laugh. "Kidding—she's twenty-three and lives in the Haight and works for a law firm downtown. But she really is organically fabulous—I had little to do with it."

He relaxes, and budges a smile. "So, if it's not an advice column per se, what will your new column be *about*?"

I hesitate. I'm still not quite sure—there are so many things I want to accomplish with it. I want unmarried women my age to know they aren't alone, and I want to make fifty as sexy as possible so it won't seem so scary when I get there.

I want to articulate the hazards and glories of romance, praise the human trait that makes us keep getting up off the mat, even after love has sucker punched us for the eightieth time. I want it to bolster my strengths so a strong man will consider me.

I want to strike a blow for single mothers like me, and make Erin proud. I want my mom and sister to smile down from heaven, where they will put in a good word with the Entity Upstairs, who's probably given up on me by now.

I want it to make me a San Francisco name, so that I can walk into Tosca and get preferential treatment from the owner who doesn't like me much, so she'll offer me the use of the secret backroom pool table, like she does Francis Coppola and Sam Shepard and Lars Ulrich.

I want to stir up the waters of discourse and help dignify my own lifestyle.

I want to piss off Rush Limbaugh, who will curse my name on the air and question my American values.

I want to work out some of my own shit. And risk getting some in return.

"I guess . . . I just want to make a difference," I hear myself saying. Then, aware of the Hallmark-cheesy nature of that statement, I quickly add: "That, and maybe get a movie deal."

Fudd chuckles. "And what will you call this enterprise?"

That part is easy. Much as I can't admit it, I also want it to lead me to Leo, whom I have yet to meet. But I know he's out there.

I smile. "I think I'll call it 'Looking for Leo.' "

Rosalind sighs and shakes her head; she has about given up on me, too. But she should know it will take me a little longer to give up the fantasy. And it surely won't be to a man with creased jeans.

"Hey, Baby, I'm a Leo!"

Oh God, I think, as my eyes open like creaky storm shutters, it's Sunday. It's morning. Get up and look at your column. It's showtime.

Hung over after last night's annual New Year's Eve debauch at the home of my most glamorous married friends, Dan and Dayna, I trip over two out of three cats in my haste to find the paper wrapped in yellow plastic behind my garage. Not checking to see if my robe is adequately covering my nakedness, I blearily grab the package and carry it upstairs again. Settling at the breakfast table, I whip to the Living section, and there it is on the cover: *Single-Minded, by Jane Ganahl.*

I flush with prickly nerves. I don't want to read it. I might suck. Also, I lost the battle on the name. The paper's brass wouldn't go with my name suggestion, "Looking for Leo," saying it would confuse readers looking for Sidney Omarr.

Plus, my editor had to sneak it into the paper past the new associate managing editor of features, a corporate goon of a woman who dresses for success and thinks morale building is supplying us with ice-cream cones on Friday afternoons. She had decreed that There Shall

Be No New Columnists in the Land of *Chronicle*. Besides, Mrs. Married A.M.E. just didn't get it: a column about single life? Who cares?

So I had to use my ace in the hole: my very old friend (who is also my semi-new boss) Phil. It was his goddamn idea anyway; years ago he said I ought to be chronicling my dramatically misadventurous life in the paper. So I took up his challenge—and ran headlong into a brick wall wearing a Talbot's suit. Phil had to wade into the fray and tell Mrs. Married A.M.E. that the column was already in the works before she came and to give it a try—at least for a few weeks. See if there's a response, he cajoled her, perhaps a readership to be tapped?

Its debut has been cleverly squeezed into a section about New Year's resolutions. Polls always show that the second-highest aspiration people have of a new year is a new relationship. Next to working off the pudge, of course. I, it seems, am doubly challenged this year.

I make coffee, open the window for some fresh sea air in hopes it will help with the hangover, keep shooting looks at the paper but avoid plunging in. Come on, read it, you big weenie, I tell myself. Erin will be reading it in her Haight-Ashbury apartment (as will her roommates, who will tease her about her mother), and your seventy-nine-year-old dad, and all your ex's, and all your friends. Don't you want to remember what you said? Didn't you *ask* to become a columnist? Deal with it.

Sighing in nervous resignation, I sit down with the page.

What does it say about the human race that no matter how many times we're bitch-slapped by love, no matter how many tire marks are indelibly etched onto our backs, that we pick ourselves up like punch-drunk boxers and keep trying to find that perfect mate?

Every year, year after year, we make that our New Year's resolution, "This year, as God is my witness, I'll find The Right One!" we tell ourselves, with an innocent hopefulness that belies a lifetime of debacles with Wrong Ones. And I'm right there with the masses: still thinking I'll find the right combination of genes and habits. And hey! Why not in 2002?

This isn't bad, I say to myself. You can write after all. I remember the head of the copy desk wanted to take out bitch-slapped; she said it was inappropriate for a family newspaper. Oh, please.

I find that my reasons for wanting to mate at my age (the, ahem, over-40 age bracket) has less to do with marriage and procreation and more to do with quality of life issues—you know, quality time, quality sex, quality coffee. In fact, as much as I would welcome a Quality Relationship with open arms, it would take a lot for me to get married again and give up the single life that I've come to love.

Oh Jesus, am I laying it on a little thick here? Being disingenuous? I would totally get married again. More than anything I'm freaked out about dying alone. But saying so won't make good copy.

Finding a like-minded tribe isn't hard. And when you are thickly in the bosom of one, as I am, loneliness is kicked to the curb. Even when you're not dating anyone, neither unescorted Friday nights nor unfamilied major holidays is cause for a pity party.

Well, unless it's *me* throwing the pity party on a night when I'm PMS'd and horny, in which case all standards are lowered.

Even though I hear women loudly complain about the lack of SEs (single eligibles) in San Francisco, I'm more concerned about my type of man—the species artisticus humanitas—the enlightened, not crazy, creative guy who is not about money, no. But successful enough to be able to afford a weekend in Mendocino. And it's a lot easier to hunt my species here than it would be in, say, Elko, Nevada.

Hmmm, I wonder if Sean, my last serious and full-time beau, will be offended, since we had a fight about him never being able to afford a weekend away since he gives all his money to his talent-free ex-wife and petulant daughter. I had to pay for everything, including that weekend in Mendocino. Oh, whatever, I doubt he's even reading it.

There are always men available for Quick Relationships. For those moments when, as my friend Claudia puts it, "We need to check in with our sexual selves."

I wonder if Lenny will be reading this online from New York. He was the last . . . Oh God, but my dad will be reading this in his morning paper, after church. I'm not so worried about Erin; she knows how I am. But this will take my dad back to my tarting-around years in college, and my missing curfew every night and making him and my mom insane. He will not love it. But my mom would have. My mom . . .

The column meanders a bit and then lurches for its conclusion.

I keep one eye open for Leo, but he has yet to level my gaze across the produce section. And I'm not really tapping my foot anymore. I figure he'll show up or he won't. In the meantime, there are so many opportunities out there for romance and scandal. What's a woman to do but answer the call?

My eyes water, my heart thumps. Oh, don't get all tearful, you big baby. There will be someone soon. When you're ready; when you're worthy.

Reading this makes me feel like a trout laid out on a plate: gutted, filleted, and begging Eat Me. I may be wearing a bathrobe, but it's only a token cover-up of my nakedness. What am I opening myself up for? Humiliation? Excoriation? Oh, well, it's done. Let the chips fall.

The phone is eerily quiet, and I don't have the guts to look at my e-mail yet. It's close to noon when I finally do, and—pow!—my work in-box is full of unread e-mails. Among the fifty or so subject lines: "Thank You!" "Finally!" "Date Me!" (which I'll open first), and "What a crock!" (which I'll open last).

Mr. Date Me puts it on the line: "Hey, baby, I'm a Leo! You sound like a sexy gal! Maybe we can get together sometime I work in Fremont but I like you're style you're funny and I like funny women! So how bout it? I could come to 'Frisco for drinks and we could gab!"

Ack, I frown. Where is Pablo Neruda when you need him? I may be looking for one particular Leo, but I'm pretty sure this ain't him.

There are several like this from men, which I expected there would be. It's why I didn't let them put a photo of me with the column—it would have only aggravated the situation and appeared too much like a Match.com ad. *Date this woman! She is so very lonely!*

Because really, what caliber of men might be hitting on me? Lonely ones sitting at home with only their Sunday papers and memories of love. And possibly stockpiles of porn.

Thankfully, there are a few charmers: an architect from Alaska who takes good-humored exception to my suggesting all men from up North have oil in their fingernails, and one from a lawyer in Louisiana who says he spends a lot of time in Baghdad by the Bay. He asks, with incisive wit, "Do you really mean all this or are you just trying to give feminism and middle-aged women a better image than they deserve?" The audacity makes me laugh out loud. These two, I shall answer.

It's weird to think that these guys have no idea what I look like. They are drawn to my brain, what I have to say—not my blue eyes, pale skin, and red hair. Oh, if only this were the way of Real Life. And thank God they can't see me right now, in my ugly fleece robe, Noodge the cat purring on my lap, my hair twisted up in a bad ponytail.

The majority of the e-mails have praise for the paper for "bringing a needed new perspective to its pages" (those will be printed out and saved for the dubious A.M.E.), for me "being willing to regurgitate publicly" about my own issues, and looking forward to more of same. Hmmm, perhaps Single-Minded is too refined for what I'm doing here. Perhaps Sunday Morning Gut-Spilling would have worked better.

Phil e-mails with a nice attagirl: "You owe me a drink when you sell the movie rights." And there are e-mails from salon friends, who give me the huzzahs they pretty much have to in an effort to be supportive. Still, they seem genuinely excited. Rosalind teases me, asking if this means that all our girl-talk conversations from now on need to be preceded by her saying "off the record . . ."

And I get choked up at Po's missive: "I think this is it—I think you've really found your voice."

And there's one from Marco, my Most Special Ex, who congratulates me—and then asks if he should consult his lawyer before I go any further. I laugh out loud. "Hey, anyone who treated me well in my life has nothing to fear," I type back to him. "Sadly, you do not fall into that category. . . ."

But there are some really ugly ones—one woman tells me I'm not doing my sex any favors by "playing a man-crazy, aging Carrie Bradshaw," and another suggests my contradictions make me sound just this side of dysfunctional. These missives would hurt more if they didn't contain a kernel of truth. Still, it's hard to just shrug them off. I knew I'd end up on the receiving end of flamethrowers like this, but I'm not sure I'm equipped to handle it emotionally.

And—yikes—Sean was reading the paper today after all. "I can only assume that your pointed, bitchy comment about poor men who can't pay for trips to Mendocino was aimed at me, and I don't appreciate it," he fumed. "I hope that in the future you aim your arrows elsewhere. Or, since you have about a thousand ex's, at least you can spread your venom around."

The phone rings, startling me, and I realize I have been reading and responding to e-mails for two hours already. It's Erin, groggy after a night of hip-hop at some sketchy club on Divisadero.

"You're a columnist," she says. "My mommy is a columnist. This is so good. I got all *verklempt* reading it. Allison and Joy loved it, too. Are you getting any responses?"

"You could say so," I say. "Like, maybe seventy-five so far today? Pretty incredible. Some of them hate me, but most of them love me. Some of them want to date me."

"Eeew! Please tell me you will not be taking anyone up on it. You have no idea what these guys might be like! They could be ax murderers—or Republicans!"

She always makes me laugh. A dose of Erin in the morning is better than pure Kona coffee. I ask her if she is joining me and Grandpa for dinner down the Peninsula; I need her moral support in dealing with the parental weirdness the new column might generate with the old man.

"I have an early meeting tomorrow on the Genentech appeals court case," she says. "But I can come if it's not too late."

"What the hell? When did the little paralegal girl get so fancy? You're only twenty-three, for chrissakes. Too busy to have dinner with your grandpa . . . ?"

"Mommy." She always says it firmly—a sentence unto itself—when I'm yanking her chain and she wants me to chill. "I'll see you tonight. And don't forget we have a date to go to the movies Wednesday. Try not to be late this time—I hate missing the previews!"

My better self forces my weaker one to turn off the computer after too many hours of sending and receiving. It's addictive is what it is. I feel woozy from the assault, spun by my own impact, but pleased about it, too.

On my way to Woodside my cell phone rings and I recognize the number. "Girlfriend, you are a trailblazer!" It's Peter's comforting voice, a funny/sweet mix of street toughness and Proustian eruditeness. "You've now begun your inversion of the female paradigm. You are so brave!"

Peter has been my friend longer than anyone I know except Phil. A writer of street-punk novels hailed as brilliant by the mostly underground press, he taught himself to write while squatting in abandoned buildings. We met at a reading in the early nineties, and despite a discernible lack of anything whatsoever in common, he has been my cheerleader like few others in my life—with the possible exception of my mom.

"Man, you don't even know the crazy-ass e-mails I've gotten today," I sigh. "I seem to have really hit a nerve—or pinched one, perhaps. Lots of cranky people, lots of guys who want to date me. I'm a little freaked out."

"Listen," Peter responds. "Anytime you start to break down a wall you're going to take heat. This is a brave new world for you, are you ready for it? It's going to take some getting used to, so take your B-vitamins—and your echinacea."

"Yeah, thanks, lovie—I gotta go. I'm meeting my dad in five minutes for dinner. That could be awkward to say the least."

Peter laughs richly. "Aw, honey, doesn't your dad always surprise you? I'm sure he'll be cool."

Erin and I meet my dad and Barbara at Buck's, his favorite, dependable Woodside eatery, scene of countless dot-com deals when the boom was on, now resuming its low-key country-chow-palace profile. I so worry that my dad will not be around long that I make time in my insane life to have dinner with him once a week. I see he is without his cane again, which causes him to walk with a scary list to one side. Makes him feel old, he always shrugs, to carry that appendage around. For an ex–Pan Am pilot, for whom the world was once a playground and the skies a proving ground for his athletic flight records, aging must be a rotten trick.

But he is getting up there—just a few months shy of eighty—and he knows it. He jokes often about death, with the joviality of one who is both religious and excited about seeing my mom again, with whom he is still in love—even though she died five years ago. Theirs was a great marriage, and one of the reasons I historically compare my own relationships poorly to what I saw with my own eyes growing up.

He has already ordered his first glass of wine—always the cheapest on the menu—and rises to his feet to greet us.

"Well!" he says awkwardly, after an embrace. "Well, well . . ."

"Congratulations!" interjects Barbara, Dad's constant companion since a golf date a year after Mom died. "Your new column was just . . . great."

"But what does my dad think?" I say, looking at him pointedly. Erin looks down and suppresses a giggle.

"It was . . . good." He chooses his words carefully. "But I was a little embarrassed when people brought it up to me at church this morning. Do you really have to put all that in there about your sex life?"

Zap! Time warp to the wild times, the summers between my college years, when I attempted to throw off the shackles of my protective parents, learned about serious partying and sneaking around, resulting in my dad banging on my locked door and shouting in anger that he knew I'd come in late last night, us not talking for days . . .

"Robert," Barbara interrupts. "It's her column, let her write what she wants."

My dad shrugs, smiles, and changes the subject to the Giants' latest acquisition. Collision averted. I could try to explain more about my motivations with this column, with my life, with everything to Dad and Barbara, but they wouldn't get it. My family never has. It's okay, I am well loved. But, as big a blabbermouth as I am, I am also the least vociferous in my family because I am the least listened to. It's the curse of being the former rebellious daughter/double divorcée in a family of big-personality overachievers. I don't compete with Anne the actress and Rob the photographer for stage time at family dinners; I take what time is left over after they're done telling of their latest opening and newspaper article.

Lisa used to be the quietest one within the family, but she died four years ago, eleven months after my mom. Her circumspection was due to a missing gene—the show-off one—that the rest of us have looming large on our DNA ladders. It made her all the more dear. Instead, she commanded us with her stealthy humor.

On our way to see *Last of the Mohicans* in 1992, with Anne and a preteen Erin, we were discussing the attributes of Daniel Day-Lewis. I admired his acting in *My Left Foot*. Anne, his skill with accents. Lisa said more than anything, she admired his "long, thick dong." Erin blushed, then giggled—and we laughed until we thought we'd pass out.

Goddamn, it would be perfect if Lisa and Mom were around to see me now.

I want to tell him, *Dad, I wrote this column for Mom and Lisa. I've been a chronic underachiever most of my life, and have neither fortune nor lover to show for it. So what I'm after is pride, from you, from them. From me.*

"Anyway," I tell my dad after dinner is over, "I'll try not to embarrass you. Too much." I wink.

He chuckles and hugs me. "You write what you want. I can handle it."

Erin notices my quiet on the way back to her car. "What are you thinking?" she asks.

"I miss Mom and Lisa. And I think I'm a little overwhelmed."

She hugs me as she says good-bye. "You'll be fine," she says. "You always are. What are you going to write about next week?"

I sigh. "Not a clue."

The phone rings as I'm falling asleep.

"Were you thinking of me when you wrote this about 'checking in with our sexual selves'?" rumbles the bass voice on the other end.

"Lenny, wow," I stammer, pulling myself up in bed. "You read it online?"

"Yeah, it's good. Very good. You know I'm close to being a Leo."

"Well, you're on the cusp, but you're a Virgo." I laugh. "That means you're missing a few critical Leo traits." Like attentiveness, romantic spirit—all the good ones.

"So . . . am I gonna get body-slammed at some point?" He chuckles.

"Hell yes. You knew the job was dangerous when you took it."

There is silence.

"Kidding, of course," I add. "Sort of. Where are you tonight?"

"Cincinnati. And then Madison. I have a week or so of college gigs lined up."

"God, Lenny, you are never home."

Lucky for me, or I'd never get to see him. We met on the fly three years ago when he was doing a concert in town. I met him in the afternoon before the show, interviewed him for a story in the paper—and began an affair the next day. It would have been immediate, possibly outside the North Beach bar in which we had postshow drinks, but for the shred of journalistic integrity I still had in me that night. "Let me go back to the paper and write my story," I panted, as we made out madly on Columbus Street, "before my objectivity vanishes." I wrote until two a.m., came back the next morning with the story primly in print, and the only time we left his room for three days was so he could limp back onstage. I was astonished to be attracted to someone five years older than me, since younger men (sometimes much) were my standard; he usually went for women half his age rather than close to it. Nothing about it really made a lot of sense, which was why it was—and still is—so delicious.

At first I thought it could be something—we talked on the phone every other day, had torrid phone sex, I flew to L.A. to see him. But within a few months it was clear that it was not to be. His life was too crazy to make a decent stab at a relationship, and I didn't have the kind of money required to go see him in cities around the country. At that point, Lenny made it clear that as long as I could accept a no-expectations rule, I would always be his West Coast woman. He valued me—even treasured me—but it would go no further.

This sent me into grief; damn, I really thought this might be Leo. And he was a rare someone I could have loved—if I'd been allowed to. *Maybe I just don't deserve him,* I recall thinking, pity party in full swing. *He's so amazing and you're so . . . middle-aged.*

In the years since then, I've gotten better adjusted to the nowheresville in which we live; still, every time I see him it's always a game of Romance Roulette. He comes to town every few months for gigs; I've seen him in New York a couple of times, too. Once we didn't sleep together because I was involved (briefly) with Sean; another time he was making a stab at a relationship. My friends describe it as "off and on," but it's never completely off—nor completely on.

They can't understand why I don't end it completely, cut the lifeline between us. I think it has to do with the image I carry around of him in my mind. It's never him falling asleep smoking or not kissing me good-bye in the morning. When I think of Lenny we're in North

Beach shopping at City Lights, back when we were new. He's looking gorgeous and gray-haired in his dark overcoat, he takes my hand quietly as we look through the bookshelves, we kiss softly and frequently, his eyes smile into mine with the look of a man falling in love.

If I could replace this image—which seems indelibly burned onto my hard drive—with something resembling reality, it might not be so hard to quit him and move on. It doesn't help that the sound of his voice—a honey-soaked bass etched by cigarettes—does things to me.

"So are you coming out or what?" I asked, hating myself for even asking.

"Maybe next month. I'll let you know."

"Okay, well . . ." *For Chrissakes, don't say anything else needy.* "Good night, Lenny."

"Good night, Jane. Or should I say, Madame Columnist?"

I settle into the pillow, exhausted. Clearly, I won't be at a loss for material.

The Mama of Reinvention

"Po, how do you handle this? The crazy nutbag readers?"

"Uh-oh, bad morning?" says my friend on the other end of the line. He is clearly dealing with his baby; I can hear Luke mewling in the background. And yet he's never too busy to listen to me whine.

"You could say so! Weird propositions—this one guy said he wondered what kind of underpants I favored. There's breathy worship from some readers, which is nice. And then utter hate from others! This one woman dissected my last column—down to my sentence syntax—and told me I was trying to be Bridget Jones for the hormone-replacement generation."

I can tell Po is stifling a chuckle. "Hey, that's not half-bad," he jokes.

"It's not funny!" I sputter. "And it gets worse. I e-mailed her back and suggested she needed to go out and get laid—and then she forwarded it to my boss, the robo-A.M.E., who already thinks I'm a loose cannon!"

"Come on, Jane, you know better than to let them get your goat."

"I know. But I'm so fucking rattled. It's been more than a month now and this gig is not getting any easier. People love me, people hate me. I think I liked it better when I was a grunt reporter covering fires and public utilities commission meetings. How do you handle it with the hate mail?"

Po gets a fair amount, too, for his articles and books. I think he might be too handsome and successful.

"First of all, you know I never read my reviews, right?" he says. "I had to stop reading them because I was obsessed and anxious all the time. E-mail, too. You can usually tell by the subject line. I kill out anything with a subject like 'you suck' without even reading it."

"But I feel compelled to read everything that comes at me," I sigh. "Partly because it's kind of addictive—knowing I'm getting a reaction. But also because I know I'm sort of on probation with the column; I need to collect all this response to make the case to keep it going."

"Jane, you don't owe your readers to take that kind of crap," he insists. "You've been writing for twenty years. You know what you're doing. Give yourself a break. I'll see you Sunday at salon. And don't you have a birthday coming up?"

"Yes, in a couple weeks!" I laugh, tension alleviated by the warmth of his tone. "My forty-ninth—the last birthday I ever plan to admit to."

I hang up, profoundly grateful for knowing Po, ground zero for the complete reinvention of my life over these last five years. Between family deaths, the breakup of my several-year relationship to George (aka The Shallowfuck Lawyer), and Erin's departure for college, I was flat on the earth, devastated, and rethinking my entire life. I didn't want to leave my house, cried all the time. Po was the strong tractor who dragged my sad self into a new circle, a new life.

We'd bonded over writing and Giants and loss (he was just out of a postcollege marriage and I was an old pro with two under my belt), he invited me to Writers Grotto lunches, and so it went—blooming into

Tuesday writers' dinners, literary parties, eventually my own salon. He's now married again—this time to a doctor who shares his passions for sports and literature—and has a cute little boy, for whom Erin babysits. It's lovely when things come full circle.

And as hard as I crashed when Erin went off to New England for college, she actually did me a fat favor. If she'd stayed here, I'd have continued to smother her with my micromothering—and even though we have always been the very best of friends, I suspect once she unloaded her trunk in Maine, she danced a little jig. The focus of my maternal energies has now become my friends, and unlike Erin, they don't wait until I'm away for the weekend to throw a party at my house with guests who barf on my carpets.

It's been an excellent trade-off: maternity for hostessing. In fact, I think I've discovered a truth about aging gracefully. Find your inner busybody and get her involved in as many people's lives as possible. Although, sometimes, the time commitment can be excessive.

When I get to work, I have several nonwork-related e-mails. One from Dayna, who is a documentary filmmaker, asking for the number of Marc, a musician friend who might do a soundtrack for her next work. Another is from my friend Tamara, editor of a literary magazine: she wants to talk about organizing a reading between her organization and Litquake, a literary festival I founded and still help organize. My friend Elsa, a digital arts activist, is asking how to e-mail the salon group about a benefit for her women's organization. And Po's best pal, Ethan, is interested in finding photos of the salon for possible use on the cover of his new book, a treatise about urban tribes.

I haven't even opened my snail mail yet.

It's only natural that I would start something like the salon—I tend to collect and connect people, and gathering them all together one Sunday a month is a time-saver. People can talk to each other face-to-face without employing the skills of Ernestine the telephone operator in the middle. Still, I spend plenty of time doing just that.

"Dayna, Marc is in Japan on tour with Virgil Shaw, but here's his e-mail and I know he gets back in a week! Are we still doing the ballet thang on the 12th? Can you get us in for free?" I e-mail her back.

It struck me recently that despite my sketchy relationship history, and my lack of future romantic prospects, I'll never be alone, thanks to my coterie of creatives. My life revolves ever more around them, and rightly so. Maybe I had to lose a lot of people before I learned how to properly treasure them.

Still, at times this strikes me as yet another prank by Mother Time. How come we can't feel this fully engaged, this richly alive, when we're young? I suppose if we did, we'd be impossibly smug.

I turn back to my e-mail and in the last fifteen minutes have gotten six more. This time I am more careful to kill out the obvious flamethrows. "Feminism = immorality?" is one that I spike without reading. But I'm curious enough to open one that leads with "I worship you."

"Jane Ganahl—I worship your exquisite hilarious writing. RJ. (Available for boffing, maybe)"

Boffing? God, I sure am attracting 'em.

I also hear from the Alaska architect ("I come to San Francisco on business a few times a year and would love to meet you") and the Louisiana lawyer, who says, "I find you refreshingly candid. Tell me more: what are you looking for, Miss Ganahl? Marriage? More kids? White picket fence?"

I want to respond, *Jesus, right now I'd settle for a cuppa Joe with someone resembling Leo. Or sex. Sex would be nice. I can't always count on Lenny riding in on a white horse to rescue me from Chastity Castle.*

But I answer the lawyer coolly. "Well . . . I don't want two out of three of those things." I add a wink for mystery's sake.

Dieter and Rosalind are the first people I see when I arrive at the restaurant for the monthly salon. They are always maddeningly on time—Rosalind runs her French artist on an American timetable. "*Félicitations* on the column," he says in his brisk accent. "Are you getting a lot of response?"

"*Mais oui!*" says Rosalind, who is progressing nicely with her French lessons. "She's even getting marriage proposals!"

"Not quite," I laugh. "More like *propositions.* Weird, considering there is no photo with the column. I could look like Phyllis Diller for all they know!"

"Phyllis who?" Dieter says blankly.

"Never mind," Rosalind tells him, not wanting to engage in a lesson in American pop cultural history. "Have you heard from Mr. Louisiana again?"

"Yeah, he's becoming a regular. This one has potential."

"Hey, if you end up getting married out of this, do I get a finder's fee for getting you the gig?" Phil announces his presence with the usual alpha-male gusto. He is without his actress wife, but that seems to be the case more often than not lately.

"I don't care so much about getting married as getting a *lover* before I'm fifty next year," I sigh, hugging his beefy shoulders. "And if you can tell me what the finder's fee on *that* would be, we can negotiate."

Phil, besides being my boss, is my oldest male friend in The City. It's never been an easy friendship; we've veered in and out of closeness depending on our respective romances. We've also had some doozie fights—probably because we always think we're right; it's the journalist's curse. Lately, I've all but lost him completely, to a wife and a life that's split between here and L.A. (which he hates) and the fact that he's a dad for the first time in his fifty years.

"Hey, wait," he smiles, and raises his voice for all to hear. "Aren't you turning fifty-five soon?"

"Oh . . . stuff it," I sniff. "That's *your* next birthday, not mine."

These gatherings started two years ago during the dot-com boom, when artists were being forced out of their studios en masse. My friend Jon, who owns this restaurant, was moved by the plight of the creative class and opened his doors for this monthly feast, which he asked me to organize. I always hesitate to use the word *salon*, which is way too precious for this group.

Those expecting these gatherings to be stuffy, with pompous intellects jockeying to toss off the evening's best bon mot, are always surprised at how base we can be. We might be dining at a swanky eatery, but our conversation is more fitting of a roadhouse at times.

There are seventy-five people in the group now. Most I met through writer friends, who are the salon's beating heart. And some were interviewees I met while doing entertainment features on them—like Mark and Patty, both singer/songwriters, and Dan, the city's only big-name Japanese DJ, and David and Adam, filmmakers. And my darling Dan and Dayna, whom I met ages ago with the debut of their second documentary.

There are some noncreatives as well; people like Craig who were so interesting, even visionary, that I wanted their voices at the table. I met him at a Webbys party, standing there at the food table looking utterly disconnected from the craziness around him. When I learned this shy, sweet nerd was the founder of the world's largest online community, I was fascinated and had to drag him to dinner. And I've tried to find him someone to date, a process that hasn't been terribly successful since he's holding out for Julia Roberts.

And after two years of this mostly-hit-sometimes-miss invitation process, the group has become like a big, sprawling, noisy family. And a loving one: a few months ago, after 9/11, there were no toasts, no gaiety, but a lot of hugging and tears and gratitude that we had our safety and one another.

If there is love there are also arguments—the most colorful being when the new *Chronicle* entertainment editor fled in tears after a novelist told her she was out of touch with the local arts scene—as well as romances, babies, weddings. Drop-ins, drop-outs. People conscripted and people bounced. So far, that's only been a few, and they were either rude to the long-suffering staff or guilty of going off the deep end in a not-funny way. (One painter pal, given to illicit substances, got up on the table one month to do a turkey dance for the upcoming Thanksgiving.)

We celebrate one another's successes and soothe wounds rendered by failure, the likes of which creative people have by the dozen. And the talk often turns to sex.

"How good is the show gonna be?" I can hear Mark, the city's gay singer/songwriter icon, about his show next week at the Great American Music Hall. His words are loud and boisterous, signaling his pre-salon cocktails were many. "It's gonna be like one long jizz shot!" At this stage of the evening, everyone thinks this is uproariously funny.

I've brought a few dates to these events in an attempt, I suppose, to throw them into the deep end of my pool and see if they'll swim. Sean came with me for six months—as long as we dated. And when we broke up, he asked to be taken off the e-mail notification list. "I really don't want to hear how much fun everyone else is having," he snarled.

I have never brought Lenny, since when he comes to town it's only for shows, and we literally never go out and socialize with my friends. It goes like this: room service, screw, go to the show, come back to the hotel, screw, more room service. Not terribly imaginative but a routine that's always worked for me.

Peter catches me around the waist with one arm and draws me close. "Hey." It's all he says, smiling affectionately. He always looks the same: knit cap pulled down over shaved head, eight or ten tiny gold earrings marching up the outside of one of his ears, Carhartt construction jacket, military boots. "How are you adjusting to life under the spotlight?" he asks.

I smile and study his perfect skin—the result of his macrobiotic diet no doubt. "I'm overwhelmed. But happy the column's hitting a nerve."

I'm always amazed at Peter's ability to make conversation with anyone about anything, having come from poverty and not hovering too high above the line even now. I recall an animated conversation he got into at one party with Billy, the scion of a famed oil family, about their mutual interest in sustainable agriculture.

"Hey, babe!" Sexy Claudia embraces me. "I'm going to give you two hugs—one for your fabulous new column and one for your birthday coming up!"

Her arms are soft but athletic as she squeezes me and smiles. Claudia looks amazing for being just a couple of years shy of forty—a yoga fanatic and sometime Buddhist with a couple of interesting tattoos, she has an addiction to Pirates to match mine. We went to see her lover recently, a singer/songwriter of some renown, and I was duly impressed that she got to go home with the guy that all those women in front of the stage were swooning over. She worries she is fading, but compared to me, she still blazes a hot trail. Just ask any of the string of young lovers she's had in recent years.

As the thirty of us sit down, and as I do every month, I toast the various accomplishments of the group in the last month: Dayna and Dan just got an NEA grant for their next documentary; Cameron was approached about turning her book into a TV series; Po's son turned one. There are cheers, and Po stands up to make a toast himself.

"To Jane's upcoming birthday—and to her new column. May it make her famous . . . and get her laid!"

There is another roar and a clinking of glasses. I sigh theatrically. "What has become of my life that my lack of sex is becoming a salon joke?" I demand, before taking an undiscriminating swig of Sancerre.

Hours later, as the group is dispersing, I get a call on my cell phone from a New York number I recognize. "I'm sorry I didn't call sooner, but I'm in town just through tomorrow to talk to Clear Channel about a tour," says Lenny. "Do you want to come over?"

Amazing, from Po's mouth to God's ear. I shouldn't go. He should have given me more notice. If I had decent self-esteem I'd say no.

"What's the address?" I ask.

The Baby Buddha vs. My Sex Life

"Where are you? I tried you at home just now but you're not there. You're never gone by now. . . ." Erin's voice on my cell phone is all at once breathless and demanding. She gets impatient when I call too often, but if more than one day goes by without hearing from me, she'll track me down.

I wince, feeling hungover as I drive toward home, sunglasses pushed high up on my nose to protect against the advancing morning light of spring. I glance down at my outfit—the same one I had on last night at salon. "Uh . . . Lenny came to town unexpectedly and I spent the night with him."

I always feel like a wounded gazelle after a visit with Lenny—exhilarated by the passion of our tango, but physically pummeled and emotionally unsatisfied. I always hope for a return to the early days of passion, but on an emotional level he withholds himself like I'm the IRS.

There is a pause while she digests the sordid information. "Oh, okay. You sound wiped out. How was it?"

"Not great, actually. It was late when I got there after salon and he fell asleep smoking. Not charming."

"Mom, when are you going to give that guy the pitch?" she demands. "Wasn't he supposed to *call first* if he was coming to town? I don't care if he's famous, he can be pretty lame and irresponsible."

"You're right," I sigh. "It's annoying how right you always are."

When Erin was born, a friend gave me an astrological reading for her as a present. I have recalled a million times how the astrologer chuckled, noting that this baby was "such an old soul—much older than her mother." He also told me that our life together would be equal parts her learning from me (her ABCs, pet care, the names of the Beatles) and my learning from her (how to live, how to relate, in a humane and spiritual manner). This, I came to learn, was not New Age bullshit. My brain is stocked with memories of ways in which the Baby Buddha would hand me my errant ass. We must have taken a hundred road trips during her childhood—road trips that required detouring to McDonald's because there was no other food to be found, ordering her the usual Filet O' Fish, and trying to sneak in an order for a Big Mac without her hearing me. "Mommeee!" the Buddha toddler would shriek, "Don't forget we're *veg-a-tar-ee-ans*!! What about the *cows*?"

She was so adorable—and so from another planet. None of the parenting guides applied when it came to her. Most parents hide their youthful transgressions out of fear that their kids will follow suit; I, on the other hand, made sure she heard most of them so that she could learn *what not to do* from her mother's bad behavior. One of her favorite stories had to do with why I attended my high school graduation on crutches. The night before, I'd been to a graduation party at one of my wealthier friend's homes in Atherton. No parents were there, and I drank a ton of cheap red wine. Someone put on the Dave Clark Five and it was all over. I climbed up onto a four-tiered cement fountain whose water cascaded into the pool below to go-go dance, cheered on by my friends who were frantically boogying below. During "Any Way You Want It"—still one of the great rock tunes of all time—I slipped and went over the side, hitting the cement on my way into the pool below. I lost a layer of skin on my right thigh and had to limp, hungover and in major pain, to collect my diploma.

As a middle-schooler she liked that true story as much as the ones I made up when she was tiny.

Her dad moved three states away when she was three. Fearing she'd feel alone and defenseless, I made up some fractured fairy tales, putting twists on some old legends. Her favorite was about Tarzana, a little girl who lived with the apes in the jungle and rescued a crashed plane full of people, including several brawny men, by swinging through trees and being strong and smart. She ate it up. "Tell me Tarzana again!" she said over and over. I needn't have worried that Erin couldn't find her strength—I think I underestimated how much there was in my family. Including Lisa, who told me once, when I was in tears that Erin's dad was so seldom in touch: "There's a reason Erin picked you as a mom: you come from a family of strong, independent women."

I thought at the time she was referring to herself, Mom, and Anne.

Nowadays, I tell Erin stories not to entertain or share cautionary tales, but because I love getting a reaction. "Anyway . . ." I say slowly, intent on further ruffling her feathers, "he may have passed out last night but when he woke up this morning he was fully ready to party."

"Okay, Mom, you need to stop now," Erin says in exasperation, stifling a giggle. "This is a case of seriously TMI."

"Too much information?" I tease. "If you really loved me, you'd be pleased to know that my romantic drought was momentarily halted."

Not that my ten hours with Lenny had even a shred of romance or emotion attached. This morning wasn't even all that great, truth be told. But sometimes it's enough, more than enough, to just smell him on my clothes afterward.

"I'd be more pleased if you actually found someone to be *involved* with, not just sleep with," she huffed. "Anyway, I'm at the office now so I have to hang up. Can you get some sleep before you go to work? You sound terrible."

"Yes, Mom," I say to her, not yet done teasing. "Thank you, Mom . . . I mean, Erin."

"And we need to talk about your birthday!" she says, ignoring my taunts. "Should we try that new place down the street from you? And I'm making you another CD—I hope you don't mind but I found some more tunes from the early nineties!"

"Are you kidding? I play the one you gave me for Christmas all the time!"

Rock 'n' roll has been the Great Equalizer in our relationship, as religion or knitting or sports are for other mothers and daughters. No matter how alienated we occasionally became during her teenage years, pop music would drag us back together. It was hard for her to stay mad at me when I was dangling Pearl Jam tickets and an invitation: "Want to come help me review the show?"

To get her to appreciate the finer points of rock, I started her off young, with a one-two punch of nature and nurture. When I was pregnant, I would stand with my belly close to the speakers in the living room and swear to anyone who'd listen that she jumped around to the Eagles' "Hotel California." And soon after she was born, she began to groove. I recall so clearly driving with her in her baby seat in El Paso, where she was born, with Heart's "Straight on for You" on the radio. I glanced over at her and she was bobbing in perfect rhythm to the song. She was five months old.

And when she got old enough to sing, which she did pretty much constantly ("Does that child ever shut up?" my mom wanted to know), I would hear her in the living room singsonging the words to Bruce Springsteen's "Born to Run" while she played with her blocks.

My eyes welled with tears. She was really mine!

My mania was acceptable then; I was still in my twenties. And I think I always assumed that my tastes would eventually change; that the gene would kick in that would cause me to suddenly stop loving the Stones and turn on to Jimmy Buffett or John Tesh—the same disease that had befallen some of my best friends like they'd been invaded by body snatchers. But it has not happened, and at this point I doubt it will. I still listen, at ear-threatening volume—usually in the car, where I can damage no one but myself.

My refusal to budge from rock camp started to wear on Erin when she got old enough to notice I wasn't like all the other moms. I'd pick her up in eighth grade—the year during which any variations on my part from the June Cleaver prototype were met by her with shudders and chagrin—and when her classmates heard Black Crowes blaring from my speakers, they were mightily perplexed.

She got over her mortal alarm eventually—about the time I started covering music for real. We went to dozens of shows in the next few years—Spin Doctors, Green Day, Soul Asylum, Counting Crows. It was so cool: I didn't have to try to find a date and she didn't mind being seen with me as long as (a) she got to take a friend, and (b) I didn't act like we were related.

When she went away to college and my heart all but broke, I sent her tapes of songs that reminded me of her. I let Uncle Tupelo express my anguish: *"If I break in two will you put me back together? / When this puzzle's figured out will you still be around?"*

I used to delight in clutching her sweet-smelling babyness and dancing around with her in my arms, singing loudly to rock 'n' roll while she erupted in enchanting toddler giggles.

Nowadays I turn her on to my favorites—Jay Farrar, Franz Ferdinand, Owsley—and she keeps trying to get me to love hip-hop. It's a more grown-up type of mother-daughter sharing—and much more rewarding than wiping her baby barf off my blouse twenty-three years ago.

I pull into my garage, which is full of not only hundreds of my CDs, but hundreds of hers as well. Not to mention all the rest of her crap; since she graduated almost two years ago she is half in the house and half out in the world as she wrestles with her future.

There are boxes of her baby clothes, with dresses handmade by her late grandma, complete with antique Irish lace around the collar and perfect hand-smocking. If my mother was in "grandma overdrive" when it came to Erin, I was enslaved to her. I didn't have much else going for me.

I so clearly recall my mother saying, more than once, that she worried what would become of me "if something happened to Erin." I thought that was a pretty hideous thought to entertain even momentarily; I would, of course, lay down and die immediately. It took Mom actually dying and Erin leaving home for me to realize what my mother was saying: I had no idea what I was good at, nothing to fill the void. Thank God reinvention is always possible, even in one's forties.

But God, I loved being a mom when my name was Mommy! It was like having a doll, one wearing handmade dresses. She was such a beautiful little girl that we were bothered in supermarkets all the time by gawkers, dismaying the shy child endlessly; she was even recruited when she was ten by a top modeling agency. The Buddha-preteen turned down their hard sell, shrugging: "Mommy, it's just a cheap way to make money—off my face."

It was all a rehearsal for being the beautiful and maddeningly modest young woman she has become. With her wiry surfer's frame and natural blond hair (both gifts from her father's Swedish side), worn like a wild horse's mane, loose and unprimped, cobalt-blue eyes and pale skin with freckles she's always hated, she's been told, possibly by admirers looking to get into her pants, that she looks like Uma Thurman. Of course, that makes her laugh. "In my dreams!" she sighs incredulously.

She's better now about my less-than-stellar behaviors when it comes to men, but there were days when she was young and I was younger that my normally charming child would turn viperous. I'm the first to say it was all my fault. I hadn't a clue about how to draw boundaries, and she would let me know, vociferously, if I had transgressed.

When we first moved back here after her dad and I split up, I was so needy for attention that I would put her to bed upstairs and roll around with my date on the couch downstairs. The wispy-thin line I drew was that I wouldn't bring them upstairs. But she always knew, and would howl for mama in the way a three-year-old does when they mean business and won't shut up for all the tea in China until you come and lull them to sleep a second time.

I have no idea what I was thinking in my twenties. But how do I explain situations like last night?

Realizing I've hit on a good topic, I race upstairs and pound out next week's column on my home computer.

Being a single mother is a bitch. Any mother who's been relegated to that role, by virtue of a divorce or widowing or the decision to not marry, can tell you so.

I can tell you so.

The struggles are daily and unending: making ends meet, holding a job (since most single mothers must), trying to be active in the child's life despite the job, dealing with the lack of a co-parent.

But if being a single mother has been one of the toughest jobs in the world, it has also handed me some of my highest highs. No matter what harsh craziness was dealt me by life, ex-husbands, boyfriends, or work, Erin was there, a chatty, nutty, cheerful little jewel who painted watercolors for me, brought home stray cats, quoted Monty Python, and thought pretty much everything was enormously funny.

Except when I tried to date.

Dating, for all single mothers, is a big issue. Even when you do have the option (since men often equate a woman with children to a woman with a heroin habit), you run headlong into the brick wall of your child's attitude. My own daughter was prickly and sullen with any new beau and resented when I'd leave her with her grandparents for weekends.

Before my eyes, she would transform from the angelic light of her teachers'/grandparents'/friends' lives into, as my second husband came to call her, "the changeling." He also did a mean (literally) imitation of her becoming Regan, the devil-afflicted girl in The Exorcist.

Ah, my charming child.

And then, just when your daughter finally begins to accept you as a real person, a sentient woman with needs, she becomes one, too. And things can turn a bit upside down. The teenage Erin became not only more understanding of my need to date, but actually encouraged me to. No mystery there: when I was out, she could have the house to herself. There were times when I found myself calling home, driving back after a date, to give her and her boyfriend time to straighten up before I walked in the house.

Oh man, I hope she doesn't kill me for that one.

But the best, the very best part of the single mother/daughter continuum has been lately, as we have evolved into girlfriends. At 23, out of college, managing life in San Francisco, and working full-time, she doesn't need me for much anymore—a fact she likes to bludgeon me with when I try to give her advice.

But that also means we're free to have fun.

We see each other often, and when we do, a healthy amount of time is spent scoping out males in the vicinity. I try to pick out her type and I'm usually pretty spot-on. Scruffy, countercultural, big smile, surfer type, no Gap/yuppie clothes.

That one, I'll gesture.

"Oh, yes . . . hellloooo?" she'll murmur, always too shy to let me forge a better introduction. ("I'll kill you," she hisses when I suggest I try.)

And in turn, she listens patiently while I whine about my lack of prospects, poignant/dismal drinks with an ex, or occasional setups. Occasionally, though, the shoe does slip onto the other foot. The last time she started using the b-word in reference to someone she was dating, it ended poorly. The phone rang at work in the afternoon.

"Can I come home for the night and will you make me macaroni and cheese and tell me he was a bastard?" she said.

Maybe she still needs me a little.

Just to make sure she won't freak out, I send her the column copy in an e-mail before I turn it in. The next day she responds simply: "Mom, I still need you *all the time,* you silly!"

What nobody realizes is how much I still need her.

"If You Lived in Sudan, You'd Be Dead by Now"

I wake up on the eve of my forty-ninth birthday with a vicious cold-flu. Snoggy-nosed, puffy-eyed, and pale, a Phyllis Diller look-alike greets me in the mirror. But it's not the end of the world: I have no major plans that would require my being seen in public, since the salon doubled for my friends-birthday and since I am, as I have been for the last few years, date-free. Except for dear Dad of course, whom I'd seen last night for an early-bird dinner at Buck's.

So tonight is for Erin. As it so often is.

It's been our routine: dinner somewhere nice, then a movie or ballet. So we're altering this a tad given my sickly state: take-out Mexican chow from Tres Amigos, and a video at home. Most likely an oldie-but-goodie; our home library is stocked with cheesy romantic comedies like *Romancing the Stone* ("You're the best time I ever had!"), *Overboard* ("Every time with you is like the first time!"), *Moonstruck* ("Everything seems like nothing to me now, 'cause I want you in my bed"), or *Sleepless in Seattle* ("I was just taking her hand to help her out of a car and I knew. It was like . . . magic!").

And other paeans to female wishful thinking.

But first there is the e-mail to read this morning, which is becoming my obsessive Sunday morning ritual. I don't have as many this week; I guess my take on sleeping around while Erin was a youngster wasn't scarlet enough to unleash a fundamentalist backlash on my ass. "Thanks for bringing this topic to light . . . ," "Women need to think carefully before subjecting their children . . . ," "Hey, baby, how 'bout it . . . ?" The usual. I see a few hand grenades—with subject lines like "irresponsible twaddle" and "poor role modeling"—but I refuse to open those.

I smile when I see one from Louisiana Lawyer.

"You seem critical of yourself for your behaviors as a young mother," he writes. "But weren't you only in your twenties? What twenty-something doesn't need sex as much as food?"

I like how this man thinks. I really do.

"It may be presumptuous to ask," he continues, "but is there currently a recipient of your considerable passions?"

I hesitate before I write back. "No," I type in slowly. "But I'm taking applications . . ."

I pause before hitting send. And then shudder at my lack of restraint and apparent neediness.

I also get a birthday salutation from Chris, my second ex-husband and by far my favorite of the two: one of the funniest men on the planet, if not the most difficult. (It's no wonder so many of my friends said he reminded them of Chevy Chase—not only in looks but because he was tall, deadly sarcastic, and brilliant.)

"Remember," he writes, "if you lived in Sudan you'd be dead by now." In other words, cheer up, you're forty-nine but you're not yet planted. Sigh.

There are also several others from pals who remembered the date. None from Lenny, but he's terrible at e-mailing—and perhaps he'll call at some point . . . ?

By dinnertime, he has not. But I've gotten some nice voice messages, which, along with e-mails, are the greeting card substitutes of the twenty-first century. Rosalind leaves her trademark cheerleader-on-speed greeting: "Happy birthday to my darling Jane! I hope you and Erin do something fun tonight!" Yeah, blowing my nose is always a good time. Phil leaves me a funny one: "Hey, are you older than me yet?" Click. But Peter's message is, as always, my favorite, with his Elizabethan grammar and rush of uncensored emotions: "Girlfriend, I know this year will be the best of the best for you. You will blaze a trail as you climb the heights and over the mountain. Just know you are cherished, sweetie. Bye-bye."

I might save this one, to bolster me on some cold night when I wonder what in the hell I'm doing with my life.

Erin throws her stuff on the armchair breathlessly. "Guess what?" she says, hugging me as I turn my head to the side to avoid spewing germs on her. "You know that junior partner I told you was so cute? The one who does pro bono work with Greenpeace? He asked me to a party at his house tonight!"

She frowns. "Of course I told him I couldn't come since it was your birthday. . . ."

"Okay, first of all, who is this one?" I ask. "I've kind of lost track. There have been so many lately. . . ."

She gives me The Look. "Mom, I know I told you about him. He's been stopping by my desk to chat, which is something lawyers never do with paralegals. He's super cute, looks like a Gap ad."

"And . . . this is a good thing?" I ask wearily.

She ignores me, scratching Bunnykitty, the youngest of our three, under her chin. "He also offered to help me with my personal essay on my law school applications! He got into Boalt so he must know what he's doing."

"Oh jeez, is it that time already?" I groan, feeling suddenly worse. "Law school is still more than a year away! Can he get you into Boalt, too? I promise to let him marry you if he keeps you close by. . . ."

"Mom, I doubt I have the grades for Boalt—and I won't know where to apply until I take my LSAT this summer! And before *that* I have to take my LSAT study course. So can we not stress about this yet? Please?"

I sigh. "Okay, well . . . you should absolutely go tonight." And I do mean it. Unlike the relationships most of my friends have with their mothers and children, passive-aggressiveness has never been part of this one. I emit a spastic, thunderous sneeze. "Besides, I won't be much fun here."

She looks unconvinced. "Well, maybe after we eat dinner. . . . But I hate to leave you by yourself! I think one reason you don't get weirded-out about birthdays is because you surround yourself with people all the time who tell you how fabulous you are!"

She laughs at her own amusing observation. I laugh, too, and dab at my red nose. "Oh, right, so you're worried that one night alone is going to plunge me into the depths of despair? Please, give credit for at least a few ego-strengths."

We speed over to our favorite burrito joint, where I keep my head low and covered, Unabomber-like, in my hooded sweatshirt, hoping not to run into anyone I know who might expect a conversation. Erin, of course, immediately runs into a robust young blond god she apparently used to see when she went surfing. "Did you ever date that guy?" I ask. She rolls her eyes: "No, Mom!" "Why not?" I ask, giving him the twice-over and feeling my blood rush a bit more warmly.

She grabs our burritos and heads for the door. "You'll never change!" She laughs.

But that's just it, I think, settling into the couch with Erin and our dinner on trays. I am changing, I have changed. I am forty-nine and have not been hit on in any serious way in a coon's age. I ain't got it anymore. It's fucking discouraging.

I won't burden Erin with this, she is fully loving her vegetarian burrito and laughing hysterically at a *South Park* rerun. Saddam Hussein is chasing Cartman around the same way Elmer Fudd chased Bugs Bunny when Bugs was dressed as a girlie rabbit.

Fudd! God, maybe it's time to start considering the creased-pants wonder. Kill me.

Erin is done with her burrito in record time; soon we're tearing into the cupcakes she brought over and she's singing to me for the third time today. I unwrap some sweet earrings she found at a Union Square sidewalk table, and a newly burned compilation CD entitled *Songs That Remind Me of My Mommy.* But I can see she is antsy to head off to meet Mr. Wonderful Do-Gooder Lawyer, so I tell her to beat it. As she collects her things, I holler up to her in the kitchen: "Honey, I'm all plugged up! Will you make me up a hot toddy before you go?"

She appears at the top of the stairs. "Mom, didn't you already take some cold medication? That's really going to knock you out. Are you sure you want to do this?"

"It's not like I'm driving!" I laugh hollowly.

She returns with the drink and her purse on her shoulder. "I still don't think I should go. . . ."

"Go!" I tell her. "I'll listen to the new CD and watch television while wearing my new earrings—it will be a rich, rewarding night! But I want a full report in the morning."

"Deal." She embraces me, her thin body practically vibrating, hummingbird-like, with energy. "I love you, Mom. Happy birthday!"

And she is gone. And ugh, how alone I suddenly feel. I take several long sips of the whiskey, which tastes magically marvelous, and channel surf. The kitties gather around solemnly as if they have arrived for a wake. Alpha-male Noodge positions himself on the throne (my lap), Bunnykitty and Boo drape themselves on top of the couch like fluffy gargoyles.

It's my birthday and I have my booze, my television, my wilting hormones, and my cats. And with this, I become an instant single woman cliché.

Foul Play is on—a movie I always loved for the chemistry of Chevy Chase and Goldie Hawn. But tonight I'm finding it immensely irritating. Why does she have to be such a ditz? As if the gorgeous young Goldie would ever be a lonely hearts as she is supposed to be here. And the attitudes! When Goldie's character tries to theorize about the crime to which she's been subjected, Chevy's detective character shushes her. "I play detective. You play lady in distress."

Yecch! Is this really what I was raised to think was *romantic*? No wonder I'm not the most emotionally mature person I know. To illustrate my own point, I find myself shouting at the screen: "Fuck you, Chevy! Let her be whoever she wants to be!"

Clearly, the whiskey has taken hold and is helping to boil—or perhaps curdle—my blood. Not that I've ever needed help in that regard; several men in my life have told me I have a bad temper, which I have always joked was required of a redhead. Some have even suggested anger management problems, but I reject that. I just got involved with jerks and then reacted as anyone would.

Or not.

But there were times when I was more than justified in throwing things and screaming. The best one I can think of was when I was in the Stanford Hospital parking lot after visiting Lisa, who had just lost a lung to cancer. It was just a little more than a month after my mom died of cancer. My boyfriend, George, the Shallowfuck Lawyer (who was so shallow he thought it was funny when I called him this), asked if

I wanted to go out to dinner. Feeling shattered, I demurred, saying I just wanted to go home. He got huffy. I recall his words were "You never want to go out and have fun anymore!"

I had been with him five years, and I held up my index finger to his nose as if it were a gun. "Go away," I said, my voice quaking. "Now. Or I will kill you."

He didn't need to be told twice. A month after that, we were exchanging possessions in a parking lot, including a long, pale blue silk dress he had bought me, thinking it would make a beautiful wedding gown. I put it inside his Smoky Joe barbecue as I gave it back, thinking oil stains would make it less useful for his next victim. Immature, I grant you, but I was enormously lost at the time.

Even now, as a more mature Jane, a less tragedy-plagued one, I still have to keep my anger in check, especially for the sake of the column. If I wrote what I really think about men sometimes, they'd blow up the *Chronicle* building. They still run the world, they're terrified of losing power, they smack down any female whose head pokes up above the surface. They only look at young women because their egos are so fragile they don't want to date their equals.

And don't even tell me this romance shit is not all about looks. There were Valentine's Days when I'd get several cards and bouquets, from both current flames and exes for whom memories of me were rosy. The gifts I had then, such as they were, are even more honed now: my wit, my knowledge of music and film and current events, my ability to tell a joke like Margaret Cho, sing like Bonnie Raitt (even better on the high notes), and drive like Parnelli Jones.

But what's that all worth? Nada. Zero. Not a fucking thing. Men don't want talent, they want tits. Young ones.

Okay, I sit up a little straighter on my pillows, *maybe I am a little mad at men these days. I can't help it. They stopped looking at me.*

Maybe it's harder for me to accept being suitor-free after having so many for the first forty-five years of my forty-nine on the planet. It's enough to make a well-balanced woman go off her nut—or at least become bitter. Besides, shouldn't I have something to show for all those slutty years? All this experience and no one to give joy to—maybe it's God's punishment. I'm sure Pat Robertson would agree. Is this the penalty for being a tart: lots of stories but no love?

Good lord, this whiskey has done its evil—I'm really hammered and ridiculous. Maybe if I just lie down for a moment I'll feel better.

Ahhhhh. Lenny, lying warmly on top of me, kisses my nose tenderly. I let out a sigh and open my eyes. Noodge is sitting square on my chest and is licking my nose. It's two a.m. and I'm freezing. The phone's message light is on—I didn't even hear it ring. But it's not Lenny.

"Mom, just checking on you." Erin's cheerful voice. "I hope you had a nice night watching TV. And guess what? I really like this guy! He's faaaabulous!"

Well, I'm glad the romantic action was positive—and real—for one of us tonight.

Days later, feeling much improved, I undertake to put my birthday pity party in perspective by writing about it.

Any woman who claims that being alone and single is a self-fulfilling joyride 100 percent of the time is a liar. Just a few weeks ago, as I was trying to cheer up a recently-made-single friend, I heard myself declare: "Look at the bright side! There has never been a better time to be single. There's hardly any stigma attached to it anymore, and there are so many opportunities to have fun, meet men. I never feel like I'm missing anything!"

If I were Pinocchio, my nose would have stretched forward about a foot with that last statement.

Wow, this is really laying it on the line. How about a few warm-up lines first? My bitter stew from the other night must still be simmering beneath the surface.

> *For the most part, I—and all my single friends—love our lifestyle. And I love the luxury of living alone, of suiting myself and my own whims 24/7, without regard for the needs of someone else. But occasionally, those old-as-history arguments for coupling up zoom into sharp relief. When being single and living alone sucks big-time.*
>
> *A week ago, I was felled by an ugly flu bug. Woke up one day with my throat swollen almost closed. Even drinking orange juice felt like swallowing spikes. I don't get sick very often, so I didn't take it very well. In fact, I'm a world-class Big Baby when I do get sick—as bad as any man I've known.*
>
> *(And pretty much every man is a Big Baby when he gets sick, but that's a whole other column.)*

Hmmm . . . I wonder if this will provoke a reaction? Men are so goddamn touchy these days.

> *In addition to being physically ill, I felt inexplicably morose and emotionally distraught. Nobody loves you, I thought. You've spent your life taking care of other people and now you have to take care of yourself? Man, you must be an unworthy human being.*
>
> *Of course, these thoughts are the product of a sick (literally) mind. There are people who not only love me but who also, if I would just allow them to, would come and make me a cup of chamomile tea. But my problem is that I've set it up with the people in my support system to protect them from my truths. Call it 20-plus years of being a mother—a mostly single one—but I have a hard time letting anyone take care of me.*

I really sound like a martyr. The truth is, I could have asked Rosalind or Claudia or Po or Peter to bring me some soup and they would have gladly done it. Next time, maybe.

Despite the myriad great times to be, there are, sadly, other times when it really, truly, sucks to be single and living alone. At the top of the list: major holidays. In descending order: Thanksgiving (not so bad if you have family around), Christmas (ditto), New Year's Eve (about a 9 on a scale of 10 in suckiness), and Valentine's Day (a fat 10).

Okay, and birthdays. But I don't add that. Hey, a woman is entitled to a few tiny secrets when she lives her life nakedly on the page. And my age is one of them.

By the time the column runs, I am feeling one hundred percent better. Make that fifty percent better. My nose is no longer stuffy, but there's still an ache around my solar plexus. And no amount of vitamin C will fix that.

Of Death and Recipes

As if I weren't already down on the male species, with Lenny having stiffed me on anything at all birthday-related, my column about being single and sick seems to have brought the scariest male troglodytes out from under their rocks.

"Dear Ms. Ganahl—I just had to write and say fuck you, you fucking bitch. Men are babies? Who the hell are you . . ."

Zap—I send the offensive e-mail into space. I am astonished at the torrent of response to my comment that all men are babies when they get sick. Not only are men miffed, they are obscenely pissed off. Eschewing my own rule against reading flamethrowers, I am so fascinated by the reaction I provoked that I scroll through, reading at least the first lines of several. There are lectures on misandry (the opposite of misogyny, the hatred of men, which I am apparently guilty of), numerous retorts on how women are actually the big babies, and more obscenities ("and you wonder why you don't have a goddamned boyfriend!").

This every-Sunday battle is getting exhausting, even makes me want to throw in the towel. It's only a tiny bit easier now to get these hideous missives than it was when I started a few months ago. Maybe

I'm just setting myself up for endless assault, and I don't know if I have it in me. I want to call Po for his buck-up lecture, but I'm afraid I'll burst into tears.

I vow to stop reading e-mail, but can't resist this very last one—subject line: "A word of encouragement"—from someone named Tom.

"I don't take offense to your remark about men, but I am disappointed that you resorted to it for subject matter," he writes. "Your words go forth. The *Chron* is a regional paper, your words come to rest in places you might never imagine (in this case, Redding). As you develop a perspective and deepen it, you develop a following. You begin to speak for others, who begin to rely on you to keep speaking for them, to transcend their isolation. It's not something to be taken lightly. You've reached up and figuratively swung a leg into this saddle, now ride it. You've got the beginnings of a readership, a constituency. So keep the big issues on the table."

My eyes well up. Jesus, he gives me more credit than I give myself. I respond to him: "THANK YOU—your e-mail was just the boost I needed today."

Energized, I go back to my screen, and start flicking the offensive e-mails out of my in-box. *Out! Damned jerk!* The phone rings, startling me out of my Sunday-morning morass.

"Can you remember how to make Grandma's strawberry shortcake?" Erin asks brightly. "I just remember that she used Bisquick, and there was sugar involved. I'm making dinner for Alex tonight and I'm on my way to Whole Foods."

Right, Alex, the new man, the junior partner. She must actually like this one to cook for him. Most of the others have warranted only party dates before she has graciously, sunnily, moved along to the next hunk, trailing her commitment vs. abandonment issues behind her.

I hesitate. "Honey, I never got that recipe from Grandma before she died. She started with Bisquick, but she altered the recipe. And she never wrote it down. I've tried faking it a few times but haven't ever really gotten it right."

A pause on her end. "Oh, right. Hmmm . . . Maybe I'll just buy those little angel food cups, but they're not the same. Nobody made it like Grandma."

"No, you're right about that." I'm momentarily lost in a blurring of memories and guilt.

"Anyway," she brightens, "that was a good column today! Although I felt kind of bad after reading you had a hard time being by yourself. You told me you'd be fine, you poop! I should not have left you—"

"Nah, nonsense," I cut her off. "I was just being a big baby. You were right to go and meet Gap Ad Man. I can't leech off your life force all the time. Unfortunately."

"You should get some good mail today—I bet there are a lot of women who feel the same way," she says encouragingly. "My dad is a huge baby when he's sick, and so was Chris, remember?"

I don't tell her about the assassination e-mails I've gotten today because of my errant and bitter line about men. Why yank her head out of the clouds?

"And you should see what I'm cooking tonight!" she says. "Mushrooms in sour cream on brown rice, artichokes, and I'm making a salad with pears and Gorgonzola. . . ."

I want to blurt out *Good God, how did you learn to do that?* but instead I manage some words of praise: "My little girl! All growed-up to be Alice Waters."

God knows she got no help in that regard from me.

Being the parent of an older child is often a wrestling match between feeling good about what you've done right and guilt over having failed to pass along certain essentials. In Erin's case, I do think I did a lot right: she says "please" and "thank you," puts gas in the tank when she borrows my car, doesn't smoke, and is kind to animals.

But where did I fall short? On pretty much every domestic skill there is. Cooking, cleaning, laundry, car maintenance (hey, it ought to be a required class in high school), sewing—although she learned that from my mom, sitting eagerly at her knee while Grandma worked at her Elna sewing machine, starting at about age four. I'm pretty sure she did it just to make me look bad, since I rejected all of my mother's attempts to get me to follow her down the Martha Stewart path.

Actually, all the domestic skills Erin acquired were from my mother, the Queen Mother of household arts—especially cooking. I was the family's big disappointment in that area, the Sister Who Never Cooked a Turkey or Hosted Christmas Dinner. Interestingly, my mother never threw herself on the dogpile when the family hassled me about my lack of cooking or homemaking talent. As I got older, I realized she was far more interested in my developing the skills I did have. When my first story appeared in the paper, she smiled at me radiantly.

"Well, there!" I remember her saying. "This is your gift."

Anyway, I do believe that the most important pass-downs in a family are not culinary skills, but traditions that leap silently like skipping rocks from Mom to me to Erin. They morph with every generation, but what remains? Holiday practices, religious beliefs, principles. And certain genetic personality traits: a grassroots feistiness, a love of music and art, and the ability to burp on demand.

My mother did her best to stifle that talent in us all, and Erin lags terribly in the competition. At her age I could belch BUSCH-BAVARIANBEER without stopping for breath.

Lisa was also a queen—not just of belching (she could burp the opening lines of Boston's "More Than a Feeling"!) but of domestic skills. She was a great cook and home decorator, but also a killer seamstress. When Theo, her little angel boy, was little, she made his tiny clothes, including a lined overcoat. And she designed and made hats. *Hats*. With her own hands.

I still have two of them hanging in my bedroom to remind me of my clever sister. Well, to remind me of the happier memories. Days on the beach near her SoCal home, her blushing announcement that she was pregnant at last, phone calls that would *start* with her salutation: "Bitch!" She was so funny, so wickedly clever.

There was a reason everyone called Erin "Lisa" by accident when she was growing up: they not only looked alike—fair and freckled and blond—but seemed to be cut from the same crazy quilt. Erin auditioned for the Shakespeare play at her private Middle School for Brainiacs (as we liked to call it) by reciting Monty Python's "lady of the lake" soliloquy from *Holy Grail*:

"Strange women lying in ponds distributing swords is no basis for a system of government! Supreme executive power derives from a mandate from the masses, not from some farcical aquatic ceremony!"

And Lisa, in turn, knew how to do a wicked rendition of Python's Fish-Slapping Dance, although she'd use whatever else was at her disposal—wet dishcloths, tennis rackets—in place of the dead Piscean creatures used in the original sketch.

She, whose romantic history was sketchier even than mine until she met her husband, Terry, told me once that she didn't understand why I kept falling for short-term, dead-end relationships. "I know being single is a drag, but you ought to value yourself more. Being married is not the pot of gold at the end of the rainbow; you should stop worrying about being married and focus more on being loved by someone right for you."

It was excellent advice—and one of these years I plan to follow it.

And if anyone could have remembered Mom's strawberry shortcake recipe, it would have been Lisa, Mom's clone, born on her thirty-second birthday. That dessert was good in a completely unfancy, Southern way, as befitting my mother's poor childhood in Central

Florida: sweetened Bisquick biscuits sawed in half, filled with chopped-up summer strawberries, also sweetened, topped with both (sweetened) whipped cream and milk.

I've tried it dozens of times in the past few years but have never captured what it was that made hers so good. Something was always missing. The biscuits fell apart, or weren't sweet enough, the strawberries got too soupy from sitting. By the time we realized how ill my mom was, there was no time to ask her to write down the recipe. Or it hardly seemed the most important thing to talk about.

In fact, strawberries were key in my realization that Mom was doomed. Dad was away on one of his incessant walkabouts—his trips to the desert to play golf or visit his sister in the Tetons—so I went over to have dinner. I was startled to find her sartorially proper self disheveled (had she suddenly become a wino?) and the entire house in shambles. Especially the kitchen: there was leftover food everywhere, including some TV dinner trays *(my mother?)* with scraps still clinging to the tin.

And by the sink: a basket of strawberries that she'd left out on the drain board for so long that they had nearly liquefied. There was a river of strawberry juice running like blood across the counter.

The fact that she, the compulsive kitchen neatnik, didn't consider this problematic told me she was in dire straits. When I pointed out the potential health department violations in the kitchen, she just sighed, and looked at me with ill-focused eyes. "I'm just tired, that's all."

I called Dad immediately and he headed for home; Anne, Rob, and Lisa all agreed Mom had sounded loopy on the phone lately. Could someone get advanced Alzheimer's in a week's time? Should we hire a caretaker immediately to prevent future strawberry rivers? We talked breezily, tight as siblings can be, to hide our terror.

A few days later the tests revealed a brain tumor the size of a golf ball on the lobe of her brain that governed personality, hence her descent into slow speech, the diminution of her sparkle, and the loss of her fashion sense. Surgery was hastily planned for the next day. "Well, at least we'll now have irrefutable proof that I have a brain," she joked haltingly to Erin, who laughed bravely in Mom's company but sobbed herself to sleep that night. Just like that, there were no more family dinners, no more strawberry shortcake.

God, I should have asked her how she made it while she could still talk. Or Lisa, who'd have known it. But there was no time. No time to breathe, let alone have recipe-exchange parties. I remember the tender look on Lisa's face when she flew up to see Mom at the end and came into her sickroom at home. Mom had lingered in a coma for a week—long past the time we expected her to slip away. Lisa took her hand, and I heard her whisper: *"It's okay, I'm here, we're all gathered. You can go now."*

And so she did, within hours, at the behest of her most-adored youngest. Who, it turns out, had her own crisis in the works.

When Lisa told me, just three weeks after we'd buried Mom's ashes in the garden at church, that she probably had cancer, too, that she'd suspected this for a while, I just stared at her.

"If you leave, you're taking me with you," I told her evenly, despite inner screaming. "Because I can't bear to be left behind again."

She smiled, looking pale but of course elegant in her handmade hat and perfect Ralph Lauren outfit at Puck's cafe in Manhattan Beach. She came to need those hats when she lost her hair. But she never lost her sense of humor—or her commitment to being the perfect hostess, much like our mom.

I went to Manhattan Beach to visit her when she was about a month from dying, and she had put fresh flowers in the guest room, where the bedsheets were turned down. When she died eleven months after Mom, leaving me behind (and saying there was much I still had to do), in a fit of grief I vowed to take up her love of all things Martha Stewart: gourmet meals, a perfectly decorated home, and neat-as-a-pin attire. But then reality, as it always does, interrupts my self-improvement plans. Grief makes me a slob, not a princess, alas.

I let everything go to weeds: my house, my body, my boyfriend. I didn't want anything or anyone to love me, and I sure as hell didn't want to love anyone. Only Erin understood my raging withdrawal; only she stood staunchly, like a blond angel with a mighty left hook, between me and a deeper depression, refusing to let me slide. She could have spent that summer working on the East Coast, but instead she came home to me, her flawed and grieving mom, to charm me back to life. I suppose I could have used that summer to learn to cook, but, I figured, why start now?

So Erin got the short end of the domestic stick. No sitting at my side while I taught her the fine art of crocheting, no whipping up cocktail dresses on the Elna, and for sure no cooking lessons. But I did the best I could. And crossed my fingers that Erin would look to my more worthy family members for role modeling. So far, it's working out pretty well.

"Hey, I have an idea!" Erin says. "I'll just keep it really simple and do like you used to do for dessert: cut a cantaloupe in half and put strawberries and ice cream in it!"

Ingenuity and the ability to think on the fly: this she gets from me.

"There you go!" I respond. "And, hey, honey, how old is Alex, anyway?"

"He's twenty-five—the oldest guy I've dated yet!"

"Wow, the same age as Graham, that musician I dated from Austin," I marvel aloud. "Remember him?"

"Ewww, Mom, I'm hanging up now! I really don't want to think about this. Love you."

I don't blame her for being grossed out, but she ought not be surprised. She knows younger men were my vice for many years. And why not? At that age, they haven't yet figured out that the world revolves around them. And they sure as hell aren't babies when they get sick.

Of Tadpoles and Locusts

The monthly salon is over—well, nearly. This month's attendees are up from their bench seats on the patio at Foreign Cinema and milling around, eager for the kind of intimate chitchat that comes with free wine and close proximity. As a gaggle of women congregate, the talk turns to *Tadpole,* the film just out about a forty-year-old woman who sleeps with her best friend's fifteen-year-old son.

Everyone seems to agree that sleeping with a teenager would be (a) morally bankrupt, and (b) with all the groping and what-goes-where confusion, about as thrilling as watching those ninth-grade sex-ed films again.

A few women defend the film on grounds that *Lolita* is considered a classic. "Why the hell should women deny themselves the thing that men have made acceptable—dating someone much younger?" Claudia demands. "I think one reason women turn to younger men is that men their age are off trying to get laid by co-eds!"

Everyone here has a story about a romantic relationship with a younger man. How much younger? Eight years, twelve years, fifteen years. But I trump them.

"Twenty years," I say. All eyes turn to me.

"I know, ladies," I sigh, looking at their incredulous faces. "It's hard to believe with my recent run of bad luck, but it did happen! Some of you would remember Graham, that young musician from Texas. He was so cute and brilliant—and hot to trot. I was forty-five or so and he was twenty-five. It didn't last very long, but it was a great ego booster while it did."

Rosalind, who's known me longer than anyone here, laughs. "I remember Texas boy! You guys don't realize Jane was a serial cradle-robber for years. Remember that young KQED intern? He was a hottie, too."

I can't help but smile at the memory. Yes, that was certainly a major phase—wrought by crisis. After the Years of Death and Departure, my emotional lights were punched out to the point that I sought help from a therapist. She suggested that I was continually hooking up with younger men as a way of guaranteeing that any relationship I got into would be temporary. That commitment scared me worse than societal judgment. I knew she had a point, but I didn't care. I didn't want to love anybody deeply anymore. I said bring on the temporary fixes, the Band-Aids on my heartbreak, and make 'em cute.

"He always said he wanted to go with me to Paris when I turned fifty," I tell my bug-eyed friends. "That was, honestly, one of the sweetest things any man has said to me!"

"Well, there you go!" Claudia laughs. "There's the date for your fiftieth you've been angsting over."

"Yeah, I wish," I sigh. "I told him at the time that I wouldn't hold him to it, that my fiftieth was still a ways in the future, and that I expected him to find someone his own age before then. Damned if he didn't do it."

I didn't hold it against him that he didn't wait for me; there was no future tense in our relationship, so there was no reason to hold out for me. Oh, but how I used to enjoy the present tense—and not just with Graham, but with all younger men. I was addicted to their smooth bodies and uncomplicated ways. And all it took to force me into rehab was falling in love.

"Anyway," I tell my friends, "that's ancient history. You guys know I've wised up. There's too much risk involved."

"Marco . . . ?" asks Rosalind.

"You got it!" I sigh. "The perfect blend of Pirate and Nice Guy—and the only one since I was in college to really break my heart."

Not that it ever had much of a chance, given the fifteen-year age difference, and the fact that Lisa was only three months gone—and Erin six months away—when we hooked up. I was such a mess! The dancing wounded. Acting like I was fine during the day, but crying or drinking myself to sleep at night. That was before I had friends like these, who would have wrapped me in their arms and shortened the grieving process.

"I'd forgotten that someone actually broke your heart!" says Peter, interjecting himself into the all-female chat circle with a sly grin. "That doesn't seem possible for my tough girlfriend."

"Ah, well, and yet it did happen!" I chuckle bitterly. "He ended it, saying he wanted to find someone his age who could give him kids."

Everyone winces as if chewing lemons.

"Sounds like a column?" Claudia smiles. "Damn, I wish I had your job so I could vent a few male-related frustrations myself. . . ."

Hmmm. Marco and I are still friends. I wonder if he could take a little ribbing? I decide to give it a go; he probably won't recognize himself anyway.

The one time a boy toy became a boyfriend, our relationship provided an ongoing target for needling by friends and family. His sisters asked him if he had to cut my food for me when we dined; my friends asked me if I picked him up in the family station wagon after football practice. Har har har.

But eventually, when the inevitable where-are-we-going-with-this discussion came to pass, it ended predictably. He wanted kids; I had been there/done that/couldn't do it easily again. I wanted some kind of free-form passionate relationship on into the sunset; he wanted a traditional marriage. But not with me. I was, it seems, too old.

It still hurts a bit when I read this, sitting at my table on Sunday morning, four years after the fact.

At least this time it sent home the message: if you are going to dally with someone younger, make sure you don't fall in love, unless he wants the same things as you! And nowadays, when I consider what to look for in potential dates, gray hair and laugh lines are high on the list. Who says you can't learn from experience?

I fold up the newspaper. Ah, that was satisfying—a good purge, as it were. Maybe this will make it so I can stand to be around him now with his dates, since I still see him all over town. He always looks so damn happy.

The next day my cell phone rings and I recognize the number. "Hi, Marco."

"So that was me, right?" he teases. "The one you were crazy about but who wanted kids?"

Suddenly irritated, I think, why should I give him the satisfaction? "You're not the only younger man I've dated, Marco."

"Yeah, but didn't you tell me I was the *last*?"

Pause. "I refuse to answer on the grounds that it's *none of your damn business.*"

Laughter on the other end. "Okay, how about you? Who are you dating these days? Have you found your Leo?"

I used to needle him about being a Pisces and wishy-washy.

"No, not even close," I sigh, suddenly feeling one-down since he always seems to have a date and I don't. "Who are you dating these days?"

"No one lately," he admits. "Are you going to the Writers Grotto party tomorrow?"

"Yeah, so I'll see you there, *younger man* . . . ," and I hang up abruptly, determined to get the last word.

The phone rings immediately and I figure it's Marco again. "*What?*" I bellow, without looking at the caller ID.

"Mom? Are you having a nervous breakdown? Because I can call back . . ."

"Hi, honey! No, Marco is just pestering me about whether he was the guy in the column Sunday. He seemed a little perturbed about it."

Laughter on the other end. "Well, I kind of don't blame him. How many years has it been now since you and he broke up? You really need to give it a rest."

"Fine," I say. "You can take this position because you have men falling at your feet. And I am becoming more of an old maid every day. How is the new guy, anyway—what's his name? Alan? Alex? Shmo-lex? This has been going on a couple months now. Are you in love?"

Silence.

"It's Alex, Mom. I don't know how I feel about him. Can we not talk about it?"

I can always tell when my daughter's emotions are getting involved in a tryst because she gets prickly and unsure of herself, just like so many women.

"Can I still come home for dinner and spend the night tonight? I need time with you and the kitties. Can we go to Tres Amigos for burritos?"

"You only like to go there because it's a surfer hangout and you always recognize some cute guy from the jetty break. But sure, if you don't mind being seen with this wizened, grizzled geezer . . ."

More laughter. "I'm hanging up now! Love you!"

Actually, this Grotto party might be just what the doctor ordered. I am in need of both a jump-start and an ego boost. Lately the only men to flatter me with attention are e-mail suitors like the Louisiana Lawyer. It seems like ages since I've been laid—I don't really count that time with Lenny a month ago because it was sleepy morning sex and not high on the satisfaction scale—and this dating drought is reaching biblical proportions. I keep looking toward the sky waiting for the locusts to appear.

But I need to buck up and put on my party face. Most of my good friends and a million colleagues-in-writing would be at this rooftop soiree. I would feel loved and not like a loser. I would exude confidence and sexuality. I would perhaps flirt with Diego, that distinguished, older writer friend of a friend I met recently, since we would both be outsiders in this predominantly thirty-something crowd, and since I think he was into me last time we spoke.

I might even leave there with a date on the horizon.

Here's the thing: there's a huge difference between being single by choice—making a conscious decision to not date for a while, to spend more quality time with your friends, your family, yourself—and being single because no one's calling. One is empowering, whereas the other starts wearing on you after a while. Like a nagging doubt. Like the one tire on your groovy-sports-car life that keeps going flat.

I arrive at the party, appropriately about an hour into it. I'm looking for Diego, who is nowhere to be seen, but run smack into a gaggle of friends, including Dave and Vendela, who are too gorgeous a couple to not be in the movies. She tells me she loves the new column; he looks confused and obviously hasn't read it. "It's a chick thing." I smile with absolution.

"Uh, what does that make me?" asks Craig, entering the circle. He has one hand in his pocket, another is gripping a tortilla chip heaped with guacamole. There is a green spot on his sweater. "Because I read it, too! Thinking it might help me . . . you know . . . with the fairer sex. I guess I'm seeking enlightenment."

"Okay, then I guess it's for chicks—and single men!" I laugh, using a napkin to casually dab the dollop.

"Not true. I read it every week!" says filmmaker Dan, my most-admired married friend next to Po, laughing and giving me a hug.

"He really does!" adds Dayna. "But Dan is . . . rare among men!" She smiles at her partner of almost twenty years. He smiles back, and strokes her back gently in the chill wind. God. Marriage is so good for some people.

"You are such a sweetie," I say. "It's nice to hear that my Sunday riffing appeals to the occasional man."

"Why shouldn't it? Good writing is good writing!" huffs Phil, coming from the bar with a plastic cup filled with brown. I sniff it. "Whiskey," he says grimly. "Don't ask."

I reckon it has to do with his marriage, which I fear is fraying. She never seems to be with him anymore. Before he can say another word, his cell phone rings and he checks the number and winces. He goes off to talk furtively, out of earshot. Marriage really sucks for some people.

I distract myself by feasting my eyes on the sea of young trout up here. So many young men, none of whom would deign to leap upon my carving platter.

And of course, I run smack into Marco.

"You look great," he flirts, kissing my cheek chastely. "Are you sure you're not seeing someone?"

"Well, you this minute!" I flirt back, pleased that he still thinks I'm pretty. I certainly still think he's attractive, not handsome, really—he's too short and stocky for that. But beautiful coloring: blue Irish eyes and Middle Eastern dark hair and goatee ("I'm all terrorist," he used to joke), and a smile bigger than the Golden Gate.

I add quickly, realizing I don't want to sound like a complete loser: "Well, I've had that ongoing thing with that musician, Lenny; I told you about him. But the jerk didn't call me on my birthday, so I don't consider him really an option these days so . . . no, I'm not seeing anyone."

For a moment, I wonder if Marco is experiencing a resurgence of interest, but he abruptly changes the subject.

"So that was me in your column, right?" He smirks.

I roll my eyes. "What do you *care*? What's the matter, aren't you getting enough attention these days? Do you need a hug?"

Rosalind thankfully interrupts our conversation by walking up to us, looking her usual va-va-voom self. "Hello, sweet thing!" she teases Marco, whom she will always view as a child. She sweeps back her hair dramatically with a well-manicured hand.

"Where's Dieter?" I ask her.

"He'll be along in a minute." Rosalind leans in, out of Marco's earshot. "I am so ready to kill him. We had yet another fight about setting a date, and he just can't. It's always something—finances, the art market—both of which I *know* are doing just fine!"

She shuts up when Dieter bounds over, shakes Marco's hand, and gives me the Euro-kiss on both cheeks. He looks around. "Who's your date tonight?"

Before I can answer, Marco interjects for me: "She says she's not dating anyone! Can you believe it?"

"I have to go now," I say, flushing.

I see Claudia in another group of friends who are all raising their glasses to a couple I know—a gorgeous and talented duo involved in art and film production. "What's going on?" I ask.

"We're getting married!" she says, smiling. "We got engaged in Paris."

Her forty-ish fiancé, clearly smitten, notes that he waited awhile to tie the knot. "But she was worth waiting for."

Oh gawd, another couple off to the altar. I wrestle with alternating feelings of jealousy and pity, wondering whether their marriage will be painful or great, and raise my glass politely. And then I notice that Claudia is looking a tad blue. "God, where's *mine*?" she sighs. "I really thought this last guy, the artist, might be going somewhere, but that went belly-up this week. He's got a lot of problems—bipolarity least among them. But God, he was hot. Why can't I fall for someone boring but nice?"

"I hear you sister. Pirates—they're a weakness."

I spy Marco in the distance. He's talking to a group of women that includes my friend Elsa. I didn't know he knew her. But it makes sense—she is politically involved and, damn it, his age. I feel a rumbling of jealousy in my gut. Sigh. Why can't I accept it? There is no cheese at the end of that particular mouse maze.

Still, I can't resist interrupting. "So, you two know each other?" I ask, after greeting Elsa with a kiss. They look slightly embarrassed. No, they both say at once. So I make introductions, and they are quickly back into lively conversation, causing me to feel like a creaky third wheel.

Thankfully, I finally spot Diego and he's talking to Peter: perfect opportunity to insinuate myself. "Girlfriend!" Peter greets me. It's good to see him out and about; he tends to isolate himself. "Are you feeling better? I know you were sick. Are you taking your B-vitamins?"

Peter: the closest thing I have to a Jewish mother.

"You know I am, but at this point I think my age is just as much to blame as the flu bug," I sigh. "How about you? How are you doing?"

"Well, I hardly want to put this out for fear of jinxing it, but my agent tells me that a film company might be interested in my first book. They approached her about buying the rights!" He flashes a crooked smile, pulling his Carhartt coat closed as the fog starts to crash like waves across the rooftop.

"That's amazing!" I throw my arms around him. "That is huge! Diego, you've been through this, maybe you can give him some pointers?"

Diego laughs. "The best pointer I can give is to keep your guard up. Hollywood will fuck you for a nickel."

With his distinguished gray hair, ubiquitous hippie vest and beret, Diego seems quite out of place here; perhaps I do, too, but I just don't know it. When Peter leaves to seek out Rosalind and Dieter, Diego asks me how I feel about being a decade older than the average attendee there.

"I think we need to start a writers' workspace for writers with gray hair, or at least with some goddamn *talent*!" Diego grouses, his jealousy over the splendor of the Grotto as plain as the large nose on his face.

We laugh about the fact that we both participated in San Francisco's antiwar protests during the Moratorium year of 1969 (I was in high school, he in college) and danced around in a giant circle in Golden Gate Park, smoking pot and making daisy headbands. And in his charismatic presence, I don't mind so much being this age; it gives me a sense of history, perspective, and dignity.

Diego excuses himself to get a beer, and when he doesn't return, I peer over toward the bar, where he is leaning into a woman with half my years and twice my breasts.

Okay, can I go now? I think my tie-dye is done cooking.

Marco reappears, breathlessly. “Hey, would it bum you out if I gave Elsa a ride home? I really like her, but I don’t want this to become an issue. . . .”

My stomach twists, but I go into gracious hostess overdrive. “Oh, don’t be silly! I can deal. It’s fine. She’s closer to your age. Then again, most of the women in the world are!”

Ha ha ha! I laugh without a shred of joy. And my darling boy kisses my cheek and heads off into the night, where his future looks a lot different—and a lot younger—than I do.

Po finds me a few minutes later, offers a hug and a kiss. “Who are you with tonight? Did you bring a date?” he asks, looking around.

I draw a breath. “Well, no. But you know, it’s great to be single! It is! So much fun to be had!”

He senses my irony. “You really, really ought to try online dating. I don’t know why you haven’t already,” he admonishes. “If nothing else, you should do it for your column! Set yourself up as a human guinea pig!”

“A human guinea pig?” I sigh. “Wow . . . so it’s come to this.”

“Hey”—Po puts his arm around my shoulder and gives it a squeeze—“I’m just trying to help.”

I peer into the night sky, and the stars seem to form a constellation in the shape of the number 50. The fog clouds are beautiful racing by, but can the locusts be far behind?

SWF, 49, Seeks Leo

With Po's advice ringing in my ears, and the phone not ringing at all, I'm considering fishing in the virtual love pond. My pals are urging me to shop the online personals—where I might find at least a few handsome, brilliant, bohemian Pirates mixed in with the deviants and insurance salesmen—and take my chances with total strangers.

It's also a write-off, I realize. I can plunder this gold mine for a kick-ass column.

But I'm hesitant. I've always equated cruising for dates online with scribbling your name on a bathroom wall ("For a good time call . . ."), or standing on a street corner wearing a sandwich board that proclaims "DESPERATE! WILL GO OUT WITH ANY GEEK!" Neither modus operandi is likely to lead me to Leo. And it's also hard to interpret this action as anything other than a complete and total capitulation to the fact that I can no longer attract a suitable suitor in the flesh.

"Oh, please, could you possibly be any more 1990s?" chides Claudia in an e-mail. "You are hopelessly stuck in the previous century. It's certainly better than waiting for Lenny to get serious or for men like Diego to get their heads out of their collective asses."

She started "doing the online thing" after 9/11, when those purveyors of virtual love really started to flourish. She found it less intimidating than going to a SoMa martini bar or the music venues she and I frequent, which, after all, might be targeted for an al-Qaeda attack. But because she's stunning, she's frequently hit on by men, so why would she go online to find quarry?

"Because when you do find someone right, it's a total rush!" she writes back from her desk at the publishing company. "And it's like a smorgasbord; you can scan through 100 men in an hour. But don't forget—whether you find someone has everything to do with *where* you look. Match.com is like Wal-Mart—the meat is far from gourmet quality. Nerve.com is like Whole Foods for shopping—a more interesting, countercultural menu. And Jdate.com is like shopping . . . I don't know . . . in a kosher deli?"

I notice that the younger my friends are, the less chagrined they are to be playing this game. Those in their thirties, like Claudia, think *I'm* weird for thinking *it's* weird. Those in their forties had to get past the same associations I have: equating online personals with those psychosexual pleas for intervention found in free weekly papers. You know: "SWM seeks SWF for sunset walks on the beach, romantic dinners, and illicit acts with Wesson oil, rubber chickens, and Ping-Pong paddles."

My friends who tried it met with varying degrees of success. Two met men they ended up dating for quite a while; the rest have had many one-date encounters; none found Mr. Right. But neither did any of them come away from the experience any the worse for wear, or needing to file a restraining order. And all of them got laid.

"You really should do it—if not for yourself, then for your readers," Claudia continues her selling job. "Consider it investigative journalism!"

"Oh Christ, I'm tired of hearing that. Po said the same thing," I type back testily. "I already spill my guts for their reading pleasure; now I have to embarrass myself as well? . . . Oh hell, why not?"

Maybe I'm just wigged out by this because it's such foreign territory. I've always done my flirting in person. It seems strange, and a little sad, to be courting someone in writing rather than face-to-face. *Hey, baby, what's your font?* It's the new millennium, I guess.

Putting a toe in the water, I first go to Wal-Mart—aka Match.com. But, as I find with all of these, you need to register if you want to do any serious trolling. And in order to register, you need to prepare a profile of your own. Glancing at the profiles by other women, I can see there are delicate equations at work here. If you're getting older and show it in your face—for example, laugh lines and poochiness—you should have a great body if you want to get dates. *Forty-nine-year-old gym Nazi who worshipped the sun offers knowledge of the Kama Sutra—and a 24-inch waist . . .*

Clearly, if it's all about equations, I've messed mine up.

It was always: skinny frame + great hair − no tits = attractive.

Nowadays it's: blubber on skinny frame + great hair − no tits = unattractive.

At least the hair is still pretty fabulous—more so now than when I was young. I was born with the wrong hair color—mousy light brown. It was only when I started going gray at thirty-five and Nikas kept boosting the red when he covered the gray that my birthright was restored. I was supposed to be a redhead! Look at my pale skin and freckles, for chrissakes.

That's it! Red Writer. This shall be my handle. No photo of course—I am a (ahem) public figure now. I don't need my readers knowing of this little experiment. And I have so little privacy as it is.

So I set forth on the search and am, of course, quickly addicted. I slog through a dozen Web sites, and hundreds and hundreds of smiling male personals, convinced that any minute now, someone I might actually be attracted to might appear. The biggest problem is finding someone even remotely close to my type. The vast majority of men over forty-five on these sites seem to lack even the teensiest bit of an edge—it's as if they'd sprouted from the ground wearing Izod shirts or sincere-looking ties. Those who list their sign as Leo get bookmarked; those who say they don't believe in astrology get passed over. Long hair is the first eye-catcher, but in general this is one sad-looking group.

The photos are a shameless plunge into cheese: men pose shirtless by their sports cars, take photos of themselves in mirrors (allowing the camera to show), appear doing all manner of sports, the more macho the better. It's all rather sickening.

"Look at this one!" I point to the screen, as Erin walks by eating a Popsicle from my freezer. She is home to look at online brochures for LSAT review courses and use my home printer since she doesn't want her employers to know she's abandoning them a year from summer for grad school. She peers at the profile and bursts out laughing. " 'I'm So Lonely?!' That's how he advertises himself? God, that's so sad! I wonder who he'd attract with that headline?"

"Women who are also 'so lonely,' I would imagine. And look at this one." I pull up another profile on my screen. "This guy gives 'No STDs' as a point in his behalf."

"This is tragic, Mom. Please tell me you're not going to actually meet any of these people! They might be ax murderers or rapists. And anyway, they're all too boring for you."

She knows my addictions too well. How I wish I liked men who were nothing but *nice.* But nice all by itself, without an even slightly rough edge to scrape myself against, isn't enough to turn me on, or even have date number two.

Part of me hates that I'm hardwired this way. Part of me thinks I'm entitled to that dichotomy. Is it too much to ask for a man who has a foot in both worlds? Who is both exciting and edgy, yet kind of heart and gentle of nature? Perhaps a Formula I race-car driver who shows up at your door with fresh-picked daisies? Or a world-traveling photojournalist who has long hair and scars but who starts conversations with "Can we share our feelings for an hour or two?"

This is Leo personified. Am I crazy to think someone like this exists online? Judging by the mugs I'm perusing, I'd say that's a big yes.

I can also see that I am missing the love boat by spending my evenings at literary events. If you can believe these profiles, everyone else is off "dancing till dawn," "kayaking the Russian River," "watching the sunset at Ocean Beach," and "training for triathlons." For some reason, no one ever lists his or her hobbies as sitting around the house in their sweats on weekends drinking beer and watching TV, or surfing for porn on the Internet.

I do, however, manage to find a few guys who look like they might have a few Pirate genes—and are fairly attractive to boot. So I send them each an e-mail—promising to send a photo if they respond—and then sit back with fingers crossed, that they might in some way resemble Leo, or at least be interested in being my fiftieth birthday man, or at the very, very least be someone to make me stop wondering when I get to see Lenny again.

One of the potentials is a Marin-ite (5 points) who has a film production company (10 points), is politically active (10 points), and has longish hair (100 points). Because the fall 2002 election is coming up, he makes it clear that his time will be limited by his political activity. He writes that he also makes plenty of time for his hobby: solo dancing. Solo dancing? I write back.

"Yeah, I drop in on classes. I put on my leotard, we light candles and incense, and shake our booties to world music!" he writes proudly.

Okay. . . . Next? I mean, I love a sensitive man, but not one in spandex.

I hear back from Bachelor #2—a guy whose photo includes a little puppy dog (cuuute!). His writing is crisp, he seems smart and funny, is involved in the arts, and he's my age and dates women my age—that is, he's not looking for Lolita. For the first time, I get the rush Claudia promised.

We meet for lunch in downtown San Francisco, but he is late, he says apologetically, because he had to circle the block until he found a parking space in the shade so the blind toy poodle in his car would not get overheated. During our hour-long lunch, he has to go to the car twice to let Boopsie out to wee-wee. He's also older than he said in his profile—close to sixty—and is, in fact, unemployed.

Now, being penniless has never been a deal-breaker for me—many of my Pirate lovers were less than solvent. But I don't know that I could ever compete with a blind poodle. Please, bring on Bachelor #3.

This one is a writer, like me, who lives on the Peninsula, as I do. My age, or so he says. Good sense of humor. And our e-mail chemistry is red-hot. Because our profiles are anonymous, there is a lot of guessing going on as to who the other might be. We figure we must know each other somehow. He will allow that he is a sportswriter, both freelance and AP. He tells me his first name, as a tease to having lunch on the weekend.

I go talk to a friend in Sports the next day—does he know someone by this first name who writes for AP, lives on the Peninsula, and covers San Francisco teams? "Oh, yeah, that's" so-and-so, he says. "Great guy. Nice wife, a couple of kids. Why do you ask?"

I catch myself before the words *are you fuckin' kiddin' me* leap from my mouth. "No reason!" I smile. "Just curious. I met him . . . the other day . . . and, you know, forgot his last name. . . ."

When I e-mail him to ask what the hell he's doing, he confides that he has been surfing the Net for women to have affairs with for a couple of years now. "My marriage is very unhappy," he writes sheepishly. "She barely notices my absences."

"Call a marriage counselor," I respond. "Or a call girl. But don't call me." I don't hear from him again. Where married men once had a certain no-strings appeal, they now only represent hassles, and who needs more of those?

I am fuming at the amount of time I've spent in this enterprise, which has lurched over the line from investigative journalism to an ego trip. And worse, when I think about writing what I've learned about these guys, I realize I can't. I just don't have it in me to torpedo my unsuspecting respondents (even though Dude #3 deserved it); I don't mind baring my sordid life in print but it's not fair to strip them naked as well.

But my column is due, so I decide to write about the generalities of what I'd learned, and finish it with a list of advice for the men out there who use online personals sites to seek "that certain special someone." Most of them do it very, very badly.

- *"No STDs" is not a romantic description of yourself. It's creepy.*
- *"A friend put me up to this" makes anyone answering your ad feel as if they're twisting your arm.*
- *If the word "lonely" appears in your self-description, you're probably bound to be just that a while longer.*
- *Smart women are attracted to offbeat names (i.e., the one you give yourself when you register). Bad: "Normal Guy." Good: "Sartre Devotee."*
- *Try to find a photo that doesn't look like a mug shot. The most popular, least-threatening photos seem to be of men doing manly things: sailing, skiing, etc. The least effective: a photo of yourself taken in the mirror, which makes it appear that you have no friends. Extra*

points: the yoga devotee whose photo made him look like a pretzel. Hmmm, promising!

- *Very few women use the word "gal" anymore, or "lady." We are women. (Or at least girls, or grrrls, until we become women.) Hear us roar.*
- *Honesty is the best policy. Men whose ads claim that they're superhuman ("Handsome! Sensitive! Strong!") make most women immediately suspicious.*
- *Bonus points for describing your dream woman as a pushing-50, pushy redhead.*

Oh, yeah, and don't be a self-absorbed Marin County New Ager, keep your blind poodle at home, and if you're going to fuck around, get a divorce first.

After the column runs, I get a ton of responses—many from people who have juicy horror stories to share.

One guy met a woman with a "Marlene Dietrich voice," and was in full make-out mode when his date confessed she was really a he. A woman from the East Bay was being fully romanced by a dreamy doctor she'd met on Match.com, when a friend pointed out to her that he was cruising chat rooms for anonymous B&D sex. (Amazingly, when confronted, he didn't think this ought to be a deal-breaker.)

Another woman had planned to meet her anonymous date on the Embarcadero, near the Ferry Building. She was there at the appointed time, saw a man get out of a car, look her way, and nonchalantly get back into the car and speed away. She stood in the whipping wind and fog another half-hour before she realized that had been her date, and he was not impressed enough, or kind enough, to even say hello.

It made me recall the words of Richard Brautigan, upon whom I hazarded my senior thesis in college: "This might have been a funny story if it weren't for the fact that people need a little loving and, God, sometimes it's sad all the shit they have to go through to find some."

It reminds one that celibacy, while occasionally lonely, is devoid of the bullshit of dating. That grass looks browner, not greener, after this little trial.

I do get a sweet e-mail from Louisiana Lawyer, who chides me: "So you'll go out with total strangers in your hometown but you won't let me come to Frisco and meet you? Don't you know me well enough by now to know you'll like me?"

I frown at the screen. As much as I'd love to meet someone, I'm still not ready for the pressure of him flying two thousand miles to see me. And based on what I've learned in this little experiment, how can anyone trust what they read in e-mails? Especially from someone who uses the tacky word *Frisco*?

"No," I answer. "I don't know you well enough yet. But some day . . . Just give me time. Keep talking to me."

I suppose it's possible that the lawyer would rock my world if we ever do meet, but I'm tired of online romance. I guess I haven't given up the fantasy about the magic that happens when you clap eyes on someone in the flesh. In person. As it happened when I met Lenny.

And as it apparently happened when Marco met Elsa.

I get an e-mail from him, asking shyly how I would feel if they went out on a date? The lump in my throat threatens to throttle me. What the hell? Where's *mine*? I want to write. But instead, I collect myself a minute before responding carefully: "I think that's wonderful. I love you both and why shouldn't you date? The only thing I ask is that you let me know if this is gonna become something more serious. San Francisco is too small a town and we run in the same circles. I just don't want to be surprised. Okay?"

After I click the send button, I sit back and unconsciously put my hands on my own throat, perhaps trying to keep the lump from getting any bigger. This is a Good Thing I've done. And if we'd had this conversation in person or over the phone, I would probably have said something clunky or imperious.

So I guess as much as online relationships can help us lie, e-mail can also allow us the time and thoughtfulness to be our best selves.

Still, I can't help but feel old—older than I've felt in a long time. *You kids go run out and play! And date and fornicate! Grandma is fine here at home—all alone with her computer!*

Third Person Singular

"Mom, that guy was a jerk. And drunk, too! You're not old, you're not invisible, and you're beautiful. You are!"

Erin holds on to me a minute longer than usual as we hug good-bye on Mission Street, the smells of spring citrus blossoms and taquerias wafting past. She looks squarely in my face to see if I'm buying her statements of fact, with an expression that's half anger and half close-to-tears sorrow.

"Honey, I'll be fine. Really!" I say lightly, attempting to convince us both. "I had a great dinner and I'm glad we came. Now go home, you look tired!"

She gives me one more minihug before she heads north to the BART station and I head for my car that will take me south to the coast. If it's possible, I think she feels worse about tonight's little aging-based embarrassment than I do.

This aging thing is inescapable and in-my-face as I lurch toward fifty: it's the elephant in every room of my house—at least those rooms with mirrors. On most days, I have an uneasy truce with the calendar. I've managed to cheat the Frump Gods by being genetically (thanks,

Mom!) graced with younger-looking skin than I'm entitled to, and staying at least moderately current on attire. I'm not sucking down the hormone replacements—yet. I'm hardly out to pasture; in fact, I'm busier than I've ever been.

"I'm doing great! I'm looking good!" I think to myself most days.

But then come the increasingly frequent boots to the head that remind me that the double whammy of aging and being unmarried is torture worthy of the Tower of London. (Anne Boleyn! Get thee to the loneliest tower, gain thee fifteen pounds, and never get thy knickers peeled off again!)

The other night at dinner, my dad said, "Honey, have you gained weight? After Aunt Mary visited last week she said she was worried about you after being so nice and thin your whole life." I handled it well in the restaurant—meaning I didn't stab him in the ear with my butter knife—but burst into tears as soon as I got in the car.

I couldn't be angry, unless it was at my dad's lack of sensitivity. He was right. Some days I barely recognize my body: my wiry frame covered by some kind of fleshy cushioning ("At least I'd live through the winter if I were in the Donner Party!" I recently joked to Erin) and my cute, perky butt now resembling a pair of square, padded ottomans. Sometimes my once-sexy ankles swell to where I can't see the bones, and the tops of my thighs touch for the first time in my life. And if my body is no longer familiar, neither is my brain: I often walk into a room and have to pause, dumbfounded, because I've forgotten my mission.

Chubbing-out and senile! Such a catch!

At the same time, I hate that I even care about this shit. My higher mind knows that for our species to evolve, we have to accept body changes as we hit them, think of every age as beautiful, and quit trying so goddamn hard to stay young. I mean, I see these young women on TV and in the movies and at parties and am unnerved by their perfect bodies—perfect, because every single part has been dissected and surgically reassembled in the image of some *Playboy* fantasy. Sure, they're beautiful, but isn't that cheating?

It all partially explains why I'm becoming invisible to men these days, I think, taking my time getting back to my car and looking in store windows. Luckily it's taken years for me to become invisible; it was so slow enough in coming that I'm barely shocked by it anymore.

Well, almost never.

I pause to look at my car, my red Sebring convertible, before getting in, and wonder if perhaps a Buick sedan would be more appropriate. Once seated, I replay the last hour in my head. It feels a bit like a post-traumatic-stress flashback.

I'd taken Erin and her friend Martine out to dinner at Bruno's in the Mission—a nice middle ground between her need for a happening place and my need for decent food—which is also owned by my friend Jon. He put us ahead of the line and showed us to a sweet corner booth, where we settled in to enjoy the Rat Pack ambience and *calamari fritti.*

Before too long we had company. The two young guys were really, really hammered. They weren't invited to sit with us but here they were, sliding wordlessly into our booth, clutching shot glasses of Jägermeister, the fortification of choice for frat boys everywhere.

They were transfixed by the girls, both symbols of early-twenty-something all-American beauty. Now, both these girls can take care of themselves—when she was just twenty, Erin did a semester of environmental studies in Venezuela, sometimes traveling alone, sometimes having to bat away aggressive men like pesky mosquitoes. She's learned to roll with the inconveniences wrought by her looks.

And this time, she was amused—at their mumbling words of praise, at their idiotic behavior—turning to me with a silent roar of laughter that showed me she wasn't offended. And then, one of them raised his shot glass in a toast. "Here's to you two beautiful girls . . ." he said, leaning flirtatiously in their direction. And then, suddenly realizing I was also there, he turned slightly to me, glass still raised: "And here's to . . . the third person."

The third person? Is that what he said?

I felt a strange flush—and a twinge as if someone were prodding my brain stem with a hot poker. Ay-yi-yi! Hello God, thanks for the reminder! I am in no way, and on no planet, or in any parallel universe, in the same league as my daughter. Nor will I be ever again. I've become *the third person,* which I would guess is neither feminine nor masculine but some kind of mutant life form.

Erin, who has always had the ability to feel my emotions even before I do, suddenly became an angry hornet. "Get out of here!" she hissed at the confused guy, giving him a little help with an elbow as he slid back to the aisle, leaving his shot glass behind.

And then I burst out laughing—the involuntary response to an event both stunning and embarrassing. Martine, though clearly mortified on my behalf, chuckled along with me. Erin was not so amused and wanted to leave.

"Honey, it's okay," I said. "He was too drunk to know he was being insulting."

"He was a *jerk,*" she fumed, cursed as she is with her mother's temper. "But if you're okay, I'm hungry."

I convinced her I was fine. And so I was. Sort of. We finished our food in a haze of awkwardness. And now, driving home, tears get the better of me.

The next day I find myself pouting on Phil's office couch as I tell him the story.

Despite our oft-tumultuous friendship, I get better advice from Phil than from almost anyone I know.

He pauses and looks directly into my eyes. "So let me get this straight: some drunk frat boy insults you by accident and you're all down in the dumps about it?" he demands. "Shake it off! You've had plenty of men around you your whole life. Rock stars and comedians and authors."

"Yeah, just not recently," I sigh. "I'm afraid I ain't got it anymore. It's my ass, I think. It's gone completely south."

"What *are* you talking about?" he asks, exasperated.

"I'm just falling apart. I'm invisible to men, I'll end up going to my fiftieth birthday party alone, and someday they'll find me dead in my kitchen being eaten by my cats. They go for the lips, you know. . . ."

"Just stop," he demands, heading out for an editorial board meeting. "And go write about it. You always say it helps give you back your perspective."

"Okay, fine," I groan. "But that's cutting it a little close to the bone."

One reason Phil, and many of my guy friends, can't hope to empathize is that aging is such a male-friendly process. It seems to make no difference in terms of their ability to be attractive to the opposite sex. I mean, in twenty years of friendship Phil and I have seen each other through a combined four marriages and innumerable relationships. He's also seen my options dwindle to barely finding a date for New Year's Eve, while his never did. His significant females only got more gorgeous as his hair got grayer.

The female friends with whom I shared this incident were, understandably, more sympathetic than the males, and were offended on my behalf. Since most of them are younger than me by a good decade, perhaps they were freaked out at what their own futures might hold: invisibility, mutation, and loss of ass.

"Oh my God, how did you not slap him?" asks Rosalind, who's

about a size six, the size I hovered near my whole life, until the hormone fairy smote me at age forty. "Besides, you still look so great. It was probably just dark and he didn't get a good look at you!"

I pause before I respond. After all, we're in line at the *Chronicle*'s coffee bar and it would break some kind of journalistic brass-ball code to dissolve in tears while waiting for a latte.

"Aw, you're sweet," I sigh. "But you've known me for ten years and you know I'm not the cutie-pie I used to be."

"That shouldn't matter!" says Rosalind, genuinely believing what she says. "You are so good to everyone you know, people love you, you're on a roll with this column, so fuck that guy! And go and write about this. Your experience will probably speak to lots of women. It's all grist for the mill."

"Yeah, that's what Phil said. It freaks me out to expose myself this way and this will be my most personal column yet. But hell, there's not a lot of difference between being half-naked in print and going for the full Monty."

So I pound it out, replacing sadness with anger as I let loose each word.

> *It's really pretty simple. When you get older, you also get smarter, more sex-savvy, and better at relationships. And then the opportunities dry up. Sometimes it feels as if it's all part of a giant cosmic practical joke. But one with which I've become, curiously, almost OK.*
>
> *At least on my good days. On my bad days, I feel like the sky is falling.*
>
> *I'd hate to think the only solution is to age disgracefully—pinching butts of men who are embarrassed by and for me. Let's hope it doesn't come to that. But after years of turning heads and now being referred to as "the third person," the likelihood seems pretty good.*

At least that story has an amusing ending. When my friend Jon, who owns Bruno's, heard about the annoying dweebs, he took action. His bouncer found the offender barfing up his Jägermeister in the bathroom and tossed him out. Who says there's no such thing as instant karma?

There, I sigh, reading it in print. I feel better. I do. Phil was right, and I don't think I come across as a whiner.

"Ms. Ganahl—why don't you stop whining and accept it?" says the first e-mail I open—marked with the subject line Column Feedback (got me again!). "The reason men don't look at you anymore is because you're an aging white woman. The reason so many men have moved on to Asian women is because they're NICER. You might as well quit. . . ."

That one goes straight to the shitcan reserved for psychos. Luckily, there are others—many from women who say I have moved them to tears, or made them feel they weren't so alone. It makes getting e-mails from the likes of the Asian lover less painful. And there is the usual assortment of ill-written mash notes.

"Hi Jane I bet you're a babe you write like one so what was that guy's problem anyway? I'm a good guy work for U.P.S. and I like Jagermeister too. How about joining me for a cocktail?"

I forward this one to Erin. "He clearly doesn't get it," I add.

She responds, from her desk at the law firm. "It was probably that same guy at Bruno's and he's trying to make amends. I think you should go for it!"

Louisiana Lawyer e-mails me yet again, challenging as always. "Why do you think women have the market cornered on rejection? Try being a man of fifty-five who is losing his hair, and see how quickly the interest fades."

I respond by telling him this is bullshit; most women I know don't give a crap about hair. That we are far more interested in character, style—the intangibles. I'm not lying. At the same time, I wonder if he has either.

"Then you are a gem of a woman and I really must insist you meet me. I'm sure I would think you're beautiful no matter what your age. I'll send you a ticket, or I'll come out there," he responds.

I sigh and stare at the keyboard, my eyes suddenly welling. And I find myself typing: "Okay, come out. I give in. I would like to meet you."

The next day I'm back in Phil's office with a new spring in my step.

"I can see you're feeling better now." He chuckles as I flop in his armchair and boldly put my feet up on his desk. "Didn't I tell you it was a win-win? You exorcise your shit and we sell some papers."

"Yeah, yeah, I drop my panties in print and you make a few quarters." I laugh. "And guess what? I may have even gotten a date out of it."

That's right. With someone who is falling for my character, not my baby blues nor my seen-better-days backside. Someone who has enough character himself to leave the twenty-something girls to the twenty-something boys. Someone—God help me—who might be Leo.

Of Closets and Crackers

So the Louisiana Lawyer is coming out tomorrow night. Since we decided two weeks ago to come face-to-face, he's been filling me in on all the salient points about him: he's rich, he's a semi-retired lawyer who made a shitload of money on a nationally known insurance fraud case, has two homes, a wine cellar, and, oh, he's rich. He'll be staying at the Fairmont, thank you very much.

He knows all about me, he says, from reading me for lo these several months. This is not something I bargained on with writing this column: meeting someone for the first time who thinks they know me already! He gets a glimpse of my inner life every week, but he is still a mystery to me—short of what superficialities he's told me via e-mail. I feel exposed and vulnerable, but what else is new these days.

The e-mail chemistry has been major—he is a deft writer, and deft writing turns me on—and we've even had a few phone calls. His Southern accent is disconcertingly, but also charmingly, hayseed. He's sent me a photo of him from ten years ago when he settled the Big Case; he has longish blond hair. I sent him a jpeg of a promotional photo they took of me for the column, which has hardly been used. I worry that I'm a lot cuter in the photo than in real life, especially after he reacts to it with great excitement.

"If the face is a map of one's life, you must have led a perfect life!" he writes. "What a dream you are. I can't wait to hold you. I swoon with hope."

And his words make *me* swoon. I'm hardly a schoolgirl, but his e-mails make me feel that way. I'm willing to take Springsteen's "walk out on the wire." I'm more than ready to have my world rocked.

But first there is the gnawing issue of what to wear. This lame question is rattling me beyond reason. This is by far the hardest part of any date these days. Why? Because walking into my closet can be like entering a Chamber of Horrors. Didn't this used to fit me? Was orange mohair really in fashion two years ago when I bought this? Who the hell did I think I was buying this skintight brown-and-turquoise Custo T-shirt? Britney Spears?!

I'm running laps around the hideously common conundrum: does this make me look older . . . *because I'm trying too hard to look young?*

Every woman knows that how she attires herself for a first date is of huge importance. What's the old cliché: you only get one chance to make a first impression? But for women pushing fifty, certain options are just immediately out of the question. Miniskirts any higher than an inch or two above the knee, punk-rock T-shirts, pink feather boas—all of which I admit to having sported before.

Nowadays, I feel the pressure to conform. It sucks because I'm clearly still a teenager at heart.

In fact, one of the greatest injustices in a woman's life is that when you're young and skinny enough to wear sexy/snazzy clothes easily, you're too poor and too clueless about what looks good on you to capitalize on it. Seriously. I look at photos of myself in the eighties (granted, the Dark Ages of fashion) and cringe at my clothes. I just wore anything that struck my fleeting fancy, without a thought to color, proportion, or whether it even flattered me. And now that I'm acutely aware of all those things, it's hard to find fashion that walks the line between gracefully hip and abjectly teenybopper.

Sometimes the best you can do is choose an outfit based on the occasion. Like, for example, the "I'm Meeting a Rich Lawyer Who Is Coming All the Way from Dead Possum Louisiana to Possibly Sleep with Me" occasion.

I choose a simple black dress, above the knee but not much, which should disguise both my pudgy spots and my undersized chest. I also choose some interesting patterned tights and midcalf black boots. Can't dismiss the Boho in me completely.

Erin calls while I'm getting ready. "Where are you meeting him?"

"At the bar at Big Four restaurant in the Huntington. *Lord love a duck*, why did I get myself into this?"

She laughs. "You know, when you get stressed, you always talk like Grandma."

She adds soberly, "And remember this saying, too: 'I should hope to kiss a pig!' It might come in handy. At least you're meeting him in a public place—he could still be a creep."

"Yeah, I suppose," I say, ineffectively trying to put on my tights with one hand. "Although the odds of that are lowered by the fact that he has money."

"Mom," she says firmly. "Many creeps are rich. Look at Hugh Hefner, Donald Trump!"

"Okay, okay," I sigh. "But he has been nothing but gentlemanly and romantic in our e-mails. I'm holding out that he'll be the same thing in person. And these days I'm obsessed with finding a boyfriend before my fiftieth birthday, you know."

"Mom, it's still almost a year away!" She laughs. "You have plenty of time for that. I hope he's romantic and wonderful—you deserve a break."

The phone rings again as I'm walking out the door, and a rumbling bass greets me. "On your way out for the evening? You sound breathless."

Lenny. How is it that men seem to sense when your obsession with them is on the wane?

"Hi, Lenny." I pause to regroup from the headspin I get from hearing his voice. "I am breathless, but because I'm late getting up to the city."

I pause again, torn between wanting a heavy catch-up conversation and the desire to hang up on him for not having called in ages and for missing my birthday lo these five weeks ago. "How are you?" I ask, sighing.

"I'm fine. You know I've got a gig there in a few weeks. Was just about to book my hotel and wondered which one you'd prefer?"

As if I didn't know he was coming to town. As if I don't obsessively check his tour dates on his Web site. I stop myself from saying what I really think. *You fucker, you haven't called me in six weeks and four days and you're presuming we'll be sleeping together? This must mean you're fresh out of babes to bang.* I clear my throat. "Uh, can I answer this question later? Like, after tonight? I'm not sure whether you and I should have a sleepover visit or not."

"Fair enough." He chuckles. "It's my own fault for not calling sooner."

"Yes, I'm glad you realize this!" I snap back. "There's an old Chinese proverb that goes, 'Those who do not remember Jane's birthday do not get to sleep with Jane!' I mean, generally speaking . . ."

There is hearty laughter on the other end. "I'm sorry, kiddo—did I forget your birthday? Can I make it up to you when I come to town? You know you like my presents. . . ."

"I have to go now," I say, refusing to be swept away by his flirtation. "Ta ta! I'll call you later about your visit."

That felt good. Why is it that knowing we have options—in this case a handsome lawyer who's dying to meet me—frees us to be the dazzling bitch-goddesses we were all born to be?

When I walk into the Huntington, stomach atwitter, I see someone who might possibly be Him, but for the fact that his hair, what there is of it, is short, and he's wearing glasses. "Jane?" he says, standing and smiling. We hug awkwardly, and he immediately snaps his fingers at the waiter. A martini glass, empty but for the toothpick, sits in front of him. He orders another, and I request a gin and tonic. Tonic's always good for queasiness, which I'm experiencing in spades.

We make small talk for what seems like ages—the weather, my job, his flight—while he drinks rather quickly. All the while he's looking at me in the strangest way: face tilted down, eyes tilted up, and grinning, like a coquettish high school senior posing for her yearbook photo, thinking she's being alluring. The net effect is strange and off-putting.

Finally, he puts down his drink, sits back in his comfy chair, and slaps his thighs. "Well," he says, in his thick drawl, "what do y'all think?"

I am taken aback. "Of . . . ?"

He doesn't answer verbally, but swings his hands out to the side and puffs out his chest, in the classic, Neanderthal, get-a-load-of-this pose.

"The evening's young!" I mutter, attempting to smile while looking for the nearest exit in case it gets any weirder.

He lets out a roar of laughter. "Damn, darlin', you sure play hard to get! Your e-mails made you sound rarin' to go!"

"Yeah, well, it all depends on the situation, right?" I smile, realizing I'm sounding icy, and that I seem to be dealing with a near-drunk person. "Maybe we should go to dinner. I'm pretty hungry, aren't you?"

We walk a block to the Stanford Court, and while we walk he continues to look at me with this foxlike grin, as if expecting me to suddenly launch into a striptease. But he is physically gentlemanly, not touching me, opening every door, taking my coat, pulling out my chair. I really am trying to be open-minded.

And even as I'm being so, I think, why are you giving this guy more chances than you'd give the average guy? Because he came all this way to see you? Because you've invested several months of e-mail courtship in this already? Or because he has money? God, I'd be disappointed in myself to discover it's the latter. I've never had much money and have always thought that someday it would be a nice commodity to own, but the day I fuck a man I'm not attracted to for his money is the day I don't want to know me anymore.

He peruses the wine list with some disdain; he had thought it might be of higher quality, given the circumstances. "I told you I have my own cellar, right?"

He tells me that he sometimes flies to France to order wine to be shipped home. He also regales me—after our first bottle is consumed, mostly by him—with a tale from his disastrous last trip there. It seems the lovely twenty-two-year-old daughter of a French pal threw herself at him and they had a torrid affair, much to the upset of her father when he found out. And now she is pestering him to fly her over to the United States for a visit. Hearing this feels like having a lemon stuffed in my mouth.

"Wow, a man your age with a twenty-two-year-old?" I sputter, realizing I have little to lose at this point. "Is this a father, or maybe a grandfather, complex at work?"

He laughs. "Honey, what man my age wouldn't go for that?" he drawls, leaning in close.

When the waiter disappears, he begins snapping his fingers impatiently at a Hispanic busboy. "Hey, José, over here!" I want to crawl under the nice tablecloth, and bite his cracker ankle while I'm down there.

Dinner mercifully over, we walk back to the Fairmont, where my car is with the valet. There is stilted silence, and he suddenly pulls me close and kisses me, which is actually okay with me, because sometimes a kiss can tell more about a man than all his blustering buffoonery. This one only furthers the buffoonery. It is ravenous with sloppy lust, all tongue and no lips. I pull back, beyond disappointed but not at all surprised.

The fog is whipping across the top of Nob Hill, and I pull my coat more tightly across my chest as I fumble for something to say. "Why hide those?" he asks loudly, as if addressing passersby as well, pulling my jacket back open to expose my chest area. "Why hide those big boys from the public?" He laughs heartily.

My face flushes and stomach twists. "I have to go," I say. My car arrives by valet that very moment, and I climb in, watching his dumbfounded face in the rearview mirror as I drive away with my life, if not my pride, intact. And I burst into tears within a block. *Stupid, stupid you,* I lecture myself. How needy do you have to be to let something like this happen?

I leave two messages, one for Erin ("Lord love a duck, I should hope to kiss a pig that I just did!") and one for Lenny. I try to control the trembling in my voice. "Sorry I was rushed on the phone today. When you're here in a few weeks, can we just play it by ear? I'm just not sure what I want to do. But it will be good to see your friendly face."

My friends, knowing how much I was betting on this being a great experience, sympathize when I tell them about it—and then, of course, tell me to make a column out of it, just to give the creep some comeuppance. But for once, I can't. It's less about not wanting to hurt his feelings than it is about my own feelings; I can't stand to look the fool yet again.

The Spittin' Image of Betty

"Honey, get up! We need to be out of here in an hour!" I call into Erin's room, still decorated as it was when she left for college: with surfing posters, a cork bulletin board boasting photos of her friends, and a Greenpeace bumper sticker, a framed autograph by Eddie Vedder on her unused desk. The troll stirs. "*I need ten more minutes!*" she hisses, in a strangled tone resembling Regan's before the exorcism.

"Okay, fine, but I need your help on attire. And hey, how about a little 'Happy Mother's Day,' huh?"

"*In . . . ten . . . minutes!*" she growls her final warning. So much for breakfast in bed.

This day has been hard on me since Mom died, and since the fiasco with the lawyer a week ago, I haven't needed any help in the depression department. Even though I adored my mother, the feelings are mixed on this day. She was supportive and loving as world-class mothers are. But I've been dragging a cross bigger than Jesus' my entire life because she was so damn close to perfect.

The four of us kids had a lot to live up to, so high did she set the bar for graciousness, manners, big-heartedness, and general gorgeousness. But I was doubly cursed: I was also, as I've been told by my Southern relatives since childhood, "the spittin' image of Betty." I had her Irish-blue eyes, pale skin, slightly crooked smile, cheeks that plumped up like peaches when provoked by laughter. But that's where our similarities ended. For one thing, she had better taste in men, having married only once to a gem of a man.

But then, there was always a huge gap between my wanting to be like her—wanting her grace and wisdom and je ne sais quoi—and my ability to pull it off. This photo on my bookshelf tells my childhood story: My mother in a Halston-type suit and pillbox hat—a California Jackie Kennedy—smiling determinedly like a model or a political candidate, ushering her four children around at a church function. I was off to one side, tomboyishly awkward at six or seven in a frilly, handmade-by-Mom dress that matched my sisters' but was worn far less elegantly by me: my skinny legs sported socks at different levels and I was wearing one glove instead of two. My sisters and brother were all smiles at the camera, but I, the defiant second child, was impatiently focused off somewhere else.

In my ungainliness, I saw no place where my mother and I intersected as females of the same species. Yet I heard it even then—*you're the spittin' image!*

I can expect to hear similar exhortations several times this morning.

Erin spent the night so we could go to church with the family in Woodside. We'll pay respects to Betty, whose ashes are there under the gigantic oak tree that shades the memorial garden. I do it every year, a token gesture that seems silly when you consider I think of her every day of my life. But going to church is for the sake of the living: it means a lot to my dad, and Erin the Buddha-child has always (I kid thee not) *enjoyed* going to church.

Attire is always an issue when faced with a religious pilgrimage. I felt so comfortable last night at the Fillmore in jeans, leather jacket, and cowboy boots, but now have the heebie-jeebies knowing I need to dress in my church clothes to greet my mother's friends. She had so many. They were equally elegant. And so devoted. It's been six years since Mom died and they still get tearful when they talk to me. *You look just like her!* they say, their eyes full of wonder and sadness at the reminder of the friend they lost. *Thanks*, I usually say. I want to add, *You know, I lost her, too*. But so far never have.

I pick out a straitlaced navy blue Ralph Lauren blazer I would not normally be caught dead in—one of several I took from Mom's closet when Dad couldn't stand to look at her clothes anymore and we divvied them up. The shoulder pads are way too big, but who cares. It fits me. And it fits such occasions.

"Okay, it's been ten minutes!" I call back into Erin's room. "And I already chose my clothes, no thanks to you."

"Okay, I'm awake, I'm awake," she mutters hoarsely, sounding decidedly more human. "Happy Mother's Day, Mommy. I'm sorry Grandma isn't here for you!"

The thought stops me in my tracks outside her door. "Thanks, honey. I wish she were here, too." It's too early in the day to cry.

We arrive at church to warm greetings from my dad, for whom this place is home away from retirement home. My brother, Rob Jr.—a rarer sight around these parts than even I am—is also here, as is my sister-in-law, Julie, who is really more of a sister to me. The boys clearly could not be dragged. Rob is one of those people (found in abundance in NorCal) for whom organized religion offers far less inspiration than does a walk in the redwoods. He's always respected my parents' love of ceremony but feels no compulsion to attend.

"Great to see you!" Dad says jovially, giving us all hugs. "Happy

Mother's Day!" he adds to me and Julie, handing us single roses with plastic cups on the stems.

"Good God, Rob even wore a tie!" I exclaim, lifting his expensive silk accessory high for all to see. "Did you buy that for your fancy gallery opening so you'd look like a normal person?"

"Nice shoulder pads!" he retorts, squeezing the bulges atop my blue blazer. "Was there a sale at the Salvation Army?"

Rob was one of my best friends when we were kids, my partner on the go-kart track.

And as shit-disturbing adolescents, we were perennially in trouble with the parents. As adults, it hasn't been so easy. Rob and Julie have one of those fabulous marriages that are put on the planet to irritate those of us whose luck in soul-mate location is lacking. Being so well married, he's never quite sympathized with me as a single woman. He took me to lunch before my second marriage and asked me why I always had to have a boyfriend and wasn't I worried about the impact on little Erin? I was torn between wanting to thank him and wanting to tell him to mind his own fucking business. In hindsight, of course, I see the love that it took for him to stick his neck out, but at the time I just wanted to lop it off.

He's also one of the funniest human beings on the planet—who used to sit next to me in church and insert lines into the hymns we were singing just to dissolve me in laughter. "Praise God from whom all blessings flow . . . and I could really use some blow . . ."

I really adored him, and probably just wanted his approval.

I keep waiting for him to chide me about the ongoing indignities in the column; instead, he puts his arm around my shoulder as we're walking into church, and smiles. "The column's going great, huh? Lots of letters to the editor every week . . . You must be pleased!"

"I am!" I smile back. More than anything, pleased that he's pleased.

We all sit with Dad and Barbara up in the choir loft, where they sing every Sunday without fail, where Mom lent her gorgeous soprano until months before she died. In my preteen and teen years, I'd sit up here and ponder what it would be like to kiss whichever boy I had my current crush on. After I got my first Serious Boyfriend my junior year, it was all I could do to keep from touching myself up there in the subdued light, so hot was I for Don, a platinum blond senior at the Priory Catholic school. We would kiss until my lips hurt; and the smell of jasmine incense, which he was partial to, almost made me tremble.

I even taught Sunday school here when Don and I were dating, and I had to dress carefully with scarves to cover the hickeys on my neck. Back then the "spittin' image" reminders made me smile; I was catching up to her—if not in graces then in looks. After Don went off to college, swearing to love and remain faithful to me, only to knock up the first of many girlfriends there, I extracted my adolescent revenge on the male species. My boyfriends started stacking up around me like cordwood in the winter; I had love notes left in my locker, phone calls every day, dates every weekend. My mother never said anything, didn't try to tame me. Maybe she realized I'd waited seventeen or eighteen years to come out of her shadow, and she wasn't going to stand in my way.

The riots of spring flowers on the altar remind me of how she loved making these arrangements—the Altar Guild's most skillful craftsman. When she died, I went down to the creek that ran along the front of my parents' three acres and picked handfuls of forget-me-nots and arranged them in a white teapot on the table. "You're good at that, just like Betty," her visiting friend Peggy told me, and my spirits were enormously buoyed.

I manage to get through this morning's service and all its reminders without weeping; at the same time, why tempt fate? Before her friends corner me, which is also impetus for the showers to start, I slip off to the memorial garden with Erin. We've brought a bounteous handful of forget-me-nots that I grew in a pot on my deck, and we put them by where her ashes are. Already there is a single red rose there; my dad has made his visit today.

Erin's speech is brief. "Happy Mother's Day, Grandma . . ." she murmurs, looking down at the unmarked spot where we buried Mom's ashes. She smiles, and tiptoes off through the ivy to find Grandpa.

"So, Mom, everything's going pretty well," I say quietly to this spot in the earth under the ivy, my hands clasped. "Erin's going to go to law school next year, as you hoped she would. Always seeking justice in all things. Litquake is going to be much bigger this year. I don't have a man in my life these days but I think I'm doing pretty well on my own—I'm even getting used to living alone! And the column is doing great . . ."

"Well, if hell hasn't frozen over!" A belting alto interrupts my soliloquy. "Look who's at church for the first time in ages!"

"Hi, Hannah," I say, embracing the church's Big Character, who was a good friend of my parents. "Give me a break, you know I'm a busy career woman now!"

"I know—with that column of yours," she mutters, shaking her head. "I don't know how you do it, putting yourself out there like that. You're getting more like your mother every day."

I'm taken aback. "How so am I like my mom? She was always the height of elegance compared to me."

"Yeah, she was elegant, but she never spared you her opinion. Remember the night she broke my toe by dropping a candle on it? The night Nixon won reelection?"

I gasp. "Good lord, I forgot that story!"

"Right, well, I had to wear a goddamned cast for three weeks so *I'm* not likely to forget it!" She chuckles.

"Thanks for the reminder," I tell her with a wink. "I might have to immortalize that little episode on paper."

"Oh Lord!" she sighs. "Well, at least spell my name right! "

She pauses, momentarily serious. "You really do look like her, gal. I miss her still."

"So do I, Hannah." I smile.

Later at home, and alone, I decide to pen a little Mother's Day ode to Betty. I put my favorite French candle on my desk and light it, turning the writing into a ritual of sorts.

In November 1972, my mother bit the nose off Richard Nixon.

I wish I'd been there to see it. But I was in college, getting brought before the dean of students for riding my skateboard, drunk and disruptive, into the dining hall when our senator was visiting, and heckling students by megaphone on their way to rush parties at the Greek houses.

God, was I ever a refugee from 1968 . . . I thought I knew it all.

My mother was the only Democrat in Woodside at that time. She tolerated my father's Republicanism because, she reasoned, it gave her four children a good look at all sides of the story. Election time in the Buelteman household was a good time to practice our duck-and-cover exercises.

She thought Nixon was a crook, and would say so to anyone who'd listen. And they listened because my mother was also the town fashion plate—a gorgeous brunette with flashing blue eyes and killer taste: Lilly Pulitzer, Anne Klein, Ralph Lauren before the horse. Fashion was a goal for her, after a childhood of hand-me-downs.

She wouldn't mind my saying this, I don't think. I hope.

She came from a poor family in Central Florida, a place she buried deep in her heart by going to college, flattening her accent, and moving to California. But she never forgot the hard times. Every Sunday at church when the minister asked for prayers, she would always say, "For the homeless and the hungry."

It wasn't hunger that caused her to bite off Nixon's nose. It was a party to celebrate his reelection over McGovern, her guy. There were life-size candles of Tricky Dick's head all around her friend Hannah's home. After some cocktails, everyone began to tease my mother about Nixon's reelection, and Hannah put one of the Nixon heads in my mother's face. Mom grabbed the candle, bit off its nose, and dropped it on Hannah's foot, breaking her toe. My mother walked home. It became Woodside lore.

I sit back and stare at my computer screen. I'm not sure I'll use this for the column, but it felt good to write, maybe put things in perspective.

But I need to finish the conversation I started earlier with my mom, the one that was interrupted by Hannah. "So, Mom, everyone says I've really found my voice with this column. . . . " I say aloud to the burning candle. And I finally feel a flush, from my heart to my throat, and the tears come. "But the more I think about it, it's your voice, too."

The computer pings, signaling an e-mail. It's Lenny, clearly trying to make amends for forgetting my birthday: "Happy Mother's Day to one hot mama. I'll see you next week!"

I chuckle through my tears. "Okay, Mom, I lied when I said there's no man in my life. There is, although he's never enough in my life. You'd like him, Mom. He'd make you laugh."

Of Average Joes and Rock Stars

"Can I bring Alex to Lenny's show tomorrow night?" Erin's calling unusually early today. "He's a fan. He couldn't believe it when I told him you guys are an item."

I sigh, pouring myself a cup of coffee. "Okay, we are *so not* an item, not really. I'm trying to avoid thinking of him that way, and trying to be more like . . . friends now."

Jesus, whoever thought up the word *friend* should be taken out and shot.

"Oh . . . *friends.* Sure, Mom, good luck with that. Anyway, can he come?"

"You know, I think it's very interesting how you scold me for having anything to do with Lenny, until you want tickets to *see* him! Okay okay, I'll see if I can get another ticket. But I'm already taking Po and Michele and Claudia . . . Where are you anyway?"

"I just left Alex's house and I'm running for the bus."

"Wow, okay, scarlet harlot." I laugh. "Guess things have progressed a tad, eh?"

She groans. "Please! We've been seeing each other almost two months now. So can you get me another ticket, please? I really want you to meet him, Mom!" she says, before hanging up.

I am a little astonished at the potential ramifications of this last statement. Erin's been home from college for two years now and I've rarely met any of the guys she's dated, probably because she didn't date most of them long enough for one to "stick."

I ring Lenny up to ask about the ticket situation. "I think it can be arranged—for a fee," he teases me. "And what's happening with you after the show? I need to hang with the boys in the band a little while since we have some local folks sitting in. Maybe we can go to Tosca? And then, I'm staying at the Tuscany nearby . . ."

I take a deep breath. I've been turning the after-show options over in my head a thousand times this last week. "Sure, Lenny, of course I'll come. But it's awkward when you come to town these days. I seem to stand in line for your time. I know you're famous now and you weren't then. . . ."

He cackles. "Oh yes! So famous! I'm sick of getting hounded for my autograph!"

"Okay, semifamous at least. And you *do* have people pulling on you now, all the time. So why should I keep sleeping with you? It just makes me feel like a sycophant—or groupie. And it just makes me miss . . . you know . . . the way things used to be."

And probably never will be again.

There is a pause. "But isn't it great when we do see each other? Don't we like each other a lot?"

"Yes, yes," I sigh. "But men have a much easier time being in the moment than women do. Okay, than I do."

Plus, I have been close to madly in love with you since we met, you big idiot!

"So, can we just play it by ear?" I say, feeling like I'm spewing confessionals like a tweaked-out sixteen-year-old. "I'll see you tomorrow night. Safe travels."

Erin and Alex arrive at the North Beach venue before the rest of the group gets there, just as I'm sidling up to the bar. Seeing Alex walk through the door, I'm startled by just how . . . boring he looks. All-American. So very average. He is handsome, of course, but looks out of place in this earthy jazz venue: khaki pants, a perfectly pressed powder blue Ralph Lauren dress shirt (complete with the polo player), and loafers. Thank God I can detect no tassels or I'd have to run screaming. And Erin, who normally dresses with a bit of bohemian flare, is dressed simply in a peach-colored linen dress that I recall she bought at Banana Republic, complaining that she had to wear *preppie shite* like this to the office.

But she is grinning like a Cheshire cat when she introduces us. "Mom, this is Alex."

"How do you do?" he says in a hearty baritone, thrusting out his hand and smiling broadly. "Great to meet you, Mrs. Ganahl!"

I cringe theatrically. "Call me that again, dear, and I'll have to enter a retirement home! It's Jane, *please*."

He laughs. "Okay . . . *Jane*. Erin has told me so much about you! And of course, I've enjoyed reading about *her*."

Alex winks at Erin—and she turns to me with a didn't-I-tell-you? glare.

"Wow," I stammer, "I didn't realize this column would impugn not only my reputation but that of my daughter!"

Alex smiles broadly but Erin is not quite as amused.

"Anyway, let me buy you a drink!" I say cheerfully, changing the subject. "It's the least I can do for your taking on the burden of helping Erin study for her LSAT's. God knows she's already left me in the dust academically! What can I get you?"

I turn back to the bar to order drinks, and out of the corner of my eye I see her slip her hand into his. He looks immediately uncomfortable, as if this is unseemly behavior. And then he checks his watch—a Rolex, of course. Dear God! Where have I gone wrong? Where have I failed as a mother? To see her thus infatuated . . . with a yuppie?!

Claudia, who has known Erin since her Phish-loving teen years, arrives next and is introduced to the smiling young lawyer. She raises her eyebrows at me quizzically, and I mouth the words *Her new boyfriend!* She cocks her head and mouths back *Are you sure?*

Po arrives with Michele, looking much more relaxed than the last time I saw him, frantically finishing his manuscript. "Done!" he says triumphantly. "Now I get a break."

They give Erin a hug and meet Alex; he eagerly claims to have read Po's last two books, and that "this is a big honor." The two kids wander off to listen to the opening band, and Michele says admiringly: "She is so fabulous, Jane. You are my role model for girl-parenting."

Po adds: "Did we tell you we're working on baby number two? We have a feeling this one will be a girl." He smiles at Michele sweetly and lasciviously.

When you're a single woman without a decent suitor in sight (and no, Lenny doesn't qualify), it's irksome to see such wanton displays of worship. It's a good thing I love these two so much or I'd be looking for a Louisville Slugger.

"Yeah, she's great," I sigh, watching her near the stage. "But something has happened to her taste in men! This guy is a total yuppie."

Claudia agrees. "He seems nice enough, but jeez, I remember some really brilliant and unusual guys she used to date. . . ."

Po chides us both. "You don't know that he's not brilliant! Or nice for that matter. You two and your thing for Pirates and rock stars, where has it gotten you?"

He might have a point, but I fear it's too late to change course now. We're all just victims of our programming. And mine was completed in the sixties, when I was drawn into the antiwar movement—and lads with long hair and mustaches and body odor and a penchant for rebellion. That image remains on my hard drive—on my desktop right next to the one of Lenny-in-love—and try as I might, I can't force-quit or purge it.

Of course I lost my virginity to someone who fit the archetype to a T: the rebellious youngest son of a wealthy Seattle business magnate. It was my freshman year, and I thought this was it, that I had held out for love and now I had found it in Vince. I loved his wild partying ways and his long sideburns and even longer hair, and the fact that he dabbled in guitar playing in a frat-house rock band. Of course, Vince turned out to be a total jerk and smashed my heart, but he set the style standard—not only for my college years but for my life.

It explains my several affairs with musicians: the gorgeous-in-bed, twelve-years-younger Adam, with whom I had one torrid weekend before he went off on his first national tour and ended up on the cover of *Rolling Stone* four months later; Graham, the twenty-something pianist/composer and wild man from Austin; Warren, the borderline-insane rocker from the eighties who courted me for two months by phone after an interview, leading to one rather disastrous encounter in San Francisco. And, of course, Lenny. None of it ended particularly well.

"Truth be told," I admit to the group, "I should be glad that Erin is outgrowing the fixation with rock-star types because I never did."

"I think I know why you have always chosen guys like Lenny," says Po, smiling. "I think you're actually afraid of things working out. So you pick the guys you know are bad bets for long-term happiness."

I stare at him in amusement while Claudia and Michele applaud his bull's-eye. "I'm sorry, I thought you were a *manly man*!" I snap back, pinching his cheek. "Only *girly men* have this kind of sensitive insight!"

We're interrupted by the onset of Lenny's set; he soon has the house rocking to the perfection of his playing. When the set is done, he comes around to the bar to greet my group. He gives Erin a hug and asks what she's been up to. When she tells him she's studying for the LSAT, he growls. "Just what the world needs, one more fucking lawyer."

She laughs, and then introduces a wide-eyed Alex. "Lenny, this is Alex—a lawyer."

Lenny shakes his hand and makes no apologies.

Po and Michele excuse themselves to get home to the babysitter, and Erin and Alex head out as well. Erin gives me a hug and whispers in my ear: "I'll call you tomorrow so you can tell me what you think!"

Good, I have until tomorrow to figure out what to say.

We head down the street to Tosca, where Lenny's manager had called ahead to reserve some space for our small group. When I first met Lenny, the idea of him having an entourage would have been a good joke to us both, but it seems to grow every time I see him.

We grab a back booth and Lenny slides in next to me, shooting me a Significant Look and touching my thigh under the table. The waitress recognizes him from last time, asks if he wants his usual scotch-rocks. She does not ask me what I want, so I wave at her before she moves away. "Bombay-tonic, please." As always, we are immediately surrounded by other musicians, including tonight's stand-up bass player, a local boy who got to sit in. A tall drink of water, Jim is maybe thirty, has brawny forearms covered with tattoos, bushy dark hair and a goatee, and one gold earring in each ear. Claudia, who had said she was only going to stay for "two seconds," stops in her tracks when she sees him. Young. Tall. Cute. Musician. It's all over.

I nudge Lenny to make introductions; soon Claudia and Jim are chatting up a storm. I marvel at her ability to flirt, which I seem to have forgotten how to do. Lenny is right next to me, but monopolized by the group that surrounds and paws at him, and I feel mute to say what I really want to say: let's get the hell out of here and go somewhere alone.

Claudia finally gives a faux stretch and an I'm-so-tired line, noting she must look for a cab to take her back to the Western Addition. Young Jim leaps up off his bar stool on cue, and gallantly offers to drive her home. He fetches his (ahem) man-size instrument, shakes Lenny's hand, and they head for the exit. As I hug my friend, I whisper, "Okay, dear, this is hardly the insurance salesman you said you were looking for! But I want a full report tomorrow." She smiles slyly. "Ditto."

After ninety minutes have gone by, and the front doors are locked, and the bartenders are sweeping up, Lenny still shows no signs of moving for the exit, nor do his hangers-on, who are now chatting among themselves, waiting for Lenny to say what the next destination is. We've talked about his upcoming projects; there is interest in his doing a movie score. And we've talked about my column, which he claims to read online "almost every week."

"Hey," I finally say quietly into his ear. "What's the plan, Stan?"

He turns slightly to face me. "I don't know," he whispers. "To be honest, my life's gotten kind of . . . complicated this last week. I just started seeing someone in New York, and I'm thinking it might really lead to something. But you're here, and you look so pretty . . ."

"Wait, wait," I interrupt, so irritated I want to smack him. "Why didn't you mention this earlier when we first talked about spending the night? Why did I just spend ninety minutes waiting for you?"

"For one thing, I wanted to see you," he says, not looking me in the eyes.

He takes my hand under the table and gives it a calm-down squeeze.

"How old is she?" I ask curtly, taking my hand away.

"Uh . . . I think . . . twenty-four?"

I feel like I've been slapped. "Twenty-four? Oh, Lenny . . . why?"

He smiles, with a guilty I'm-a-shit shrug and grin. "I'm a weak man . . . ?"

Mute with hurt, I grab my purse and head for the door. Once there, I turn and take one last look at him as I walk out: he's looking in my direction, confused in his drunken state about the abruptness of my exit.

I know I know I know, we supposedly have no constraints on our so-called relationship, and I shouldn't be jealous, but I am. And it shouldn't make me feel old, but it does.

I wait a day before I write about this so I won't be so pissed—and when I do, I decide not to dwell on Lenny himself, but on my fateful love of rock stars. He'll get it.

> *I was obsessed with them throughout my youth, turned on by their bad attitudes, salivating over their dangerous sexuality—despite knowing that they were probably shallow and not too bright. It's a pattern that lasted in my relationships until . . . well, it's not really over, actually.*
>
> *Friends who had crushes in the sixth grade on the captain of the football team ended up marrying bank presidents. But that wasn't me. Those straitlaced types bored me silly. Instead, I papered my room with photos of Paul Revere and the Raiders and the Monkees, then later on the dangerous Rolling Stones. And of course, the Fab Four.*

In recent years, covering rock music, you'd think my obsession would be quelled by interviewing quite a few musicians. And it's helped to see how ghastly flawed most famous ones are. But there's a personality requirement to do that job, and God help me, it still appeals to me.

It's not as if I'm alone. Even though my friends are educated, literate, and music-savvy, along with their appreciation of a musician's craft comes an appreciation of his other assets. And if they have their choice between seeing a Tom Waits or a Jim White or Pete Yorn or John Wesley Harding, most likely they will go with the hunks of burning love.

Those who have never slept with a rock star imagine the sex would be as electric as their stage presence. I can tell you, as one who has "gone there," that there ain't no real difference between them and mortal men. If anything, they're more selfish, knowing there are women often lined up to cater to their needs.

At least my daughter's generation shows signs of better taste. Her first rock crush was Pearl Jam's Eddie Vedder—and only partly for his dark good looks. She also admired his politics, his ability to take a stand, his desire to make a difference in the world. So when I met him and asked him for his autograph for her, he wrote: "Erin, power to the people. Love, Eddie."

And when I surprised her with it, her eyes welled with tears of joy. Some things never change.

After I send in the column, I'm inspired to send an e-mail to Erin, too.

"Honey, I liked your new man. He's a little on the straight side, but I'm glad to see you've become more mature in your selection process than I've ever been. Rock stars . . . who needs 'em?! (And yes, I'll tell you later about my nonevent with Lenny that night.) Alex has nice manners and seems to think you're aces, so I give him two thumbs-up!"

I sigh as I click send. I guess I'm happy she's outgrown rock-star types; Alex may be boring, but at least he's not a jerk. I'll try to give him the benefit of the doubt. And if he takes up the guitar, I'll advise her to run screaming.

The Art of Aging (Dis)Gracefully

"So, Mom, are you ready to write off Lenny for good?" Erin asks the second I pick up the phone. "I know he pissed you off last week when you saw him, but, *jeez*, don't you think he'll be reading this online?"

"Happy Sunday morning to you, too, sunshine!" I laugh, pouring myself my second cup of coffee. "And yeah, I hope he *does* read it. I mean, come on, making me hang around for him for an hour and a half and then telling me he's seeing someone your age?"

"Oh, so he *made* you? He held a gun to your head?" she teases. "Mom, you hung around because you wanted to. And you know Lenny is a flake, so you have to accept the consequences."

I hate that she's right so much of the time. It would be sharing too much to tell her that just thinking of the other night makes my eyes puddle up and my feelings of self-worth evaporate. Lenny should feel lucky I just wrote about him and didn't hire an assassin.

"Spoken like one who has men falling at her feet!" I chide her. "Someday you could find yourself in my position—wondering where your sex appeal has gone. Then you can hassle me for being less than discriminating."

"Hey, did Alex e-mail you?" she asks brightly. "He asked for your address so he could send a thank-you for the drinks last week."

"Yes, yes, he did. Nice manners, that lad."

If only he weren't so boring.

Claudia e-mails that I am dead wrong about musicians being crappy lovers. "I am in bass-player heaven," she purrs. Clearly, her ride home with Jim turned into at least a weeklong love-in. "But what happened with Lenny to set you off this way?"

Rosalind e-mails, too: "Does this column mean you've given Lenny the pitch once and for all? I've always said he isn't good enough for our Jane!" Suddenly irritated by the fact that not only Rosalind but everyone else with a pair of eyes has been right in their observations about Lenny, I resist the urge to point out that her fiancé hasn't exactly done right by her either. I put that e-mail aside to answer later when my mood is better.

I also hear from Phil, who asks me if I'm "turning this column into a vendetta." "Well, he hurt my feelings, as you can tell," I write back. "Seems he'd rather sleep with a gorgeous (or so I imagine) 24-year-old than with me. How on earth could that be?"

"Didn't I give you the lecture about getting involved with anyone in the entertainment industry?" he writes. I can see his jaw clenching.

"Riiiiight, unlike us print journalists, who are so saintly?"

He doesn't respond.

I don't get an e-mail from Lenny, but that's not surprising. I so rarely do. But despite my flip attitude, when I think that he might read the column online—and that I might have done something irreversible in a week of acute anger—I get a pain in my stomach.

Later that afternoon, I'm cheered when Marco calls. "Man, that was brutal today!" He laughs. "Did you have a falling-out with your honey?"

"You could say that," I sigh. "I wouldn't call him my honey either. Not now or ever. It was just a casual thing."

There is silence. "Yeah, well, I can remember your saying otherwise at a party a few years ago, right after you met him. You were crazy for that dude!"

"Hey," I cut him off quickly. "Are you trying to ruin my afternoon? What did you want, anyway? Other than to tell me how glad you are that you aren't currently in my crosshairs?"

He chuckles. "I'm just wondering if you're free Friday night for a drink. Call it a belated-birthday catch-up. Maybe at Zuni?"

Zuni! Our old haunt, not far from his office at city hall.

"Sure, how about six o'clock?"

Hmmm, I wonder. What's this about? I'm intrigued, and as Friday rolls around my anticipation is piqued enough to dress up a bit. He complimented me once when I wore a short skirt so I put one on—but a denim one, not fancy, not too short, not too transparently seductive. Paired with casual midcalf boots. No need to overdo. Yes, summer is approaching but in San Francisco that just means switching from black boots to brown.

My prep work is interrupted by a call from Peter, getting back to me about his Litquake gig coming up in September. "I'm actually getting ready to go and have a drink with Marco," I tell him, finding it difficult to mask my glee.

"But you told me that you introduced him to Elsa and they're dating," he says slowly, clearly confused. "Besides, you said that was your worst breakup ever; didn't he tell you that you were too old to marry? Why would you even want to be in the same room with that guy, let alone want to date him again?"

I stop in my tracks. He's right of course. "Well, first of all, that was a couple of months ago that he told me he wanted to ask Elsa out, and I have not seen them around anywhere and you know what a small town this is! And second . . . well, I don't know why I'm so keen on having this drink."

"Honey," he says solemnly, "you are one of the most powerful women I know. And yet I get a sense that you're feeling a little . . . desperate, perhaps?"

I feel suddenly on the verge of tears. "Peter, when you're pushing fifty, and not exactly being hotly pursued anymore, it does a number on your compass."

There is a pause. "I understand. I'm sorry if I made you feel bad. You just owe yourself, and in some ways your readers, to be your best self. To realize how great you are—with or without a dude. You need a serious dose of self-acceptance."

I feel like I might lash out at him, so I excuse myself and finish dressing. I won't think about any of this anymore tonight.

The fog is somersaulting down Market Street when I find Marco at Zuni's bar—blending in with the other Civic Center suits, not looking at all like the Marco of four years ago.

"You look nice."

He says this flatly and without flirtation. Sigh.

"So do you, although I can't get used to seeing you in a suit all the time!" I smile.

"Comes with the territory." He shrugs. He's already ordered me a martini, which I never drink. He knows this, but perhaps it slipped his mind. So I take tentative sips and soon the strength of the elixir is both becalming and benumbing to my jagged nerves. He fires off his usual round of questions: "How have you been? How's the writing going? How's Erin?"

The conversation, for a good thirty minutes, becomes all about me, which is unheard of. Men sometimes need a kick under the bar to let you get a word in edgewise. He orders us second martinis, against my protestations. I'm already buzzy from the first. Finally, in the middle of martini two, I stop him. "Okay, I've told you all about writing the column, my lack of love life, Erin's law school pursuit, even my dad's eightieth birthday coming up. But what's up with you? Inquiring minds need to know."

His smile fades and he looks slightly stricken. "Well, actually, that's why I wanted to meet with you, so you'd hear it from me and not from someone in the circle. Elsa and I have been dating for a couple months now, and . . . we're boyfriend and girlfriend."

Boyfriend and girlfriend? Have I just stumbled onto the set of *Beverly Hills 90210*?

I swallow hard on the olive I was chewing. "Okay, so . . . what are you telling me, Marco?"

"I'm crazy about her," he blurts out. There is a semicomedic pause while he regains his calm. "And she is about me. We're thinking about moving in together. And we both care so much for you and don't want you to be upset. And you did ask me to tell you if this happened."

I'm spinning a bit. "Wow, okay. I'm just surprised because I hadn't heard that you were even seriously dating."

"I know," he sighs. "These things so rarely work out that we wanted to keep it quiet until we knew for sure that it was the real thing."

The real thing? Unlike what he and I had, I guess. Yeesh.

"Totally understand," I say slowly. "That was kind of you. Appreciate it."

Collecting myself for a nanosecond, I realize Peter was right: it's incumbent on me to be my best self. After all, I'm the grown-up here . . . by a decade and a half. I touch his hand. "You guys don't need my blessing, but you know you have it."

Realizing tears are a distinct possibility, I make excuses. "I gotta get home in time to get that important phone call from my broker," I joke, and try to pick up the bill, but he grabs it first. "You're the best."

He beams, embracing me quickly as I back toward the door, too quickly for it to appear casual.

By the time I get to my car I am both bubbling up with confused tears and acutely aware that the two martinis have taken their toll. Think I'd better just sit a minute and get my shit together. *Why do you care if they're in love?* I lecture myself. *They deserve to be happy.*

It's just what it *says* about my luck of late. And for God's sake, it's Friday night at seven p.m., and I certainly hadn't planned for my evening to be over so soon! But this is okay, I think, dabbing my eyes, I have a video at home I can watch. But, uh-oh, I have no food in the fridge for dinner. No cat food either. So I'll go to the supermarket on the way home. It's not far and maybe I'll buy myself a consolation prize, some Oreos or something.

I can drive safely to my favorite gourmet market, despite my overall discombobulated state.

My friends have regaled me with their own experiences of braving the supermarket while buzzed, but I have never experienced the joy myself. But here I am, pushing my cart down the aisles in my fancy boots, trying to look like an upright citizen.

In my altered state, I'm thinking: "I must look pretty hot!" But without a doubt, everyone who might be looking at me is thinking, "Boy, *her* Friday-night plans must have gone south in a big way. . . ."

I find the cat food section and choose the favorite flavors of Noodge, Bunny, and Boo. I chuck a dozen tins into the cart, trying for a little distance on the last ones, raising my arms in victory when none end up on the floor. Only then does it hit me: I am in a supermarket on a Friday night and shopping for my cats. This is really, really not good. I add more dignified groceries to the pile: bananas, spinach, milk, biodegradable detergent, a *People* magazine to make the evening's self-indulgence complete.

On my way to the checkout line, I spy a special stand of just-for-women vitamins, and pause to have a look. God, maybe if I took some, if I looked healthier, I might find a new Marco who would love me like he loves Elsa. At the *very* least, it might help with the weeping jags and the fact that I toss my covers off at night when I sleep too hotly to stand them.

I lift a large plastic bottle of a supplement that claims to be "for women over 40," which boasts "natural hormone-replacement ingredients" that aid in the reduction of hot flashes. Now we're talking! Reading the label with eyes unfocused, I glance over the top—and spy a very attractive man there in the health food section, also reading a vitamin bottle label.

He looks up to see me looking at him. Our eyes meet.

And in my haste to put the geezer-lady vitamins back on the shelf before he can see what I'm perusing, I miss the shelf by at least an inch. It thuds to the ground—thankfully without breaking—and rolls along until it stops about six inches from his foot. I gasp, and start giggling uncontrollably, but he turns quickly and continues down the aisle away from me, ignoring both my spastic display and the hot-flash remedy at his feet. This must be a very, very nice man, I think sympathetically, to pretend like he didn't just witness this witless act. Come back here and marry me!

Safely back in my car, I realize I've had a Bridget Jones moment: the character I have disparaged in print for being both tragically attached to getting a man and an embarrassment to herself, with her pratfalls and ridiculous displays. A few days later the episode makes its way into my column.

> *Ever since I started writing "Single-Minded" a few months ago, I've had several people ask me what I thought of* Bridget Jones's Diary*—both the book by Helen Fielding and the recent movie starring Renée Zellweger.*
>
> *The answer is: not much.*

I found both, particularly the book, to be major sources of embarrassment. Bridget was so desperate for a man, to get married, that she continually made a fool of herself. From public blurtings-out to private passings-out—always while intoxicated—to literal pratfalls and chain-smoking, here was a woman seemingly bent on self-destruction. And all to get a man!

Is this a serious case of the pot calling the kettle black?

Reading the book, I found myself irritated by her ridiculousness, and wanting to chide her: Look, I've been married twice. It's no picnic—unless it's a picnic plagued by fire ants and hail. But of course, single women who have never goose-stepped down the aisle to the altar think they're missing something. And everything is sacrificed toward finding it: spare time, endless self-improvement dollars, dignity.

Because even through the ice ages between my serious relationships (like, ahem, the one that's currently giving me frostbite), I always, always, maintain my sense of decorum and dignity.

I describe the chain reaction of events that led to my drunk shopping experience, and close with the following:

I hastened to the checkout line, feeling a little less superior than I had previously to my sister-in-fiction, Bridget Jones. In fact, much inferior. When she behaves this way, she still gets to choose between Hugh Grant and Colin Firth. And me? I get my cats.

Peter was right. I do need a dose of self-acceptance. But I also need a manual on aging gracefully, one that can tell me how to handle it when the men in my life fall like dominoes away from me and in the direction of young babes.

Of Fame and Infamy

"You're late! We're about to miss the National Anthem!" chides Po as I arrive, Giants baseball cap askew, at the Willie Mays statue at PacBell Park, where he and Michele and Claudia have been waiting.

"I know . . . I'm sorry! I always get so carried away on Sundays reading my e-mails," I say breathlessly. "Come on, the tickets are under my name."

We make our way quickly to the VIP ticket line. It helps to have friends in high places.

"How are you, hon?" asks Claudia, slipping her arm around my waist as we walk. "Take a deep breath, columnist lady!"

"Feeling frazzled," I groan, fishing in my purse for my ID to show the ticket counter. "I got thrashed by Bridget Jones fans, advice on natural hormone replacement therapy, and e-mails from MADD supporters telling me I had no business driving while I was high. I mean, I'm such an idiot to even tell people I did!"

"So five months into this, you're still getting a lot of response?"

asks Po. "That's great, the reading public can be really fickle. Does it translate to name recognition?"

"Not really." I shrug. "It's just one column in a Sunday section. I'm just another gasbag pontificating in print."

They all laugh. When I get to the window, I hand my ID to the seventy-ish man behind the glass. It's so sweet that the Giants give all these jobs to seniors.

"Jane Ganahl . . ." he says, flipping through various envelopes until he gets to my name. "Here you are. Wait, I know this name. You do that Sunday column on dating, don't you?"

His eyes take on an intimidating glint as he slowly grins. "That's right . . . I know all about *you*!"

"Oh, wow, really?" I stammer, flushing red. "Gosh, that feels . . . really weird! I mean, thanks a lot!" I grab the tickets and turn away.

My friends' eyes are wide and amused as we walk toward the escalator. "Not recognized, eh?" Po laughs.

"That was strange!" I say as we ascend to our seats on the club level. I don't want to be so uncool as to also admit that I enjoyed it. "Maybe I should have asked that guy if he was single!"

"So you haven't talked to Lenny since we saw him a few weeks ago?" asks Michele. Unlike Rosalind, she thinks Lenny is ideal for me. But she always had a thing for Pirates and rock stars herself, and Po walks that walk.

"Nope," I sigh. "It's possible that he's pissed at me now after I wrote my musicians-are-lousy-in-bed. I kind of lost it, but God, I was devastated when he told me he was seeing someone Erin's age."

Getting maudlin, I add: "I'm fated to die alone and unloved. . . ."

Po chuckles. "But I thought you said you were going to stop looking at the swashbuckler types. That alone should improve your chances of happiness."

"Yes, you're right. No more musicians for me. Claudia, on the other hand, is still sold on the concept of musician as sex machine. . . ."

"I know I said no more flaky artist types," she sighs. "And he *is* a flake—he's terrible at calling when he says he will. But the sex is too good for me to cut him off."

"Well, dear," I say, patting her arm as we take our seats. "Just make sure you keep a little distance and take care of yourself!"

It's always so easy to give my advice away, since I'm not using it myself.

"Speaking of tough broads," I say, turning to Po, who is pulling out his scorecard to keep score, baseball geek that he is. "I also heard from our old city hall news colleague Wendy this morning. She e-mailed to say hi—and then asked me if I miss reporting on 'real' stories like the ones we used to cover. Was that condescending or what?"

"I think you should tell Wendy that your column has made you more of a name in six months than your political reporting did in five years." Po chuckles, ordering a beer. "I mean, you have ticket-counter people recognizing your name."

"That was anomalous and you know it," I say, elbowing him. "Anyway, I have a long way to go before I catch up with you."

When I get home after the Giants masterful win, wind-whipped and sunburned, there are more e-mails that came in throughout the day. But I'm tired from drinking beer in the warm sun and don't feel like reading them all, so I scan the sender addresses quickly to see if I recognize any names. There is a Vincent A. Smith, with the simple subject line "hello." I know that name somehow, but it also looks like spam, so I flick it into the trash.

Then it hits me: Vince Smith? As in, the guy I lost my virginity to when I was eighteen? Is it possible?

I fetch the e-mail out of the trash and read it: "Jane, reading your column today I can see that the party animal girl I knew at Willamette hasn't changed too much—didn't we do mushrooms once and end up tripping in the Kmart on Congress Street?"

Good God, it's really Vince—the first real love of my life, and the first real affair. The son of the wealthy Seattle family who was brilliant and witty and gorgeous—and who turned out to be a bit of a prick.

"I hope these last 25 years have treated you well. I've been reading your columns for the last few months since I Googled you and found your columns online. You're famous!"

Oh Christ, the "famous" bullshit again.

Vince explains at great length what he's been up to: married twenty years, moved to Colorado, two college-age kids, getting divorced now, doing personal archaeology to try and understand what went wrong in his life and by the way . . . why did we break up and how do I view him when I think of him?

Perhaps I'm hormonal today, or still in a state of fuming after the Lenny debacle, but I don't hold back when I reply. "Honestly, Vince, I rarely think of you—unless it's in context with why I have a deep-seated distrust of relationships and fear of intimacy. I fell in love with you and you with me—and then you treated me like crap. After the first few months, you would go out drinking with your friends and never invite me along. And you'd come over just to have sex with me. And I was miserable for most of the year we were together. Oh, and the sex wasn't even that good. Anything else?"

I hit send, and let out a whoop. Come find me, all you errant exes who did me wrong! It's clearly time to set things straight.

To my surprise, he not only responds, but does so quickly: "Jane, I completely understand. I've often felt bad that you knew me when you did. I was immature, and insensitive. I've changed a lot, and would like to explain how."

And so he does, in gratuitous detail. He was feeling pressured by his father (now dead) to perform in school, to be the best at everything. And to eventually have the best of everything. He was a yuppie prince in the making, it seems, which got him started on a slippery slope of taking advantage of people.

"I wanted you for my girlfriend," he writes, "because you were so popular. And so infamous."

"Infamous?" I type back, incredulously staring at the word. "This is not how I thought of myself in college."

"Yes, you were notorious for always being on a soapbox about everything. You were against the Greek system, against Nixon, against our spending so much money on the football team. And you were so attractive—although you acted like you didn't know it. I know several guys who tried to get you and failed. It made me want you even more."

I could recall a few of his friends who'd hit on me earlier in my freshman year, but I'd rebuffed them, thinking I wanted nothing to do with frat boys.

"So you had to have me, but then once you got me, and made me fall in love with you, you put the trophy on the shelf and pretty much ignored me," I respond, not feeling like softening just yet. "I also recall seeing you draped on my friend Leslie at a fraternity function. It's hard to think kindly of you after the way you treated me."

I keep thinking he'll give up on this exchange soon enough, but he keeps coming back for more. He'd love to see me again, he says, so he can explain better in person. Maybe in San Francisco on his way to the Far East, where he does international consulting work, maybe in Denver if I'm ever there, maybe at his second home up in Aspen . . .

Oh Christ, Vince is rich.

"You wouldn't like me these days—rich men don't. Different aesthetics," I quip. But I'm not kidding. With the exception of Lenny, if a man gots money, he don't want Jane. Something about my lack of refined features and French manicures, and penchant for jeans and old cowboy boots.

And anyway, why encourage this? I have serious considerations about ever conducting a romance by e-mail again; not only that, my attempts in the past to reconnect with exes have proven, if not plain disastrous, then disastrously disappointing.

"I'll think about it," I finish the e-mail. "And now, I'm going to bed. We've been at this for more than an hour!"

"Thanks for talking," he writes humbly. "You didn't owe me even that much. More anon."

An e-mail-filled week after Vince knocked on my virtual door, I have a dream about the time I reconnected a few years ago with the second guy I ever slept with at college—and I wake up in a cold sweat. That particular adventure should have cured me of the desire to *ever* try to rekindle the flame with an ex. He was the sweetest, hottest, most brilliant guy in the class above mine, the one who really made me enjoy sex for the first time, since Vince wasn't exactly Dr. Kinsey in that regard. I kept his handsome picture nearby—one that I viewed often through rose-colored glasses.

But when we reconnected after twenty years, I almost didn't recognize him. His thick beard and disheveled state made him look more like the Unabomber or a Phish-head than my swashbuckling lover. But the looks weren't the real deal-breaker; he had done the unforgivable and become boring. I decide to use it as column fodder, with the punchline: *My Rodney: boring. How cruel life can be.*

I realize after purging onto paper that perhaps this was an attempt to talk myself out of wanting to see Vince. But my strategy doesn't work; he is wearing down my defenses. Probably because he's been e-mailing me all week—just charming little nuggets. Today's began with the lyrics to "Good Morning Starshine."

I stifle a chuckle—and the impulse to say *awwww.* This was our favorite musical. His missives are increasingly curious and intimate. "I've been thinking about your parents. How are they? How is Captain Bob? I always admired him so."

"My mom died of a brain tumor five years ago," I write, feeling a rush of gratitude for his query. "But my dad's still around and doing great. We're throwing him a big eightieth birthday next weekend."

"I'm so sorry about your mom," he responds. "But that's great about your dad. So . . . do you need a date for that?" I stare at the screen a moment, fighting the impulse to say YES YES YES, before typing back, "No, I think that weekend will be stressful enough, thank you! But thanks for the noble offer."

"I can see that I'm going to have to work pretty hard to talk you into seeing me again," he writes cheerfully. "But I'm patient. I've waited almost thirty years for this wonderful thing to happen."

That's nothing. I've waited forty-nine.

This Is Your Captain Speaking

The caller ID says The Sequoias—my dad's retirement center.

"Party central!" I answer cheerfully. There is a pause.

"Listen, I hope you guys aren't going to a lot of trouble!"

My dad is one of the world's best human beings and the only guy who doesn't understand why everyone loves him and wants to attend his eightieth birthday party.

"You know what, Dad? We *are* going to a lot of trouble and it's just exactly what we want to be doing! So just show up tomorrow and have a good time!"

He chuckles. "What time you want me and Barbara there?"

"How about four p.m. since it starts at five? And for God's sake, don't wear the plaid vest! We should have burned that when Mom died—she forgot to put it in her will. . . ."

"Are you bringing someone?" he interrupts, surprising me. Dad has pretty much stopped asking about my love life in recent years, most likely because we both started getting embarrassed that the answer was always the same.

"Well, I'm bringing Erin, but I know that's not what you mean.

Dad, I'd tell you if I were seeing someone," I say impatiently, and then pause. Might as well throw him a bone. "But do you remember my first serious boyfriend at Willamette? Vince Smith? You met him at parents' weekend. . . ."

"Oh yeah!" his tone brightens. "Rich kid, if I recall." Dad's always had this irrational hope that I would marry into money, despite my apparent vow of poverty—at least when it came to men.

"The very same!" I find myself feeling suddenly adolescent. "And guess what? He's gotten back in touch with me, and he might come out from Denver for a visit."

I can just imagine his baby blues twinkling.

I pause in my party prep to check e-mails, hoping to see one from Vince. Instead, I'm stunned to see one from Lenny in my in-box—sans subject line so there's no clue as to its content. I have to get up and walk around a minute, bracing myself for what might be an angry onslaught in response to my rock-star column of a few weeks ago. What I don't expect is a confused paean.

"Jane, You were and are an absolute gem in your dealings with me. And I should have done better by you. To be honest, I can't quite understand what you see in me! I'm weak and flawed. And of course this new thing is already not panning out. Anyway, I am sorry if I caused you pain and distress. I have always loved our time together. It's always joyous. You are quite an extraordinary person. I'll be back in a few months; can we try again if you're still speaking to me?"

My hand goes unconsciously to my mouth. Had he read my revenge column or not? I guess it doesn't really matter—one way or the other, contrition is evident. I'm not sure how to feel—thrilled at his sweet words, or saddened by the knowledge that things never seem to change for us.

I decide to feign breeziness. "Dear man, you did not wound me unduly. I would welcome a visit from you in a few months—*if we agree ahead of time as to what's going to happen*, so I don't get old waiting for you! And don't worry about your twenty-something, if you want one, there will be another one along soon, like the subways in your town. And if you decide you're ready for a real woman again, you know where I am."

I sigh and hit send. I sound a lot more confident than I actually feel. I go immediately to his Web site to check for upcoming dates. Nothing yet. Nothing.

"Hi ho!" I hear my sister's voice and accompanying clamor as she walks in the door, balancing boxes and suitcase, looking windblown. She never knocks; she doesn't have to. Anne has to get up to speed quickly since she only got to town this morning, having jumped off the *Les Miz* tour to come home for the big occasion.

"Hey! Dad just rang to check in . . ." I call out to her.

"Let me guess," my older sister says drily, as she arrives in the kitchen, where I am cleaning our mother's silver serving bowls. "He said not to go to a lot of trouble."

"Of course he did!" I laughed. "It's Dad, after all! How are you?" We give each other a long hug; I haven't seen her in months.

"I'm okay—I took a pill so I could deal with the cats." The singer is always deathly afraid of getting plugged up with allergic phlegm. I used to call her Peggy Phlegming in the morning when she woke up and had to do her psychotic noises *(hee hee haa haa brrring!)* to clear her tubes. "Let me show you the napkins!" she says brightly.

Anne specially ordered cocktail napkins that read: "June 23—Celebration to Honor Robert Buelteman," and on a separate line: "This Is Your Captain Speaking!" This was the running joke we made about Dad when we were growing up. My dad tended to make family announcements at the dinner table as if he were about to explain the weather conditions before landing in Singapore. "There's a high-pressure front coming in, so at 0900 hours on Sunday we will go for a walk in the woods!"

"What's the final RSVP count?" she asks, stacking napkins neatly on the kitchen counter.

"God, I don't know, Julie is the one keeping track. I think we told the caterer fifty-five?"

A pause. "God," she smirks, "that's a steamin' heap o' Tater Tots."

We share a laugh at our dad's nefarious taste in cuisine. We've decided to go upscale for his birthday party, though he would have been happy with Goldfish crackers for appetizers, and flank steak, Tots, and a wedge of lettuce with Thousand Island for dinner. If Mom had been here, she would have insisted on a higher-class menu and told him to get over himself if he pouted. So we are following suit.

"Who's picking up the tablecloths from the party-rental place?" she asks, letting loose a machine-gun-like series of consecutive sneezes. The pill is clearly not working.

"Erin is, and I'm going to the nursery later to buy flowers. And Julie and Rob are stopping by Woodside Vineyards to get the sparkling stuff."

I pause. "I think it's in very bad taste of Mom to die before he turned eighty, leaving us stuck with all this. . . ."

I expect her to laugh, but she doesn't. Anne has a hearty sense of humor, but even now the topic of Mom and Lisa always threatens to send her down the rabbit hole of grief. And Lisa's survivors—husband, Terry, and son, Theo—are coming up for the event tomorrow from L.A., so there are bound to be some tears.

"Sorry . . ." I hesitate.

"No, it's okay," she says, tossing her curly mane back dramatically. "I was just thinking she'd be proud of how we're honoring Dad." And then her eyes do cloud over.

As she starts pulling out my wineglasses and frowning at their spots—Martha Stewart I ain't—the doorbell rings. It's a florist's deliveryman with an arrangement the size of Alcatraz—a riot of roses and hyacinth and white carnations. For me? Confused, I reach immediately for the card.

You said you had to go and buy flowers today for your dad's birthday, the card reads. *I thought I'd save you the trip. Vince.*

"Who are they from?" asks Anne, wiping the glasses.

"You won't believe it . . ." I sigh. Anne knew Vince because she and I went to the same college, although we traveled in different circles—Anne with the brainy intellectuals and me with the party animals and agitators.

I hesitate to tell her about my virtual reunion with Vince; as much as I've always envied her musical talent, smarts, and grace, she's never had much luck with men. So I have always treaded lightly when it came to news of my liaisons. I would love to tell her that I'm getting excited about the prospect of seeing Vince again, that he's utterly repentant, and wooing me enthusiastically from afar, but she might be put off to hear it. Besides, I recall that she wasn't particularly keen on him back then.

"Ah . . . actually . . . these flowers are from an old friend, who knew it was Dad's birthday this weekend. He always admired Captain Bob. . . ."

Erin bursts through the door, also juggling: arms full of white tablecloths and her overnight bag. Saved by the belle.

"Wow, cool flowers!" she pants, looking at the Rose Parade float in the living room. "Are they for the party?"

"Yep, now we just have to hire a moving truck to get them there tomorrow."

She and Anne hug with excitement; they are as close as aunt and niece can be. We've taken many trips, the three of us—the last biggie was to Europe when Erin graduated two years ago. The fact that we were still speaking to each other after renting a car on the highways of Provence is a testament to family unity.

"How's the studying going for the LSAT? And that guy you were seeing—Alex, I think his name was?" Anne asks teasingly.

"Oh, that was so two weeks ago!" I laugh. "There was a guy who actually wanted to stick around for a while, so she cut him loose."

Erin sighs impatiently. "Well, it wasn't quite that simple. I just wanted to have fun for the year until I go to law school, and he wanted something more serious.

"Besides," she adds brightly, "there's a new cute paralegal at the office who's just my age!"

"Chip off the maternal block," Anne sighs, shaking her head.

"Does Grandpa know his friends are coming in from Arizona and Michigan?" Erin asks excitedly.

"I think he suspects." I smile. "He's been trying to pry details out of us for weeks."

Erin has the same hero-worship thing going on with my dad that I did when I was a child. When I was little, and would hear his VW going up the driveway on his way to the airport, I'd cry inconsolably. Pan Am flights were not one-day quickie back-and-forths; he was regularly gone a week to ten days, and would go halfway around the world and back. And he'd bring the world back to us: an arrangement of Birds of Paradise from Hawaii for my mother, weird little electronic gizmos for us kids from Japan.

And he may have looked like Robert Young—and, like John Wayne, was born to wear a uniform—but at the core he was an eccentric. Despite his roots in the frozen Michigan tundra, he'd wear this God-awful cowboy hat to annoy my mother, and insist we refer to him as "our father, the cattle baron with the pointy-toed boots and the ten-gallon hat." When he was home from trips he'd walk a mile with us to school, and on the way, we'd pause to sing in four-part harmony when the mood struck him. We were a family of singers. "Poison oak!" he would begin, in his lovely baritone, gesturing toward the green-red shrub on the side of the road. Then we'd go up the scale: Rob, me, Anne, and then Lisa's little voice on top, until we were all crooning "poison oak!" in perfect harmony and in ear-shattering volume. And he and my mom sang show tunes a lot around the house—Rogers and Hammerstein, the Gershwins. "Embraceable You" was a house favorite.

To this day, if that song comes on the public broadcasting jazz station I listen to, I have to turn it off to avoid the waterworks.

Dad could also get cranky. And we all thought it was remarkable that Erin, as a tiny girl, was undaunted by our warnings not to bother Grandpa before he'd had his coffee and *Chronicle* in the morning, when he was still coated in a layer of crotchety. When we lived with them, or if we were vacationing together or spending the night for some reason, she'd run to him first thing and climb up on his lap, pull away his newspaper, and insist he play with her. To our amazement, he always did just that. To say he had a tender spot for his only granddaughter is a huge understatement.

"Is Grandpa going on a walkabout after the party?" Erin asks, throwing dirty clothes in the washing machine, as she always does when she comes home. "Moab? The Grand Tetons?"

Dad is famous for the driving trips he's done several times a year since he retired twenty years ago at sixty. He's gone as far east as Maine (to see Erin at college), as far north as the Arctic Circle. But his favorite destinations usually involve golf in a remote (and cheap) location somewhere—often Moab, Utah, which has become his Mecca: a place he goes to chill, marvel at rugged nature, read Tony Hillerman novels. If he were Native American, he would do sweat lodges. But he is not, so he plays golf near the Colorado River, finding great spiritual nourishment there. I've referred to him many times as Carlos Castaneda in plaid pants.

"I was kind of hoping that when he turned eighty, he might give these trips up." Anne frowns.

"Do you want to be the one to tell him we think he's too old to be on the road?" I ask, sighing. "You know it'd kill him."

"Well, I did bring it up to him last time I was home, and he got upset. But I had to! I worry he might kill someone, in addition to himself, if he falls asleep at the wheel or something!"

"Ugh, can we not talk about this?" Erin, after the trauma of losing Grandma, has no intentions of letting Grandpa go anytime soon.

"He asked if I'm bringing a date tomorrow!" I tell them. "He hasn't asked me that in ages."

They both laugh. "Hope springs eternal—I mean, for Dad," Anne says, shaking her head.

"You should write about Grandpa," Erin suggests. "For his birthday."

"I already did." I smile. "It's in tomorrow's paper, so he'll see it before the party."

The column is about the ways single women look at their fathers, and how I, the tomboy, wanted to be Captain Bob when I grew up.

> *I bothered him constantly for tales of aviation, stories about the world. He told me about landing planes on the Yucatan Peninsula and narrowly missing cows on the runway, about having prop engines flame out halfway from Anchorage to Tokyo, about seeing the northern lights from the cockpit. He broke flight speed records and flew the inaugural flight into Beijing when it reopened to tourism. I didn't want my mother's life, seemingly welded to kids and kitchen. I wanted his. To travel and explore, and to be a hero, as he was to me.*
>
> *It was only when I reached my teenage years that I began to see*

my father as less than heroic. I became active in the anti–Vietnam War movement, volunteering at the Institute for Nonviolence. And our family dinners became battlegrounds for clashing ideologies. I simultaneously got in touch with my inner Bad Girl. Sex, drugs, and rock 'n' roll became the credo during my college years, and I chafed at the strict rules Dad put on my comings and goings when I was home during the summer. We alternated between angry silences and hostile encounters. I couldn't wait to graduate and have a life of my own.

I no longer wanted his.

In the spring of 1975 I watched the TV news with increasing alarm as the war that I'd protested against so vociferously was culminating in catastrophe. Americans in Saigon were fleeing the encroaching North Vietnamese, knowing a bloodbath was to come. Commercial planes that landed in Saigon—where my dad routinely flew—were shot at from the ground. And as panic set in among both American and Vietnamese citizens, fistfights erupted among people trying to get on a flight. There were photos of flight attendants being thrown off the plane by those desperate to leave.

Then I got the call from my mother: My dad's around-the-world flight had been held up in Bangkok, and he had been asked if he would be willing to off-load all the passengers from his Boeing 747 and fly into Saigon with an empty plane to rescue desperately stranded civilians.

I remember feeling cotton-mouthed when my mother told me this, but she was cool. She told me that Dad had asked the flight officers to vote, and to a man they said, "We have to go." Then he told the flight attendants—all female—that there was no need for them to endanger themselves and that they should disembark with the passengers and wait to be picked up by another plane.

To a woman they voted to stay with the plane, with the captain.

Captain? I thought with amazement. That's my dad.

And so they took off toward Saigon. They were within a short distance when they were waved off. The city—and the airport—had fallen to the North Vietnamese. When my mother finished the story, I cried. And I felt oddly foolish and small. If you're lucky, there are moments in life when you can look at your father with the same eyes you used as a child. When that happens, he is never less than heroic.

I bring the column with me to the party in case my dad hasn't seen it. And of course, he has not—having been busy all day with visiting friends. The event is a splendid success: plenty of Champagne, nice speeches, reuniting of relatives and friends. Everyone loves the napkins, and the flowers, although I end up splitting Vince's massive floral tribute into several smaller arrangements for the tables. As things wind down, I take my dad aside to share the column with him. As he reads it, his lip starts to quake, and by the time he's finished, he's red-eyed.

"Thank you," he says, embracing me. "That was my favorite part of the whole damn day."

"You're welcome, Dad," I respond, feeling sentimental from Champagne. "I wish Mom could have been here, too."

"Oh, me too," he says, casting his eyes skyward. "She'd have been so proud of you kids. And you look more like her all the time . . ."

I sigh. "So I was told several times tonight. I should be so lucky."

As we're helping the caterer clean up, Anne asks about the flowers. "Who sent them? I don't think I ever heard," she says, stacking rental plates.

I swallow. "Well, actually, they're from Vince Smith, remember him? My first boyfriend at Willamette? He's gotten in touch with me because of the column, and is really trying hard to woo me from Denver. He wants to come out and visit. I tried to put him off but he's not being put off, and he seems serious about wanting to see me."

I realize words are spastically oozing from my grinning lips, the Champagne proving to be a truth serum of sorts.

"And I'm not sure what I think about it, because it makes me a little uncomfortable, and I'm trying not to get my hopes up, but things haven't been so good for me romantically lately, so I'm trying not to get excited but I still am.

"Anyway . . ." I pause, realizing Anne is staring at me with her mouth agape. "What do you think?"

"I think you might want to think twice," she says flatly. "That guy was a world-class prick."

The Unkindest Cuts

"Did you get my flowers?"

The masculine voice on the other end of the phone is vaguely familiar; although, given my acutely hungover state, I might also be dreaming. Deep and round, but not raspy like Lenny's, this is a sexy voice indeed. Reality? Fantasy? Gods of sobriety, help me sort this out!

"Uh, hello?" is about as clever as I can manage. It's nine in the damn morning and I threw a huge party yesterday, what do people want from me? Certainly not to raise my head off the pillow.

"Jane, it's Vince."

"Oh God," I say, jerking myself up to a sitting position, like a rocket set to launch. "How are you?"

He laughs. "Better than you, obviously. Good party yesterday, I take it?"

"Very good, yes," I say, tossing off my suddenly-too-hot down comforter. "Thanks for the flowers. They were a big hit—and most unexpected."

"Well, I wanted to surprise you and take away some of the burden of this party. I know you'd been working hard on it."

Did my sister really call him a world-class prick?

"Vince, it's nice to hear your actual voice for the first time in decades," I say, unable to stifle a yawn with my excitement. "But, uh . . . why are you calling me?"

Telephone calls in an e-mail universe: strange, exotic, and not entirely welcome.

"Because I'm being unexpectedly sent to Bangkok for business next week, and I was about to make my reservations. And I thought . . ." he pauses, cutely nervous. "Maybe I could ask them to route me through San Francisco?"

Now I'm really awake. "Wow, I don't know! I mean, we talked about meeting, but I thought it wouldn't be for another few weeks, if not months. . . ."

"Well, if it's too soon . . ." he says, sounding vaguely defeated. "It just seemed like an ideal opportunity. I could stay a few days, take some meetings while I'm there. . . . "

"When would this be?" I stammer.

"Ten days—a week from Thursday."

Jeezus Christ on a pogo stick—ten days to get in shape for almost certain sex?

"Let me think about it. Just give me a couple hours to wake up and have some coffee and do a schedule check."

And a body check, too.

"Okay," he says, humbly. "I know it may seem soon. I just really want to see you."

Considering just weeks ago I'd been telling Vince to shove it, he's definitely getting points for patience and for courting me so persistently.

I climb out of bed, feeling that heady boost that only comes from being wooed, but am quickly deflated when I catch myself in the mirror—the one that should be slapped with a label: *objects appear larger than they ought to be*. Good God, it's incredible how one can let oneself go when one isn't challenged by the need to seduce.

If sex were on the horizon with *anyone* right now it would be cause for consternation: my love life doldrums and too-busy schedule have killed my desire to go to the gym and pummel myself into fighting form. The old use-it-or-lose-it adage comes to mind, and I've clearly lost it.

But the pressure is even worse because this is *Vince*—the first guy upon whose altar I sacrificed my virginal, rail-thin, eighteen-year-old body. But between that body and this one there is a difference of, oh, thirty-five pounds, give or take? How will he react? The truth is, I was scarily thin back then—maybe 105 in my sweats—even though I ate like a horse several times a day. And the truth is, I like my body better now—well, maybe ten years ago when I was in the 130s. I looked healthier, less brittle. But he obviously liked my athletic greyhound form, because he couldn't get enough of it.

Jesus, do I need this pressure?

But what's to be done? Plastic surgery has never appealed; I've always thought that was one of the least-evolved things a woman could do. I've written about this as well, haranguing women for not finding enough to love about themselves that they need a surgeon's knife to pry it out of them. What a hypocrite I would be to get something done myself. Then again . . .

"Rosalind, you know people in the society world who do these crash diets, right?" I say into her answering machine. "Can you meet me for coffee to talk about this? I think I might actually get laid next week by someone who knew me skinny and we need to talk emergency strategy!"

Erin wanders downstairs, glassy-eyed. "Good party yesterday, Mommy! And who called so early?" she asks, frowning and yawning.

"Remember I told you about Vince, my ex-boyfriend from college who had e-mailed and wanted to get together?" I say breathlessly. "Well, he wants to get together soon—like next week! He's coming through town on his way to Asia."

"Mom, that's great." She smiles tiredly, pulling back her blond mane into a rubber band.

I laugh. "Yeah, I guess so. I'm just freaked because I look like such a bag, and it's too late to do a crash diet or start going back to the gym!"

I don't even mention the remote chance of plastic surgery because she would freak out and get pissed. As I would, if our roles were reversed.

"Oh, please," she says, pouring some coffee. "Is he not the exact same age you are? Isn't it possible he might also be carrying some extra pounds? Besides, you're beautiful and you know it."

"You're so sweet." I smile. "Now I won't even charge you for that cup of coffee."

There was a time when I felt competitive with Erin, when I felt a twinge knowing that where I used to command the attention, all eyes now went to her. It was a delicately balanced time, lasting just a couple of years, when she was maybe eighteen to twenty, coming into her looks, just as I started The Fade. It took those two years to accept that she was not passing me, tortoise-and-hare style, but pole-vaulting over my head. She was the beauty, I was the beauty's mom, never to compete with her again in any way. And it's fine with me now. I take delight in the fact that she is lovely at all hours of the day and under all circumstances—even now, dressed in pjs, hair askew, mascara smudged under her eyes.

Her eyes! Okay, I have much better eyelashes. They are long and thick and curly and dark. Erin's are what blondes' eyelashes often are: so light they are almost invisible, and they have no curl whatsoever.

Okay, I'm *almost never* competitive with her.

I meet Rosalind and Claudia for more coffee a bit later to discuss my dilemma. I always know I'll get two sides of every argument listening to them—kind of a she said/she said setup.

"If this guy is worth having, you should not have to worry about your weight at all!" chides Claudia, sipping her green tea. "Like he has the market cornered on youth and fitness?"

"Well," I sigh. "He did tell me that he's an avid skier and bicyclist."

"Hmmm." Rosalind frowns, dipping a biscotti into her nonfat cappuccino. "That probably means he's in excellent shape. I think I see your dilemma. I wonder if it's too late for some lipo?"

"Liposuction? Jeez . . ." I respond. "That seems pretty radical. I was thinking more about one of those weeklong liquid diets or something."

"No, it's really not that radical," she says brightly. "I've never had it done but my dogwalker did, and she was back at work in two days! Very noninvasive. And they can suck out something like five pounds of fat! I think you should consider it! You could shed some of this," she pokes my midsection, "in an hour or two!"

Suddenly I feel queasy at the idea of someone sticking a vacuum God-knows-where. Then again, I would make Erin take out her own splinters when she was a little girl because I couldn't stomach it.

Claudia is predictably indignant. "That's such bullshit! At what point are women going to start being more accepting of the inevitability of aging? Jane, think of your other gifts. This man—any man—would be lucky to have you, as is!"

"But she would be doing this to feel better about *herself*," Rosalind interjects, "not for the sake of a man . . ."

"I always hear that and I think it's hilarious," retorts Claudia. "If we lived on a desert island with other women, do you think we'd continue to torture ourselves into shape for the purpose of pleasing *ourselves*?

Please, it's because of what we fear: not being accepted, not being loved."

"How's your bass player boyfriend?" I ask quickly, changing the subject. Her eyes narrow.

"He's gotten back together with his ex—a yoga instructor. Who's in incredible shape."

Yikes, this explains her mood. And she does have a very good point, even if it was inflicted by pain. But I've already come to my senses, knowing the idea of plastic surgery was a desperate one not based on reality. Still, an eleventh-hour recommitment to the gym might hedge my bets. So for ten days I burn it up on the exercise bike and StairMaster, even as I'm burning up my e-mail space capacity with increasingly ardent e-mails from Vince—sometimes five a day.

When I write that this feels like a relationship already, he responds: "Make no mistake, this is a love affair. More true than many in the common context. I can look in your eyes right now. How is that possible?"

And he closes another with: "Put your faith in me. Put your hand in mine."

In yet another, he broaches the subject of a vacation together in China in the fall. Despite my admittedly swoony response to such romantic suggestions, I find it within myself to remind him that e-mail chemistry does not always translate to in-person chemistry. And I suggest that we refrain from planning anything further out than Day Two of his visit.

"I know I am getting ahead of myself," he responds. "But I am a dreamer."

When the day arrives, I'm feeling remarkably calm. I think I've stressed out so much in recent weeks about seeing him that I've run out of anxiety. Either that or I've exorcised all my demons at the gym.

I valet park at Fifth Floor restaurant, which is only a block from the Palace. I find some confidence and walk into the bar with head held high. I see someone I think might be Vince but he has no hair and is wearing heavy glasses. And he gives no sign of recognition. At first. Then he stands up and waves excitedly. Oh my, it's showtime.

We hug, slightly awkwardly. *You look great no you look great how are you I didn't know your hair was so red it's been so long* . . . Trivialities exchanged, we sit down to order drinks. Vince orders a bottle of Dom Perignon; he is almost trembling with excitement as we ease into conversation. It's hard not to be distracted by the fact that the photo he e-mailed me must have been several years old (what *is it* with men?) and that he is no longer the svelte guy in the biking outfit. But, I lecture myself, this is *him* at forty-nine—keep an open mind. It's not about bodies anyway.

Is it?

As we talk, two new revelations emerge that he had not mentioned in weeks of e-mailing: he has, in recent years, joined the Catholic Church, and has become a Republican. "I didn't tell you because I thought you clearly would not approve," he says shyly. "I can tell by your column which side you're on."

I smile, fighting an urge to recoil. "I'm really just on the side of *women*—and women are not generally well supported by either of those organizations. But I know some decent people who are both Catholic and right-wing. Well, Catholic anyway."

The divine food and Champagne, followed by a bottle of Sancerre, and Vince's charming habit of touching my hand while he talks, all help him crash through my guard rails. I feel comfortable, at ease, dare I say, hopeful?

Hours later, as we head toward the elevator to leave, he pulls me unexpectedly behind the heavy drapes separating the dining room from the bar and kisses me hard and long. I am laughing through the kiss, feeling his hands slide down my back. All the way down the Market Street block he keeps stopping to kiss me, pulling on my clothes in an endearingly clumsy way. We stumble into his room at the Palace and, oh, dear, there is more wine there in an ice bucket. He opens it and pours himself a tall bathroom-glass full. I demur—"Vince, I can hardly stand up now!" But he's on a roll, swilling with one hand and using the other to flip through CDs until he finds one by Sonny Landreth, a slide guitarist we discovered that we both love. He puts it on at top volume, tumbles onto the bed without spilling a drop, and starts pulling off his tie. And, dear Lord, he starts playing his tie like an air guitar.

I suddenly feel awkward, like I really am back in his dorm room. *Hey*, I want to say, *those were fun years but who wants to relive them? Turn down the volume, Puff Daddy!* Instead I lie down next to him politely and wait to see what happens next. And that is: talk. Perhaps driven by nerves or by excess alcohol intake, Vince starts to tell me about his divorce—why he got screwed over by that bitch, how he had called her from a fishing trip in Montana to learn she was moving out, and on and on. . . . There are pauses in his slurry diatribe, during which I look over at him to see if he's passed out. During one such pause, I pull up on one elbow, lean over, and kiss him. He does not resist but neither does he melt. "Shouldn't we stop talking now?" I tease. But the subtlety of my message is lost, and he goes on talking.

Finally, during one particularly long pause, snores erupt. I sigh and look at him. Still in his suit, mouth agape, his arms splayed to the side exposing a tubby tummy—far tubbier than mine—he is neither the Pirate nor the Adonis I knew. But honestly, that part doesn't really matter. What does matter is that he's gotten, like so many people my age, angry and bitter—something I've mostly managed to avoid, except during my worst pity parties. I mean, venting your anger and fear is one thing when among friends, quite another on a *date*. The man needs therapy, not a long-distance romance. Too tired for emotion, I turn over and pull a piece of bedspread over me, and am gone.

Market Street trolley bells wake me, and when I open my eyes, Vince is dressing in a fresh suit, hair wet from the shower. "Good morning." He smiles awkwardly. "I've got to get to a meeting. Can I call you later?"

Call me later? Like I'm a chickie he picked up in a bar? Stiff from poor sleep and hungover, I'm in no mood to play cat and mouse. "What's wrong?" I ask. "Do you not have five minutes to talk?"

"Look," he stops putting on his shoes for a second. "I'm sorry about last night. I had too much to drink."

"Yes, that's for sure," I say slowly, sitting up. "But we both did. And what about today? We had not planned it at all since we just wanted to get through last night. . . ."

He doesn't look me in the eyes. "I don't know, Jane. I just feel . . . disappointed, you know? I thought we would have the chemistry we used to have. I thought you'd look . . . more like you used to! But I'd still like to see you for dinner later to see what else might develop. . . ."

He finally looks at me. His eyes are nervous and guilty and not at all affectionate.

"Hmmm, okay, got it," I hear myself saying calmly. "I think your expectations got way too high. I don't feel the same way, since I kept mine modest. And I was willing to see what developed."

And it hits me what he really said. "You thought I'd look like I *used to*? Grow up! We're both pushing fifty—and you're not exactly Mr. Swimsuit Model yourself!"

"I know, I'm sorry. It's not just that . . ." he stammers. "I'm also not sure about how well you'd fit in with my friends. They're pretty conservative and you're, well, you still love your soapbox, just like when we were in college."

I stare at him. "You know, this might have been a good thing to consider before you gave me the full-court press and invited me into your life!"

I realize I'm losing it so I throw on my shoes and grab my purse. "I've got a really good idea. Why don't you get on a fucking plane and go to Asia. And when you get home, try going to see a priest or a therapist or your Republican Party leader about your baggage before you try dating in earnest. Because you suck at it."

I take one last look at him, sitting slouched in the chair with one shoe in his lap, as I exit the door, taking what's left of my dignity with me.

Of Luck and Love

The worst thing about having several good friends to whom you tell everything is that when you have a Momentous Romantic Event they all demand to know how it went. And when it sucks eggs, as my (non) event with Vince did, you have to relive the horror by talking about it several times. There has been such a slew of e-mails and calls asking for details since he left for Bangkok yesterday—a day early—that I write one e-mail and copy it to several people. I am the Reuters of romantic debacles.

I get the anticipated, required "screw that guy" and "poor you" responses from girl- and guy-friends alike. Phil asks if "this latest debacle will see print" and I tell him not for a while—not until I'm able to process my disappointment in such a way that it can be useful for readers. "Right now I'm just feeling insulted and sad," I tell him. "But I have no insights to offer."

My dad is disappointed yet again that the rich guy and I are a no-match. And Erin all but breaks down in tears—"I had such high hopes for this one!" she says. And I realize I did, too, despite my vow of low expectations.

But even the potent cocktail of three parts sympathy and one part relief can't fix what ails me—a pervading sense that maybe I'm hexed. That my bad-luck streak is taking on plague proportions. It's the perennial question: How important is luck when looking for love? And if luck is all there is to it, doesn't that absolve us of having to look for love? And free us to sit back and wait for Cupid's arrow to hit us unexpectedly? If so, my fantasy of meeting Leo in a produce section is a genuine option, and I don't need to worry about nutrition and exercise or ever changing out of my sweats—even to go to the office.

Then again, if luck plays no hand at all, and finding love is based on hard work and good intentions, we'd exhaust ourselves looking furtively for our soul mates in every public place we go. We'd be running to Kinko's for new business cards every week after passing out every last one. And we'd work on ourselves for hours every day—exercising and therapizing and highlighting—only to wind up feeling pissed and betrayed if our soul mate didn't materialize.

If Claudia employs the hard-work formula for meeting men—with her frantic e-mailing and flirting and picking up guys like lint on a black sweater—I take the opposite tack. I expect luck to cover my drinks. Because love (or what passed for it) used to show up on my doorstep without any heavy lifting on my part, I think I'm still assuming there's no need to go after it. The net result of Claudia's pursuit and mine is approximately the same: failed marriages and crummy luck of late. So I reckon the best modus operandi is somewhere in between.

In the meantime, I promise myself to be open to ongoing possibilities, even though it's tempting to crawl inside the shell of a hermit crab and stay there until I starve myself thin.

After a few weeks of mulling over these truths and licking my wounds, I vow to take up two sympathetic friends' offers of fix-ups. And be open-minded, and flirt my ass off, which Rosalind tells me I've forgotten how to do.

"I found someone for you!" my friend Vanessa tells me breathlessly on the phone. "He lives down the coast not far from you, he's involved in wildlife rescue—in fact, he lost a few fingers to his work—and he's your age and I know he's been looking for, you know, a life mate?"

Wow, wildlife rescue—that rings my chimes as much as a mention of looks or long hair. I'm a sucker for a man with a cause. For the first time in weeks, I feel myself perking up. Bring on Tarzan. I'll be his Jane.

We set it up to pay him a brunch visit in a week or so, braving the coastal fog of August. Vanessa will bring her husband and her son to see his wild animals, and I'll be the odd-woman-out, thrown together with the odd-man-out. Then again, given the bitch-slaps Venus has been doling out lately, I should probably keep my excitement in check.

And Dieter has invited me to one of his art patron dinners at Bix, which are always studded with interesting people and boast orgiastic amounts of eating and drinking. Dieter heard from Rosalind about my recent romantic humiliation, so he sweetly phoned to tell me he's found me the perfect man to sit next to.

"Do you know the name Peter Wolf?" he asked in his crisp accent, sounding like he's smiling. "I don't know him but he's apparently a big shot in the L.A. popular music world."

My heart leapt. Peter Wolf? The hunky former lead singer of the J. Geils Band? Once married to Faye Dunaway? Now apparently single? Okay, I know I said I was done with rock stars but *come on*—not if one is being handed to me on a platter!

"Twist my arm!" I said to Dieter, laughing.

I tell Erin about my two upcoming introductions as we meet for lunch and shoe shopping near her office. God, I love having her so close by when I need reinforcement. "The wildlife guy sounds ideal," I tell her, trying on a pair of too-expensive Donald Pliners. "But I'm not allowing myself to get too excited about either one of these things since my luck has been so hideous lately."

"Mom, there's no such thing as luck!" she chides me, turning over a pair of Pumas to see the price. "You've told me that before."

Did I really tell her that? God, the full-of-shit things parents say when they want to be helpful and appear wise.

"Okay," she adds, "romance might have *something* to do with timing, but it's also about being open to possibilities! And I'm not sure you are . . ."

I stare at her. "What do you mean, not open to it? It's not like the idea of someone loving me again someday before I'm dead is repellent. I think I would like that. . . ."

"Still, I agree with Rosalind that you really don't get out there and shake your booty." She smiles. "You have all these guy-*friends* and you've gotten too comfortable with your platonic life."

"Okay, can I just say it's weird to get a lecture on booty-shaking from your daughter?" I sigh, hooking my arm through hers as we walk through Macy's. "I promise you, I'll give these guys every last chance."

"Right, because like you used to tell me, luck is really just the intersection of opportunity and preparedness!" She beams.

"Did I really say that?" I laugh. "Damn, that's pretty good!" Maybe I was a better mother than I thought.

I find myself at Dieter's dinner party fifteen minutes early—anxious, perhaps?—and luckily find Rosalind putting around the name cards. She looks sensational in a skintight black couture dress with straps that crisscross her ample chest; Dieter apparently went shopping during his last trip to Paris and brought her something from Helmut Lang.

"Does Dieter have a closet S-and-M side?" I tease, hugging her.

"I know!" She laughs. "Can you believe this dress?"

"So I guess things are okay with you two?" I ask, and she frowns.

"Well, I am this close to sending him packing. Every time I bring up marriage or children he changes the subject."

"Maybe it's a cross-cultural challenge," I joke. "Tell him that you're not sure what the deal is in France, but in this country, when a man proposes to a woman and gives her a diamond ring the size of Baltimore, *they get married*!"

She sighs, watching Dieter walk in with his entourage. He is laughing and gesturing toward the tables in the back. "I do love him so," she says softly.

I feel for Rosalind, and I'm pulling for them as a couple. But honestly, I'm beginning to question her fixation with the actual ceremony. She has a fantastic man who loves her to pieces, who will be with her forever, so maybe she should relax about the walk down the aisle. It's not like a piece of paper or a big party will validate their love. When it comes down to it, isn't a great love the best we can all hope for? Someone to stick with you through the good and bad, and hold your hair while you barf? She has that in Dieter. The rest sometimes just feels like posturing.

Or maybe I'm starting to rationalize a certain lack of diamond rings in my future.

The fifteen or so guests move around the tables looking for their place cards. I watch anxiously for someone who looks like the Peter Wolf I know—long, dark hair, brooding eyes—but no one materializes. I find my seat and sit down, and introduce myself to the man sitting next to me, a nice-looking middle-aged chap in a suit. "Peter Wolf." He smiles. "Nice to meet you!" And then he introduces me to . . . his wife. Sigh.

Dieter didn't quite do his homework: this Peter Wolf is in the music world, too, but as a record producer. We have a wonderful dinner together, despite my own personal disappointment that he's not a single-and-hot rock star.

Thanks, Venus, for another hit in the luck department.

But there's no time to brood; I'd almost forgotten that I told Claudia I'd go with her to our friend Ethan's small backyard wedding this weekend. With the way I'm feeling these days, a wedding is about the last thing I'm interested in attending, but I've known Ethan a long time and I'm happy for him. One of the original Writers Grotto founders, "E" is Po's best friend, a successful book and magazine writer, and a killer swing dancer (oh, how we all went through that phase). And, I had begun to think, destined to die a bachelor. Not because he was old—he was only in his late thirties. But because he was a die-hard romantic at heart, and his disappointments in love (which rivaled even mine) had nearly killed his interest in it. There was a year or so there where he had nearly earned the title of Sad Sack—so gloomy was he at not having met the woman of his dreams.

And then he met Rebecca, at a Halloween party I was also attending in the Western Addition. She was a resident at the University of California at San Francisco medical center, in psychology; he wrote books debunking theories of psychology. On paper, it was not a match made in heaven, but oh my, how it changed my friend. He was suddenly warm and smiling, reembracing life.

Now, in the backyard of their funky fixer-upper Victorian, with the Mission District's summer sun warming friends crowded on the lawn, Ethan waits nervously for Rebecca to descend the rickety wooden staircase. She appears, all in white, and joins him on the tiny platform. Standing back by the deck, I cannot see her face, but his is suddenly strained by joy, and he is fighting tears.

"You look beautiful," he mouths to her and smiles shakily. And they take their vows to always love and be together, looking into each other's eyes, laughing when they flub the words, applauded by friends at their conclusion. And they kiss: the sweetest, most childlike kiss I've ever seen at a wedding. It's as if they're reborn.

I feel a surge in my chest and, almost gasping from it, I back up into the shadows under their deck to regroup. "What's wrong?" Claudia whispers. I put my hand over my heart but can't seem to answer. And then the tears come, unwelcome but unstoppable, emotion bubbling over like the Champagne being poured directly above us.

"I don't know," I say, trying to collect myself. "It's just . . . so . . . *amazing*. I think I forget sometimes that things can actually work out. And what love can lead to."

I laugh through my tears at how silly I sound, and Claudia smiles into my eyes, understanding completely.

The next day, before I head off on my brunch date with Vanessa and the animal activist, I decide to turn the week's events into a column. I write about Peter Wolf, my own bad luck of late, and Ethan's wedding, finishing with what I observed:

> *Maybe you don't need luck by the bucketful. Maybe you just need it one drop at a time. That Halloween party at Tom's house? I bet Ethan was tired, late for a deadline and cross, and Rebecca was exhausted from her hours on duty. But something made them both go to Tom's house for a holiday beer. They expected a short reprieve from their lives; what they got was a permanent one.*
>
> *It's enough to give one hope to continue. I guess that's what weddings are for: a public pledge, an acknowledgment that love—and luck—still exist.*

And as for the blind date? It's apparently pretty blind to him, too: evidently Vanessa hadn't told him of her grand scheme. As we drive up to his house, we're greeted at the door unexpectedly by a woman: his new girlfriend.

Oh well, this was not to be my lucky break. But at least I know such things do exist.

Back to the Future

This week's column on luck and love provokes another outpouring, this time mostly sweet missives, with very few sour apples.

But those sour few are bitter indeed. One from a cranky older man: "Waa-waa-waa, Ms. Ganahl, another weeper. Grow up and face facts: love is wasted on the young, and the young are too foolish to know what to do with it."

Ouch.

Most e-mails are from women who have had similar thoughts, and appreciate my giving voice to them. One even thanks me for making "an important contribution to women," which strikes me as both overstated and more than I could hope for.

I read one final e-mail before I head off on my Sunday errands. "If I didn't know you so well, I'd interpret by this column that you no longer have men beating down your door," says someone named Elizabeth. "And that just simply doesn't compute. You'll have to explain it all to me Labor Day weekend."

Elizabeth . . . ? Oh good lord, it's my college friend Lisa! The tough-talking, hard-drinking ranch woman, going by her fancy lawyer name.

"Lisa! You devil woman—you've been reading me online from Vancouver!" I respond excitedly. "Sorry to say, it's more than true, but you'll hear all about my love life woes and more in a few weeks! I can't wait to see everybody! What's the news on your end? Or do you want to save it for our Labor Day drink-a-thon?"

"Let's both save it," she writes. "It's so much better over pints at The Ram."

This will be my first college reunion in five years. The timing is terrible, with Litquake just over a month away and jamming me with production duties. But being busy is not a good excuse to not see the femmes who were there with me during my formative years: who got me through both trig and countless affairs, shared pot on the rooftop at sunset, cruised for boys 24/7.

My group was always on the periphery, rebellious, forward-thinking, politically involved, disinclined to take anything too seriously. Not the kind that normally goes to reunions, which tend to be populated mostly with sorority girls and frat boys and others who embraced college life warmly by becoming cheerleaders or debaters or captains of the chess club.

I still look at those years as some of the best of my life, as confused and out of control as I often was. But God, I was also joyful and free, and so perfectly comfortable with who I was. That was, of course, before real life—marriages, kids, jobs, mortgages—came along and popped the bubble of college life. The coterie didn't do a great job of staying in touch, nor did we go to a huge amount of trouble to see each other regularly; we counted on the occasional wedding to bring us together since my friends eschewed the dreariness of college-organized reunions.

Then we started dying.

Leslie, one of my best friends, went first: a heart attack at age forty-four, just months after my sister Lisa died. That I could not bear a third funeral in two years and declined to go to Portland still produces an ache in me. Then Margaret (aka Mopsy) died after a car accident. Then Becky, in a diving accident.

"Come to Oregon," I entreated my surviving friends via e-mail a few months ago. "Before any more of us die off. While we still have our teeth."

Happy to say, they've all fallen in line—even Lynn, who is the only one besides me who doesn't live in the Pacific Northwest. There is a flurry of round-robin anticipatory e-mails in the weeks before we meet—mostly good-humored drinking challenges and reminders to bring all the old, embarrassing photos.

"Ew, Mom, I don't like to think of you as a party animal," says Erin, when I tell her that our general plan for the weekend includes a fair amount of alcohol intake. She is driving like a maniac to get me to the San Francisco airport for my morning flight to Portland, having been late as usual.

"Honey, I know you have a need to see me as more grown-up than you," I tease, "but when I get around my college friends all bets are off.

"And anyway," I continue, noticing her mascara-smudged eyes and messy hair, "you should probably just assume that you're a chip off the old block in that department. What on earth were *you* doing last night?"

"Mom." She gives the shut-up tone reserved for when she has little patience. "I've been studying my butt off for the LSATs, and so if I do go out, it's usually late. Like ten or eleven. And I did meet this really cute guy at Kezar Pub last night . . ."

Only then does a smile creep across her freckled face.

"Okay, that's enough," I sigh.

"Hey, don't despair." She smiles. "You might get lucky in Oregon."

"It'll never happen. I'm more interested in gaining some insights for the column. As long as they can be gained between tequila shots."

Erin rolls her eyes.

The first night in Salem is taken up with alumni folderol, and my friends assemble in time for the rubber-chicken dinner on campus. Too tired to party, we promise to make Sunday night the one to remember. I'm not disappointed at our lack of festive spirit; after all, I remind myself, we are now *middle-aged.*

But Sunday night we make good on the promise. After dinner at a restaurant near campus, the five of us head over to The Ram, the bar we used to lie our way into before we were twenty-one. Settling into a booth with our drinks, we dish and reminisce: the time we all took mescaline and painted our faces and ran around campus like aborigines hunting boar, the time we stole the keg of beer from a fraternity and drank it with our friends, countless tales of male-related meltdowns.

I update them on my jagged off-on love-hate affair with Lenny. "I thought you told me you weren't going to see him anymore?" asks Connie, Erin's godmother and my closest friend in the group. In my tipsy state, I close my eyes and go stream-of-conscious: "I try . . . to break free, but he's . . . too . . . *hot*!" They all laugh.

"I dunno," I add. "I think about him every day. And I keep hoping I'll meet someone to make me forget about him for good. I'd kill to have him out of my system."

"I have a sawed-off shotgun on the ranch, if that would help!" Lisa offers with a grin, her eyes slightly blurred from the whiskey. I know she is not kidding.

She talks about her horrific divorce but triumphant completion of law school; Connie is learning how to run a political campaign since her husband is running for county commissioner in Washington state; Melissa is training to run a marathon for her fiftieth birthday. "God," I quip, "I just want to have a *date* for mine!"

And Lynn tells the sweet story of reconnecting with her very first boyfriend from college—a handsome Turk who was so hirsute we referred to him as Rug Man—with whom she remains today. And, feeling like the class loser, I tell them the story of Vince, and our attempted reunion followed by his disappointment that I wasn't the gamine gal of his past. They boo in unison.

"That guy was always a jerk, but was he really the first guy you slept with?" asks Connie. "I can't believe you were over eighteen when you lost your virginity!"

A casual poll reveals that the rest of them were deflowered their junior or senior year in high school.

"Yeah, but Jane made up for lost time," says Lisa, her voice husky from lifelong smoking. "We were slutty at an earlier age, but you passed us all in numbers, I'm sure."

I'm mock-indignant. "I doubt that! I think I'm pretty normal for this age!"

They've thrown down the slut gauntlet and I'm right there to pick it up. I suggest that we reveal our numbers, starting with Lynn on my right. She admits to only five or six lovers, but she married young and stayed married until just a few years ago. Then it's my turn.

"I'd say around fifty or fifty-five, but I've sort of lost track. . . ."

There are gasps all around; their mouths are hanging open.

"Come on!" I sputter. "You guys were way sluttier than I was in college!" But as we work our way around the circle, the numbers tell a different story: eight, twelve, sixteen . . . No one, I'm chagrined to hear, is even in my ballpark.

I defend myself by noting that in my forty-nine years on the planet,

I was only married for ten or so of them. That leaves a lot of single years. "And anyway," I add, "these numbers are mere speculation. I might be way off—inflating my résumé, so to speak."

"Well, here's a toast to us sluts—some sluttier than others—then and now," says Melissa, raising her glass. "To the foxy, freaky, fabulous femme fatales . . ."

We all roar with laughter as we clink glasses—she somehow managed to remember the name we dubbed ourselves back then.

Lynn, always the sweet, sentimental one, wells up when she proposes another toast: "To our friends who are gone—Mopsy, Leslie, and Becky—who ought to be here with us tonight. And to keeping our health until we meet again."

This time, everyone toasts but Lisa, whose whiskey glass stays on the table. "Guys," she says slowly, "sorry to blow the good vibe, but there's no keeping my health, I'm afraid. I just found out . . . Well, I have pancreatic cancer."

There is stunned silence, as we all try to absorb the bomb that was just dropped. "What? When?" stammers Melissa, who is closer to Lisa than any of us. Lynn puts her hand over her mouth.

"Just got the test results a few weeks ago," says Lisa, ever tough, not wavering in her delivery of the awful news. "They're saying it doesn't look good. The average person only lives a few months with this. But I plan to be one of those people who lives for eight years for no apparent reason."

She smiles unevenly. "Anyway, I knew there was a chance that this might be my last reunion with you guys, and I didn't want to miss it. I needed to see you."

There is stunned silence. Lisa pauses, realizing she's just unleashed a party-ending bummer. "But right now," she sighs with a shaky smile, "what I need is a cigarette; who wants to join me outside?"

Connie, a registered nurse, is torn between exasperation and pity.

"Don't you think you might improve your chances if you give that shit up?" she asks her, feigning a breezy tone.

Lisa cackles. "At this point, I worry more about sending my body into shock by quitting!"

"I'll go with you," I offer, and follow Lisa out onto the wooden back deck, where water from Mill Creek tumbles sweetly by and the moonlight seeps through the elm trees.

"I'm sorry," Lisa says, before I can say a word, as she lights up a Camel. "I know you lost one Lisa already. I'm sorry to add more consternation. You've already been through a lot of loss."

"You're worried about *me*?" I say, taking her free hand. "Christ, I should be the least of your worries. Although I admit to a flashback of sorts as soon as the words were out of your mouth."

I pause, fighting tears. "But you! You're so fucking tough. How are you feeling? Really?"

"I do okay and then it will be a beautiful day or something, and then I think, I'll really miss this," she says, exhaling a plum of smoke upward into the sky. She turns to me, smiling unexpectedly, with her eyes shining with tears. "I try to be positive, and I've had a great life, but I have to be realistic, too. This is a shitty hand I've been dealt."

She stubs her cigarette in an ashtray and embraces me. "But I'm glad we got the moment to ourselves so I could tell you how proud I am of what you're doing. It's not just fun stuff you're writing, it's important. I think you should even think about writing a book."

I pull back, and look quizzically in Lisa's face. "A book? Me? What on earth would I call it?"

She smiles mischievously. "How about . . . 'Fifty or Fifty-five, I've Lost Track'?"

We laugh like we were still young, and in that moment, transported to a place without cancer or divorce or grief, we still are.

The next day, slightly hobbled by an evening that came back together joyfully despite the bad news, and climaxed with a jukebox sing-along to "Smoke on the Water" by Deep Purple—with Lisa singing the loudest of anyone—we go our separate ways after vowing to stay in better touch. Melissa has offered me a ride to the airport, and it's a perfect chance to debrief on the reunion with my old roommate. That sophomore year, we'd seen each other through times that were both joyous and horrible, gave each other man advice, fought over turf, expressed undying affection.

I thought she'd get married first, since that was a personal goal for her. Instead, it was I who married young, right out of college, and she who stayed single through most of her twenties, partying in Palm Springs and dating the rich and famous. But when she met Mike, Melissa married just-like-that, and quickly had three daughters who look just like her. I saw an entirely new Melissa then, utterly in control of her family, her work. The wild girl had found a corner of herself that was solid and domestic, and built on it. Meanwhile, I was at loose ends because I had not figured out yet what would make me happy or where I fit in.

Pretty much like . . . now.

"I just can't fathom what Lisa must be going through," I say. "And I'm thrilled that her son has been able to take time off work to come and be with her now. These are the times when it's tough to be single."

She looks at me squarely. "You seem to be doing great yourself. The single life seems to agree with you."

"Do you think so? I guess I've really started to enjoy living alone. But it took a long time before I was able to think of it as a privilege, not a prison."

"Well," Melissa says, smiling, "It's what you always said you wanted. You used to say monogamy would never work for you and you always wanted to be single."

"What? I said that?" I am astonished.

"Yes, you did. You said you wanted to be free to read and travel and go to concerts, and you hated the idea of being with someone twenty-four/seven. I remember when you told me you were marrying Erin's dad—it was because he wouldn't live together without getting married. You weren't exactly thrilled. So I'm not surprised you found your happiness without needing to be married."

The words have the impact of a thunderbolt. "Thank you for reminding me of who I was back then," I say to Melissa as we hug goodbye. "I think sometimes when we become adults we lose track of who we really are at the core."

On the flight home, I have so many things to think about. How one can learn about oneself by going back in time, and how those revelations can reshape one's view of the future. Maybe I should stop thinking of permanence and try to be happy with a series of fascinating affairs, since that is clearly my bent anyway. Maybe Leo is a plural noun; maybe the perfect man for me is actually *men.* Maybe love should have been the goal all along. And not just love of men, but love of friends. I vow to stay in closer touch with Lisa.

Feeling rich with new information, the reunion column writes itself for a change, sans struggle. And I conclude by thumbing my nose at the bitter e-mailer of a few weeks ago who said life was wasted on the foolish young: *"We may be foolish when we're young, but we're also brilliantly in touch with who we are."*

Lit Lovers Are Good Lovers

Late September is San Francisco's most glorious time—the plentiful sun is slanted and gold-orange, the mornings are crisp, and the afternoons fog-free at long last, as the ocean cools down and can no longer produce its heat-borne mist. Flimsy dresses and blouses that stayed inside all summer or were covered with sweaters finally see the light of day. If in spring our thoughts turn to sex, in the fall they turn to books and sex. Sometimes simultaneously.

Tonight is Litquake's closing-night party at an arty hotel in the Tenderloin, and the mood is euphoric after a brilliant weekend. Mixing it up on the patio and drinking free vodka cocktails are dozens of San Francisco's literary elite, from Dave and Vendela to Amy and her ubiquitous dogs. And this year we got smart and asked the management to throw in a couple of room nights as well, so I can crash here rather than worrying about crashing my car driving home to the coast.

I catch the eye of a man in the middle of the packed bar. It's dark, but from here he sure looks like Andrew, someone I was with for a few months just before I met Lenny and, thinking I was in love, gave him the heave-ho. A brilliant but struggling techie I met through work colleagues, he was an avid reader, even of classics that nobody reads anymore: Matthew Arnold, Tolstoy. He was also a dynamite cook and made dinner for me often during our several-months-long affair.

Yes, it was an affair—the definition thereof being that I never slept over at his house, or vice versa. I recall that when I told Po this, he found it strange and very male. "Why not sleep with him?" he had asked. "There is much to be learned about someone when you wake up with them and everyone's sober."

I told Po the truth: that I liked him fine, but something about him told me that he was not relationship material. Perhaps it was because he was so shy (a home-and-hearth-loving Cancer—the opposite of Leo) and disliked large parties? So that certainly can't be him I see across the room.

"Jane?" I turn around and it's indeed Andrew, grinning and cute and awkward as I remembered. "Nice event today, I was in the audience. I hope you don't mind my crashing your party!"

"Andrew! Of course you're welcome!" I hug him tightly, feeling his chest against mine. "How are you? Besides a sight for sore eyes and handsome as always?"

He blushes. "I'm doing good. Have my hands in a whole new tech venture, kind of an updated virtual reality." Andrew—one of the few techies who didn't slash his wrists after the dot-bomb.

We hit the free vodka cocktails pretty hard, chatting all the while. Po and Michele come over for hugs and huzzahs, and I reintroduce them to Andrew, inducing who-is-this-guy expressions. "You met Andrew at a salon a few years ago," I stammer, trying to refresh their memories.

Po leans around to whisper in my ear. "This is the guy you never slept with, right?"

"Right," I whisper back. "The classic no-strings affair."

By the time the party hits full stride around midnight, Irvine Welsh is playing DJ, people are dancing, Andrew and I are at the mercy of the vodka and talking so intimately that it feels like we're this close to a mouth-on-mouth situation—and suddenly there is a splash in the pool. Poet Kim Addonizio has stripped down to her underwear and dived in, tattoos shimmering as she swims the length of the illuminated pool to the cheers of the inebriated crowd around her. After one lap each way she draws herself out, with the help of three young sailors who have somehow crashed the party. She is laughing but her teeth are chattering.

"Come on," I say to Andrew, pulling on his hand. "My room's just over there—let's get her a towel."

I'm so high it's hard to fit my card key into the slot, but I manage. The room is dark and I fumble for the switch, when suddenly I find myself on the bed, tumbling in the darkness with Andrew's insistent mouth on mine. I start to laugh uncontrollably—a joyful whoop that says *Good God, I'm having sex!* It's been a thousand years! Within minutes we're naked on the bed and I'm remembering why my time with Andrew was so lovely. I just wish I weren't quite so out of it so I could really savor it more . . . ooh more . . .

As I drift off to sleep, too exhausted to make a conscious decision about whether I want to keep my record intact of never waking up next to this man, I remember how this all started.

"The towel!" I nudge a comatose Andrew next to me. "I hope Kim isn't freezing. . . ." And then I'm gone.

The next morning I wake first, and am acutely aware of the male body in bed next to me. And I wish it weren't. Or I weren't. This is at least awkward, if not all wrong. I grab my overnight bag and tiptoe into the bathroom for a quick washcloth bath. I squint at myself in the mirror as I catch a glance of this body I'm still trying to make peace with. I guess it's true that when the lights are off, a few extra pounds are pretty goddamn irrelevant. The thought makes me chuckle.

When I return to the bedroom, Andrew is awake and pulls up on one elbow, surprised to see me ready to go. He pats the bed next to him, and I obligingly, if awkwardly, put my bag on the chair and sit down. "That was nice," he says hoarsely. "I'm so glad I crashed your party." He smiles and lifts up his face for me to kiss him, which I do. In the morning light I can see the lines in his face and they are comforting.

"Well, thanks for being my party favor." I smile. "It was much better than a bag of books."

"Can't you stay?" he asks.

Andrew has never once asked me to stay.

"Sorry, gotta go," I stammer. "Cats hungry at home."

"Can I call you?" he asks, lowering himself back down to the mattress.

I want to ask, "What's the point? Isn't this just a one-night stand?" But that would seem unsporting, and perhaps this marks a new beginning for me and old Andrew, a deepening of a shallow, nonemotional affair? Hmmm . . .

"Sure," I sigh. "Why not?"

I slink out of the hotel lobby, and catch the eye of the party professional, there early to finish packing up the Litquake collateral. She tries to appear casual, smiling and trying not to raise an eyebrow at the woman who hired her, who's clearly doing the walk of shame.

Me, doing the walk of shame at long last. Sweet.

My wanton indiscretion at Litquake's closing night turned out not to be a one-night stand after all. I'm glad I answered Andrew's call a couple of days later, dubious as I was. My cats, however, are not glad. They're pissed that I've been dragging my tail home wickedly late these last few weeks, only sleeping half a night with them in my bed.

But my friends, who are sick of listening to me kvetch about my sexless life, are thrilled. And I am doubly so: I am having an affair. A real one: with hickeys and sweat and wine and laughter.

In just three weeks, Andrew and I seem to have already established a satisfying new routine: he makes me dinner, we drink a lot of wine, have sex—and then I go home. It works well for me that he's in the city near my office and my house is twenty minutes south of there; I get to be the one who leaves. Every time. I'm not left open to the potential pang of being left, which I suspect would happen if the shoe were on the male foot.

I guess, in that sense, I ought not to be *that* pleased with the Andrew Situation. Because even though it's been a few years since we left off, we have moved no farther down the romance road. I'm still taking the same exit.

But I tell myself it's okay, at least for now; I'm reveling in my lover's earthy charms. I love the fact that Andrew makes no apologies for his love of food, wine, pot—nor the few extra pounds around his middle. Nor does he seem to notice mine, which makes me feel sexy indeed. In fact, Andrew was one of my first real grown-up lovers after I quit young men: the sex has always been quietly passionate, deliberate, eye-to-eye, focused. Orgasms have never been an issue, as they were sometimes with the smoother-skinned, frantically energetic young guys I once fancied, who were all stamina and no style.

Best of all, Andrew makes me forget about Lenny. Well, not completely. But I think of him now just once a day instead of five times.

I also realize that by limiting my intimacy with him, I'm not taking Andrew seriously as a soul mate contender. Funny how I've always gotten mad at my guy-friends, Phil especially, for always looking over the head of the woman they're with, thinking a much better one is out there that would answer every single one of their nanoneeds. And here

I'm doing it with Andrew. It's not that he's unworthy, it's just that I can tell we lack something as a couple. Depth? Emotional connection? Andrew is smart and hot, but I have no desire to wake up with him, go to the Farmer's Market at the Ferry Building, plan a life together.

And even though I'd like to imagine he'll still be around in five months or so when I turn fifty, and be my date and toast my wonderfulness at my party, I realize that affairs such as this don't have a particularly long shelf life. But boy, this routine sure works for me at the moment.

Rosalind drops in on me at my office desk to demand information. "How is it going? When are you going to bring him to an event so I can check him out?" she asks eagerly. "Shall I throw another dinner party?"

I frown. "You know I don't really want to introduce him to the gang until this seems like it has some staying power. And for all I know it could be over tomorrow!"

She drops her mouth, exasperated. "How could you say that? Shouldn't you be *working on it* to make sure it's not over tomorrow? Has he expressed any feelings yet?"

I laugh. "At least for now this is nothing but casual. Feelings have never entered into my time with Andrew."

Rosalind looks oddly sorrowful. "Then you're wasting your time. You deserve someone who will love and marry you, not someone who just wants to have sex. Then again, maybe you're not giving this guy a chance! Maybe feelings *would* enter into it if you were open to them."

It's clear Rosalind is on a marriage-or-die mission, and can't conceive of a liaison devoid of all those complications. No point in arguing with her.

"Well," I sigh. "This isn't the first time I've been told I'm not particularly open to love."

"Well, there you are!" she says encouragingly. "Just watch for signs of his feelings. Be open to them—to all his signals."

"Okay, okay," I surrender. "Anyway, you know how these no-strings affairs go. They work fine until they suddenly don't. They are sweet until something sours. So I'm taking a wait-and-see attitude. And how about you and Dieter? Got a date set yet?"

"Oh, you know him," she says. "Every time I try to press him on it, he says he can't even think about it right now because finances are so tough . . . and then he brings me expensive gifts! And my biological clock is ticking! I'm closing in on forty!"

It's moments like this when casual doesn't look so bad. And off I go toward Andrew's house in Bernal Heights for, yes, more three-star cooking and four-star sex. As I zip down Folsom Street, admiring the slew of jack-o'-lanterns on porches announcing Halloween tomorrow, my phone rings and, fumbling for it in my purse, I don't bother to check the number before I flip it open and say hello.

"Still speaking to me?" says the rumbling bass on the other end.

"Lenny," I sigh. Of course, men always get the signal that you've stopped missing them every goddamn day, even when they're across the country, and have to intervene somehow. "Of course I am. How are you?"

"Thinking about you, so I thought I'd call."

I chuckle. "It's good to know you think of me every few months at least. Although I wasn't sure I'd ever hear from you again after my diatribe in print. Or did you even read that?"

"I did," he says quickly. "But it was well deserved. You've been more than tolerant with me and I really acted like a schmuck. Can I make it up to you? I meant it when I said you were an amazing woman."

"Oh now . . ." I start with a coy response, and then feel unexpectedly flushed and on the verge of tears, so I pull over and put my car in park. In a flash it's so obvious: I am not even close to over him.

"Yeah, I'm fabulous," I say, regrouping. "But you've always known that."

He laughs, then coughs. Jesus, when is he going to give up those cigarettes? "My gig there in a few weeks was canceled—my drummer was diagnosed with RSI and we're looking for a new one. But it turns out I'll be there for Thanksgiving weekend anyway, seeing my best friend in Napa that you met at the San Jose show. My parents are on a fucking cruise, if you can imagine."

His parents, to whom he is so slavishly devoted that he jumps off tours to spend every holiday at home. He can't be such a bad guy, can he?

"So that's a month away now," I say, flipping through my beat-up day planner. "Erin's going down to her dad's for the holiday weekend, so maybe we should plan dinner that Friday night in The City or something."

"Or something . . ." Lenny flirts. I look at the time and realize I'm late getting to Andrew's.

"Don't get your hopes up too high," I purr back, restarting my car. "This time *I'm* the one who's seeing someone. . . ."

"I'll take my chances," he chuckles, and hangs up.

When I get to Andrew's, feeling flustered and distracted, he is in the kitchen as always, looking cute in his chef's apron. He holds his arm out and taps his wristwatch in mock irritation. I go to him quickly and kiss him full-on, pulling his slightly fleshy frame into me. He pulls back, slightly perplexed.

"Wow, hello to you, too!" He laughs. "What's up?"

"Just . . . good to see you," I stammer, slightly embarrassed. But what I'm really thinking is: *I was just checking to see if I get the same rush from kissing you as I do just hearing Lenny's voice. I wish I did, but I don't.*

That night is less blissful by half because I can't stop thinking about Lenny; I leave earlier than usual, before Andrew is even asleep. Before I do, though, I whisper an invitation to come with me to the opening night of the Film Arts Festival this weekend. I'm not sure why I'm doing this. Maybe I want to see how he does when we're out in the world, with my all-important pals. Maybe things will deepen when we share more experiences? Maybe.

I meet Andrew outside the cavernous nightclub that is the site of this year's festival kickoff event. "You look great," says Andrew, and we give a quick hug.

This is not Andrew's normal milieu; he likes his nerdy tech friends and his books and his home with his two cats and two occasionally visiting kids. He doesn't go out much—at all. He's looking a tad intimidated by the buzz of the place, and a bit awed by the light show flashing movie images on the wall. It doesn't help that I am pulled on from the moment we get there—schmoozed-up by an author who was at Litquake and wants to read at next year's festival, and then kissed by one of our festival sponsors, the hunky head of an Easy Bay publishing company. When he meets Andrew, he nudges him and winks, "Have you been in her column yet?"

Andrew smiles but looks taken aback. "What did he mean by that?" he asks later. "You'd never put me in your column, would you?"

"You knew this job was dangerous when you took it!" I joke, but he is not smiling.

We are joined by Michele and Po, who is in his last weeks of calm before his book hits the shelves and everything goes into high gear with the publicity machine.

When I reintroduce them to a very quiet Andrew, Po is courteous, but whispers in my ear, "Is it true you screwed him at the Litquake closing party? And have you actually spent the night with him yet?"

"Shhhhhh!!" I whisper back, grinning. "Yes . . . and no!"

Dan joins us in the three-deep line at the bar, and I introduce him to Andrew. "Where's Dayna?" I ask.

"She's meeting me here when she gets done with the editor who's at our house," says Dan. He explains to Andrew that they are in the throes of editing an industrial film, the likes of which pays for their less lucrative, but more prestigious, work in documentary filmmaking. "The D's," as we call them, are the only couple I know with two Emmys sitting in an alcove in their hallway, decorated with religious kitsch.

"What kind of documentary are you working on now?" Andrew asks.

"It's about the Ballets Russes," Dan replies, balancing his two-olive martini to prevent spillage as we exit the bar area. "You've probably never heard of it. . . ."

"Sure." Andrew smiles. "You mean the troupe that toured the United States during the postwar years and established ballet in America?"

Dan raises his eyebrows. "Damn, that's pretty good! Normally I have to explain it to everyone." He gives me a "you picked a good one" wink as he turns away to scan the club for his wife. Just then Dayna walks in the door in the distance, wearing one of her trademark retro designer outfits, big blocks of color splashed across a sixties mod dress. She doesn't see us, but Dan sees her and waves excitedly.

He turns to me with a happy grin. "That's my baby!"

And he is off to collect her, as I stand there shaking my head. "Those two," I tell Andrew, "have been together since Stanford grad school. Almost twenty years, I'd guess. And look at him—he's still crazy in love with her. It's astonishing."

Andrew nods in vague agreement. And there is a pause before he makes a declaration.

"I'd like to be in love like that again someday."

The honesty of his statement, and the utter tactlessness of it, almost makes me choke on my Bombay-tonic. It's kind of like listening to a musician play a song just for you, and then saying, "Gee, I hope I hear some tunes again someday that don't suck!"

While I mull how to respond, I lecture myself: You cannot be pissed at his obvious lack of feelings toward you! You don't have any for him! But my inner child is mewling: he should love me anyway because I'm so goddamned lovable!

So I find the middle ground. "You know, you just said something pretty important. Even though we're having sex almost every night, you're not in love with me."

A little tornado of reactions skips across his face, making him look even smaller in the midst of the partying throng.

"It's okay," I reassure him, touching his hand, even though I'm not sure it is. "I don't love you either—at least not now. I guess the question is whether you think we might, you know . . . someday?"

He hesitates. "I don't know, Jane. Maybe I don't even know what love looks like anymore."

I ponder a moment. "I think, for me, it's wanting to be with someone all the time. Wanting to get up after sleeping together and go to the farmers' market, and hang out all day long, and have sex again in the afternoon, and talk on the phone late at night . . ."

I realize I'm talking about how things used to be with Lenny.

I also realize the shelf life of this no-strings arrangement with Andrew has just expired and something is smelling slightly turned.

"You know," I tell him, feeling suddenly wistful, "there's no need for us to settle, either of us. I know I used to be good at open-ended affairs, but I don't think I am anymore. Maybe my self-esteem has taken too many hits this last year to keep hanging out in a dead-end relationship where I'm not, I don't know, treasured? I do want someone to love me. I can't help it."

He smiles. "Well, if that changes, and you're willing to settle for less, you know how to find me."

He looks relieved to be heading for the door, and back to the safety of his books and his home and his intellectual life. I watch him go, wondering why I don't feel sad. Probably because this feels honest and right.

"Where's Andrew?" asks Po, as he and Michele find me standing alone.

"Ah, well, his shelf life just expired and he had to go home," I sigh. "I just think I'm getting too old and complicated for casual sex. It sounds like such a good idea but immediately it's clear that there's not enough . . . substance."

"What you're saying is that you really don't just want someone to sleep with," says Po, winking.

"Yes, I guess so." I shrug. "I want it all, damn it! Is that so wrong?"

"It's not wrong at all!" Po says softly, pulling Michele close. He didn't settle for less than real, honest-to-God love; why should I?

Thankful for the Backseat

The alarm goes off at four a.m. on Thanksgiving Day, and, lurching into vertical mode, I stagger into Erin's bedroom and sit next to her sleeping form. I put one hand on her back and press down several times rapidly, making her bob wildly on the ancient mattress and box springs, which once belonged to my grandma. When she was a little girl, she found this highly entertaining. But this morning she does not.

"Stop it . . . or I'll kill you."

"Wake up," I say wearily. "You have to get up and go to L.A. for Thanksgiving because you hate your mother."

"*Gmphrgh,*" she grunts, rolling over without opening her eyes. "Well, then you hate me for waking me up this early. . . ."

"And *you* hate *me,*" I whisper into her ear, "for choosing your father over me on the holiday."

Now she's giggling—a froggy, early-morning noise—and stretching to her full five feet five. "Jeez, have I really put up with this crappy routine for twenty years?"

Yes, God bless her, she has. But so have I.

"And anyway," she says, sitting up and looking at her watch, "you know how it works. There for Thanksgiving, here for Christmas. Next year the reverse."

"I guess that's a small consolation prize," I mutter.

"Mom, can we not do this now?" she says, words distorted by yawning. "I wish I could be here, too, but my dad's expecting me."

I need to get a grip before I say something hateful. I have a proud tradition of never (okay, rarely) slagging Erin's dad to her, even when he had not paid child support in a year and I wanted to kill him. It was only partly good parenting and altruism; Erin would not tolerate any negativity about him at all, and would cut me off at the knees if I dared suggest that because I did one hundred percent of the parenting chores, he did not deserve her on holidays.

"You're right, honey," I sigh. "Sorry. Just feeling sad; holidays since the 'death years' have always been a little hard."

A little? Try world-class crying jags. Let's hope I can avoid those this year.

"Mommy." She smiles, childlike. "I'll be here for Christmas. We'll make it a good one, okay? Have friends over? Get a big tree? Eat cookie dough? Put the reindeer antlers on the kitties?"

And she's off to shower. I make us some coffee and feed the cats. I'm thankful that I don't need to get out of my sweats to escort her to SFO for a six a.m. flight to LAX. She looks maddeningly cheerful as we stuff her suitcase into the backseat and head over the hill to the airport.

"You okay?" she asks, checking in.

"Yeah, I'm okay. Holidays just suck sometimes because they make you assess where you're at in your life and sometimes it just ain't pretty."

"Hold on!" she says incredulously. "When has life ever been better for you? You've got the monthly salon, all your many friends . . . And your column is going great—in fact, didn't you just get a monthly writing award at the paper? And didn't you just get invited by the Commonwealth Club to moderate a panel on the single life?"

All true, I admit. "It's just the lack of men," I say. "Some days it hardly matters, other days I just can't believe this is happening to me!"

"Mom," she says gently. "First of all, you've at least had options lately! The old boyfriend from college, Andrew . . . Okay, I know they didn't pan out, but you need to look on the bright side! And anyway, you tend to romanticize your man-filled years without remembering there was also a lot of chaos to deal with. It's not like having a man in your life meant things were all that good!"

I can't help but laugh. "God, you're right, you really are."

"Besides," she says with a grin, "aren't you seeing Lenny on Friday night? How can you say there's no man in your life as long as he's in the picture?"

"True, he still haunts me. But he's not exactly someone you can count on for support . . . for anything, really. And since this thing with Andrew flamed out, I've been thinking casual relationships might have outlived their usefulness in my life."

"Well, they seem to be all I have these days," she sighs. "It's been so long since I've been in love I'm not sure I ever will be again."

"Erin, please, you're not even twenty-five. But promise me you'll never settle like I have in my life. Hold out for a guy who's as amazing as you. I'm sure that somewhere in the world there is an environmental crusader who is gorgeous, doesn't eat meat, loves the ocean and the outdoors, and children and his *mom*. . . ."

Erin rolls her eyes. She's not in any hurry.

We arrive at the airport and it's already getting crowded at five a.m. In this post-9/11 era, good-byes have to be brief, with police shouting at us to move along, move along. She leans over to hug me warmly. "I'm sorry I can't be here today. Tell everyone hi. And are you sure you're okay?"

Always taking care of me.

"Fine, good. Can you call me when you get there?" I ask tentatively, knowing how lame that sounds. I look into her face and realize she is no longer five and wearing a red "Child Traveling Alone" button and holding a flight attendant's hand. So I backtrack: "Never mind." She smiles knowingly and is gone.

I want to start crying immediately but decide to suck it up until I get home, so I don't crash my car. But by the time I arrive, I am not as inclined to weep as I am inspired to jot down some thoughts for Sunday's column, which was, up until this moment, going to be something hokey about what I'm thankful for.

This one is nearer and dearer to my heart, and has been for twenty years.

Thanksgiving with him, Christmas with me. I wonder how many millions of single parents have been sentenced to that schedule year after year. What's funny is, now that Erin is 24, living in the city and applying for law school, you'd think such things would be as much a part of the child-oriented past as high school proms, ballet recitals, and school plays.

But even now, as she's dangerously close to all-growed-up, it's still the same. She loves her dad and she loves me. She knows we both want her for the holidays, so we stick to the schedule—the same one she's had since her dad and I split up when she was 4. One year, Thanksgiving there and Christmas here. The next year, the reverse. (Those were the years I'd better hope I had a boyfriend; nothing harder for me than waking up alone Christmas morning.)

It didn't seem fair that I had her all year, fought with her over homework and chores, soothed her tears over boys and other issues of teen angst, only to have him claim her on holidays. Fie on that! I would think. (OK, probably with a different f-word than fie.) I did all the parental heavy lifting! Was I not entitled to the parenting perks as well? Waking up to her shining face on Christmas every year, for example?

But, in the interest of her happiness and of furthering her excellent relationship with her dad, I did not protest. To have done so would have put pressure on this most sensitive and loving of children, who saw the world—and continues to as she gets older—as a stage for enacting relationships of great integrity and pure joy, especially when it comes to her kin.

She really *is* the Buddha offspring.

I describe our good-bye scene in the airport, with a tightening in my chest as I write. And conclude thus:

All the old ghosts that have visited me for 20 years flood the inside of my car as I drive away. When she was little, I would smile and hug her tight and rave about what a good time she was going to have, then get in my car in the parking lot and sob until I could not talk. What had I done, leaving her dad and making this her experience of the holidays? Was I a bad mother, a bad person?

There were no easy answers, then or now.

Even now, my eyes well up a little. But these are selfish tears, that the glowing candle she is will be burning in Southern California this holiday. I also smile because despite my sins and our ragged holiday routine, damned if she hasn't turned out just fine.

And so she has. Soon after I finish writing this, she calls to reassure me that she got there fine. "Sorry I was a whiny poo-head this morning," I tell her, using her favorite childhood insult. "But I'm feeling better now."

Writing it down: Phil always swears to its therapeutic value.

Speaking of the man, I get a call from him as I'm fixing my green beans with red peppers—my festive contribution to the family dinner happening later today at my brother's house. They don't trust me with anything more important than vegetables, and rightly so.

"Happy Thanksgiving, dude," I say, recognizing Phil's number. "How are you?"

"I've been better," he says drily. "But how about you? I knew you were taking Erin to the airport so I wanted to see if you'd had your annual breakdown."

"You're a doll," I reply, stirring the beans in garlic and olive oil. "And yeah, I was sad. A lot of old ghosts, single parenting drama. But I'm okay. I purged it this morning writing my Sunday column."

"Well, I'll have to read that," he says, "since there's a good chance I might be a single parent myself soon."

As I hold my breath anxiously, he explains that things have finally come to a head in his marriage, and that things are not looking good for reconciliation. He so adores his son and worries about what will be best for him. Clearly, Phil is also doing the Holiday Gut Check and is in need of my support. After having nearly lost him to marriage—his time and attention, at least—I'm pleased to be of service, as sad as I am for him.

"Dear, you will get through this," I tell him. "Maybe what you need to be is single for a while. You've never been as long as I've known you! And sometimes people hide behind relationships. Being single means you can't hide from a damn thing—it's excellent for personal growth!"

I pause. "Am I sounding like an infomercial?"

He laughs. "No, not at all. But I might need to call you every day for the next year or so to keep hearing this."

"That's okay, babe," I tell him. "How many times have you scraped me off the pavement?"

Being at Rob and Julie's house on a holiday is like sitting in the warm lap of someone who loves me. And the chow ain't bad either. Julie, our resident Martha Stewart, has done herself proud yet again: sweet potato soufflé and mango chutney and roasted beet salad and home-baked bread. And of course, turkey. Smoked. Dad has brought his usual cheap wine by the bucketful; Barbara her imported cheese. And I, as always, sautéed fresh green beans. Appearance: 8. Degree of difficulty: 1.

As we sit down to the table, this still feels like an abbreviated group. Not just because Anne couldn't get the weekend off from the show, and Erin's in L.A., but because Mom and Lisa aren't here. Is that ridiculous? It's been five and six years, respectively, but I still feel a shadow at the table where their smiles and jokes and beautiful selves would be. It's not ridiculous, apparently: Rob's first toast is to them.

"On this day of giving thanks," he says, glass raised, "I want to remember those who are not with us, but who are missed so terribly."

His voice catches with the last words.

"To Mom and Lisa."

We raise our glasses, sniffling and smiling, and have a sip of Cabernet. Sitting next to Dad, I notice he looks downcast. I touch his hand and he looks up, eyes shining. "She was the greatest" is all he says. I know he's talking about the love of his life. Barbara smiles gently; she has never been threatened by my mother's memory, knowing my dad loves her and she is his best friend.

Later, sufficiently cheered by the trough of food and the vat of wine, we do our yearly ritual of saying what we're thankful for. For Robbie and Skyler, it's pretty simple: tickets to a cool rock concert, the gift of surf camp this coming summer, good grades. For Julie, the health of her three boys. For Rob, his family and news of a new show, possibly even an artist's residency. For Dad, all of us.

"I'm thankful for Erin, and how well she continues to find her way in the world," I share, emotions threatening to brim over. "And for you guys. And the fact that the column is doing so great and getting such good response." I don't think I ever even mentioned my career in this context before.

"No new men, eh?" my dad asks mischievously.

"No, Dad. No new men." I heave a sigh. "But I'm seeing an 'old' one tomorrow night."

I have a message on my answering machine from Lenny waiting when I get home: "Hey, I'm still up for dinner if you are. I'll be coming down from Alex's house in Napa and then across the Bay Bridge into San Francisco. I'll leave it up to you to come up with a place near the bridge. Let me know where. Let's say around seven—I'm still on East Coast time."

Hmmm. I frown. He didn't say he was getting a hotel room in The City, and the restaurant is about a forty-minute drive from my house. Then again, we never discussed whether we're going to sleep together this time or not. Well shit, rather than fret about it, let's just play it as it lays, no pun intended. I think the key is to maintain my dignity, unlike the last time I saw him, when I stormed out of Tosca at two a.m.

"Lenny, I made us a rez at 42 Degrees, which is just south of the bridge and PacBell Park," I write in an e-mail. "7 p.m. I'll be the one wearing a white carnation."

Just for fun, on the way to The City to meet Lenny, I buy a white carnation at the nursery on Highway 92 and stick the blossom in the buttonhole of my denim jacket, which sits atop a long, semisexy satiny skirt. As much as I'd like to keep my guard up, and keep my expectations low, the idea of having Lenny all to myself—sans hangers-on and band members for the first time in ages—is intoxicating.

The restaurant, 42 Degrees, was a total hot spot during the boom; it's languished somewhat since the dot-bomb, which sent techies and entrepreneurs alike scuttling for greener pastures like cockroaches after Armageddon. I love the bay nearby, the abandoned-warehouse feeling, the fresh flowers backdropped by concrete. It's not the most romantic place to meet a date, but I'm neither sure this *is* one nor convinced that Lenny and I have ever been truly romantic. The place is half-empty when I arrive and am surprised to find him already there, bellied up to the industrial metal bar and having some laughs with the bartender. His laugh makes me want to fall down with happiness.

"It's me," I say, kissing him lightly and pointing to my white carnation as verification.

"You goof," he says affectionately, embracing me and flicking my flower with an index finger. "Like I wouldn't recognize you anywhere."

This is a promising start.

"So how's the new guy?" he asks, as we move to our table and start off with a bottle of Oregon Pinot Gris.

I'm momentarily startled. New guy? *New guy?* Oh lord, he means Andrew! Right, I never told him we were no longer an item. Something tells me I'd better not say so now.

"Well, he's . . . fine! I mean, he's okay. But I don't see him that much—it's kind of an open-ended thing."

Lenny chuckles. "Open-ended? I thought you said that kind of temporary shit didn't work for you anymore?"

Oh crap, I hate when men actually listen to what I have to say and then remind me of it! I decide to fall back to the offensive defense of flirting.

"Yes, that is mostly true," I say, leaning forward and letting one booted foot stray up his calf. "But if it were totally true, I wouldn't be here now with you, Mr. Temporary, would I?"

Well, yes I would, because I keep hoping he'll change.

He laughs. "This is true. I certainly never promised you a rose garden."

"Nor even roses!" I laugh.

It takes almost nothing—well, just a lot of wine and Lenny—for me to let my guard down completely; soon we are flirting madly, clasping hands across the table, playing foot games, feeling high and making goo-goo eyes. I may hate myself for thinking this later, but at this moment I am very, very thankful for Lenny.

As dinner, and bottle number two, nears an end, I broach The Subject.

"So, did you plan to stay in The City or do you have to drive back?"

"No, I didn't get a hotel room, if that's what you mean," he says, almost blushing. "But I thought maybe we could go to your house."

"Oh shit, that's forty-five minutes away from here," I say. "And it's south, where Napa is north. Do you really want to make the drive?"

He groans. "Right now I ought not to be driving anywhere. . . ."

I suggest we go outside and get a breath of bracing saltwater air, which is always good for restoring a modicum of sobriety. He smokes while I look at the moon, my steamy breath turning silver and lacy against the night sky. Damn, I almost feel young! Okay, and fairly drunk, which may explain it. I turn to him and he embraces me warmly, and we start kissing. And kissing. And pretty soon mashing our bodies together like teenagers at a high school dance. He reaches down and pulls up the hem of my long skirt until he gets to my bare leg underneath. My bare legs used to make him crazy. He freezes.

"What are we going to do?" he asks, almost desperately.

"Where's your car?" I hear myself asking.

The parking lot of 42 Degrees is huge and dark, with a few cars here and there that probably belong to restaurant staff, who must now be cleaning up inside. Lenny's big four-door rental sedan is parked off to one side. He takes my hand and pulls me, laughing, until we collapse onto each other on the spacious backseat, which is thankfully wide and flat. The door swings shut behind us.

Awkwardly but laughingly, this near-fifty-year-old and her even-older lover manage to have sex—thanks partly to my chance decision not to wear pants tonight, which would have made the logistics even more difficult. Once done, we fall into a doze on our sides, with him spooning me from the back of the seat.

We are awakened by headlights passing by—no doubt the last dishwasher leaving the restaurant. "Oh shit, it's one in the morning," I whisper, feeling suddenly awkward. What in the hell happened to my quest for dignity? Torpedoed by a penis, apparently.

He stops me from getting up, pulls me closer. "I think about you all the time, you know," he murmurs, still half-asleep.

"Do you?" I whisper, taken aback by the words I've so rarely heard him speak. "Then why don't you ever call, you jerk?'

There is silence. Has he gone back to sleep?

"Because," he drawls sleepily, "I don't want to make it worse. I can't be in a relationship, so calling makes it worse."

There is a perverse logic here. My eyes fill with tears at his admission. Clearly, he is saying he *would* be in a relationship with me if he *could.*

"I do," he continues, "get lonely sometimes."

"Even with the growing fame?" I whisper, trying not to sniff. "Even when surrounded with the hangers-on?"

"Especially then," he says sleepily. "But I'm glad for you, that you have someone in your life so you're not lonely."

"I . . . I don't . . ." and then I stop. Why spoil a perfect moment? After lolling for another hour until we're awake and able to drive, we climb out of the car, stiff and chuckling and hugging, and have a long, sweet kiss good-bye. For once, I refrain from asking the dreaded "next time" question, perhaps because I'm confident there will be a next time.

I drive home, thankful for and elated by the insights Lenny shared with me tonight. Granted, insights gleaned after screwing in the back-seat of a rent-a-car might not stand up to time. But he shared his feelings with me! It was like a miracle. At this moment, I can almost believe that this is the beginning of a new chapter for us. One that might actually lead to love.

Does Leo = Plato?

"I got my LSAT scores. I did pretty well." But Erin's not sounding as relaxed on the phone as she normally is on a Saturday morning.

"And?" I ask, taking in the newspaper, soggy from December showers.

"Mom, I'm not sure they're good enough to get me into UC-Davis."

Granted, I haven't yet had my coffee, but my brain simply cannot accept this. Davis, about seventy-five minutes away, is the only California school to which she was planning to apply. The others are hell and gone from here: Oregon, Vermont, Hawaii, New Orleans—anywhere environmental do-gooders congregate.

"How is this possible?" I ask. "If you got a good score, why can't you get into a good school?"

"Haven't you read your own paper?" she asks impatiently. "Because of the dot-bomb and economy tanking, grad schools are getting record numbers of applications. Thousands of them for just a few hundred spots. It's just bad timing."

I pause. "So the alternative would be for you to leave the state? I'm sorry, but I just can't allow that." I'm trying to make it sound like I'm joking but I'm not succeeding. "I mean, I survived your four years in Maine because I knew you'd be coming back to stay. And now you're going to leave again? And how would we pay out-of-state tuition? Does the local community college have a law school?"

"Mom, don't stress me out. I'm on my way to a Surfrider Foundation meeting," she says briskly, clearly already stressed. "Let's not freak out about it yet, okay? Anyway, maybe it's a sign that law school isn't for me. Maybe I should really think about this. Maybe I'm not even cut out to be a lawyer—"

"Erin," I cut in, "when you were *three years old* in day care you were breaking up fights and telling the other children to be nice to each other! You argue at the drop of a hat for all kinds of rights—civil, gay, environmental, animal. You were *born* to be a lawyer!"

There is silence. "Yeah, maybe so . . . I'm just feeling confused. . . ."

"Confusion is okay, just don't be derailed, sweetie."

"Anyway," she says, changing the subject, "have you heard from Lenny?"

"*No!*" I practically shout. "Two weeks and two days and counting! I'm such an idiot for thinking things would be different. And to think that we—"

I stop, realizing that even though I tell Erin almost all my sordid stories, the car-sex episode might be a good one to leave out.

"Anyway . . ." I collect myself. "I think I made a very big mistake with Lenny this time and I'm paying for it. But it's just par for the course. I'm done with men and their tender egos and commitment issues for a while. I don't care if the holidays are coming up and I have all these party invitations, I'm sick of them. I'll go with a platonic male friend instead. In fact, do you want to be my date to the big Getty holiday party this weekend?"

"I thought Phil was going to be your date," she says.

"He is, but he has his own invitation, so I can bring you!" I say brightly. "Billy and Vanessa will be there, Stephan, Phil, Po, and Michele—you'll know a bunch of my friends. It's going to be insanely opulent, like a Roman orgy!"

"Okay, okay!" she says, laughing. "Sign me up. Better than beer and fish tacos on Friday night with my friends. And I'm sick of guys, too."

I doubt she's as sick as I am. After my Thanksgiving weekend date with Lenny, I waited a week for an e-mail from him, and when it didn't come, fired off one myself. I told him how great it was that he was able to open up to me, that it meant a lot to me to know he trusted me that much. That I was thrilled to know he missed and thought of me sometimes.

And then, I think, I fucked up. "I'm not seeing that guy anymore," I wrote. "It was only a passing fancy. And since I get more excitement from just talking to you than I do in sleeping with him, I thought it was best for all concerned."

And I've now been waiting a week for a response. Zero, zippo, nada, zilch. Fucking hell. In hindsight, I was laying too much on him. Maybe the reason he was so keen on me this time was because I was unavailable. And now that he knows I'm all his if he wants me, he doesn't.

Then again, the optimistic (read: foolish) part of me wants to believe what Lenny told me in the car (granted, after having sex with me): that he thinks he would "make it worse" by communicating. But how could it be worse? And what exactly is "it," anyway? I have to face the fact that I may have been an idiot. That this image I cling to of Lenny, the one in which he's crazy about me, may be as out of date and dusty as this 1930s photo on my wall of my dad as a child.

It occurs to me that this single life I'm cheerleading for every week may actually be my lot—forever.

Okay, it's not like I have cancer or anything. I'm much better off than Lisa in Vancouver, suffering through chemo and struggling with hair loss and fatigue preventing her from doing her job. My life is pretty great by most standards, especially hers. And I don't particularly want to ever marry again. But still, the prospect of going unloved and unsqueezed for the rest of my life is enough to make me dissolve into tears.

Phil snaps me out of my self-absorbed reverie, appearing unexpectedly at my cubicle at the paper. "So what are we supposed to wear to this Getty shindig?"

"It's dressy, you know that."

His scowl threatens to turn into a thunderstorm.

"Oh come on, I happen to know you have a tux, and you look good in it," I chide him. "Don't be a baby. You can still wear your cowboy boots with it."

"It's not just that. I hear the tabloids are coming out with a story about the divorce filing this week," he says, "and I hate being topic A of gossip at these things."

"Oh God, I'm sorry," I say, standing up and touching his arm. "I guess this is one of those things about being married to a celebrity that no one thinks about ahead of time—the rabid interest in the breakup. Are you okay?"

"I'll be okay," he says grimly, "once I get this bullshit behind me."

"Well, don't bail on me. I promise you'll have a good time, and you need a good time. And Erin's coming, too, and you haven't seen her in a while. She's always cheered you up."

"Oh, that will be nice." He smiles. "And someday maybe you can give me some tips—on single parenting and on being happily single. You really seem to have it mastered."

"Ah, yes, mastered." I heave a sigh. "Well, don't believe how good I sound in print. My life's just as fucked up as the next single person's."

I'll spare him the latest on Lenny; I don't feel like getting the lecture about avoiding people in show business one more time.

Phil's got his tux in the closet, but I'm in desperate need of shopping assistance before the Getty fete, so I make Claudia come with me after work to Union Square. She is a great bargain hunter; if I took Rosalind I'd end up spending a fortune in Saks, even though my budget is more Macy's. Holiday lights and flowers and bric-a-brac have already transformed the square into a wonderland, and the wandering minstrels and giant tree in the square's center have drawn a cheerful crowd.

Shopping at this age, however, is enough to turn one's mood sour. "God, every time I look for a cool outfit, I realize they hardly make them in a size twelve or fourteen," I say, sliding hangers down the rack angrily. "It's impossible to be almost fifty, the size of the average American woman, and wear cool clothes."

Plus, even though I have Donna Karan tastes, newspaper journalists only earn enough for DKNY.

Claudia, a size eight even on PMS days, politely nods her head, clearly not feeling my pain. "With whom are you going to this shindig anyway?"

"Phil—kind of. Not as dates, obviously. But he needs the protection of my company—he always gets hassled and it will be doubly bad now that the divorce has hit the airwaves. We've done this before. If he goes with me to something, everyone knows he's just with a friend, so there is no fear of gossip."

"Hold on there," says Claudia. "What are you saying about yourself? That you're not worthy of dating Phil?"

I sigh. "Well, I have to be realistic. He dates famous and glamorous women, not borderline-frumpy redheads with mold growing on their gym membership cards."

"Jesus, Jane, give yourself a little credit! Andrew was a hottie, and Lenny is no slouch in the looks department, and he was mad for you. . . ."

"Yes, 'was' being the operative word. Past tense," I say, realizing I'm close to snapping. "So . . . platonic pals work just fine for me for a while."

"I admire your ability to have so many guy friends like that," she sighs, checking out a designer sweater on deep discount. "In my experience, platonic relationships rarely work. Someone always develops a crush, and then there are hard feelings."

"Then I guess I have evolved up the food chain; I have no desire to sleep with any of my men friends," I tell her. "Although I flirted with the idea with all of them at one point. Especially Phil, when we were much younger and we were both between marriages. Anyway, now I know too much about all of them for there to be attraction—I love them but from a distance.

"Maybe this is my new gig," I say, smiling. "Shifting from sex object to sturdy confidante. There are worse things, right?"

"You're right." Claudia smiles back. "Like no friends at all."

"Amen, sister."

I settle on a new black velvet skirt that can go with a sequin top I have at home. Though now I don't have the right earrings. Damn. Phil's right, playing dress-up is a pain in the ass.

On the night before the party, I meet my dad for dinner at Buck's in Woodside. It's been a couple weeks since I've seen him and he wants to talk to me about his next walkabout, for which he is jovially outlining plans. First stop: Arizona to see his sister at her winter home, then Moab, and then possibly . . . Michigan to see relatives?

"Dad, you're going in January. Why on earth would you be thinking of taking on that kind of weather?"

Barbara shrugs, as if to say it's out of her hands. She, not being partial to the Motel 6 or Denny's chains, wisely doesn't go along on most of his road trips.

"Well, I'd only go as far as the weather permitted." He smiles, sipping his second glass of house Chardonnay. "It's just that if I'm in Utah already, I might as well go a little farther."

"A little farther, Dad? Isn't Michigan something like fifteen states away from Utah?"

The former pilot and engineering student rolls his eyes at my lack of geographical smarts. "Don't worry about me, okay?" he demands, looking somewhat defensive. "Both Rob and Anne have made noises about how I should reconsider going. But if I can't take trips, what am I going to do with my time?"

We always knew Dad would be one of those seniors who would refuse to accept limits of any kind. God bless him, I'm sure I'll be the same way.

"So, Dad, I'm going to the Getty mansion tomorrow night for a party," I tell him. "They have it every year but this is my first time to be asked. I think it's either because I've gotten to be friends with Billy and Vanessa Getty or because the column has raised my profile some. And they like to have 'names' there."

I have to laugh. "I'm sorry, it's hard to think of myself as a name."

My dad beams. "Well, that's just fine! Who are you going with?"

"Phil Bronstein—remember, I told you he's getting divorced?" I say, and he beams even more brightly. "But it's not a date—just a platonic thing."

"When I met him years ago, I thought he was the handsomest man I'd ever seen," Dad says. "And I could never figure out why you two, who were such good friends, weren't romantically involved."

"Uh, how about . . . because I know him too well?" I smile. "This is the check-and-balance system of all platonic relationships.

"Erin's coming to the party, too," I add. "Maybe she'll have better luck finding a rich man than I've had."

I'm being utterly sarcastic, of course, but Dad just smiles, pleased as punch at the notion.

Erin has refused my offer of a ride, saying she wants to drive herself to the party—most likely so she can escape quickly in case it's completely lame by twenty-four-year-old hipster standards. So I pick up Phil at the office, where he always seems to be when his son is not staying with him. He looks absolutely gorgeous. "Okay," I tell him on the drive to Pacific Heights, "you need to decide what to do if you're hit on tonight, which you always are. If you want to cash in on it, I'm cool with that, but you'll have to find your own way home. We just need to figure out a sign, like a thumbs-up or something."

He looks at me, incredulous. "Jane, I'm still married."

"Right, but now all these wealthy single women know you're going to be free soon. I'm just saying to expect a few phone numbers to be tossed at you like you're Tom Jones."

He scoffs. "You overestimate my charm. Besides, I'm with *you*."

I give him the hard look. "You're sweet, but please, I think everyone will know that I am merely your escort! And if you do want to hook up, being with someone like me will improve your chances, because I can help steer you toward a good woman."

"Well, I'm not ready for that yet," he says, fidgeting uncomfortably in his monkey suit. "But when the time comes, you can be my escort if I can be yours."

I smile. "Ah, but I'm not thinking about men anymore! I've given up, remember?"

"Right, that will last about three days," he says. "Hey, are we picking up Erin, too?"

"No, she's meeting us there. Phil, she's having second thoughts about becoming a lawyer, and it worries me."

"She knows her own mind," he says gently. "She always has. Let her alone and she'll come up with the right decision."

He sighs and stares out the window. "I hope this party isn't a big fucking to-do with photographers and everything. I really don't need that."

"I'm sure it will be as subdued as all San Francisco soirees are. Nobody does that shit here. Don't worry!"

"Phil! Over here!" shouts a photographer after we hand over my car to the valet and face a thicket of popping flashes. I feel like the stuffed animal in his pocket; no one knows who I am. We walk quickly past them, although Phil slows for a moment to oblige the press. Name of your companion? he is asked.

"Jane Ganahl, *Chronicle* star columnist," he says tersely, and takes my elbow so we can move quickly inside.

Inside the Christmas-overdosed mansion are waiters dressed as Dickens characters poised with trays of Champagne glasses. Everywhere you look there are fir trees drooping from the weight of dazzling lights and opulent ornaments. We encounter friends immediately and get separated in the sea of partygoers. The party hostess swarms on Phil with her friends; he is among the fanciest of partygoers and she clearly aims to show him off. And I greet Stanlee the party planner, who tells me he loves the column: "All my gay friends are reading it!" Vanessa tells me Erin is already here and raves about what a beauty she is.

A forty-ish socialite whose name escapes me chats me up like we're old pals and asks if it's really true that Phil is single again. I see the moony way she's looking at him and sympathize. I've seen that look on hundreds of women in twenty years. Meanwhile, he is glaring at me from ten feet away, as if to say "help!" But I'm more distracted by my surroundings; this is the first party I've been to where security guards have been hired to make sure partygoers stay away from the priceless art on the walls. Talk about a buzz kill.

Erin finds me, and looks so stunning in her simple black cocktail dress that she quite takes my breath away. Phil's, too. "I just can't believe this is the same scruffy little girl you'd bring to staff picnics." He smiles, giving her a hug. "Now on her way to law school."

She winces. "Well, we'll see. You guys have to go downstairs—there's an indoor pool! And the bar will make you any drink you want, even mojitos!"

Ah, the trendy cocktail du jour. My party-animal daughter must be in heaven.

"Oh my, is this really Ganahl the younger?" My rock star friend Stephan embraces me quickly and then turns his attention to Erin. He puts his arm around her shoulder and gives her a chummy squeeze. "I haven't seen you in a year, since I gave you that ride on the back of my motorcycle through North Beach. You look as sweet as cherry pie!"

"Hi, Stephan!" she says, melting into him affectionately.

I first met and interviewed Stephan in 1997, soon after Lisa died and his first album came out. We butted heads immediately during our first interview, when he wanted me to let his then-girlfriend sit with us, and I said no, I don't let anyone sit in on my interviews—ever. He was not happy, but he eventually came to appreciate the fact that I didn't kiss his ass like everyone else.

We've had periods of intense closeness, usually based on his need of it. I have not seen much of him this last year, but there was a time when he was enduring a terrible breakup with his own actress—having lost her to his own commitment issues—and I was both a sturdy shoulder and a sympathetic ear. "I need to play something for you," he said when he called me at work a year or two ago, and I went downstairs and we sat in my car while he played me a special song he'd written for her, hoping to make amends and get her back. It didn't work; she even sent back a pair of skis he'd sent her as a present.

His new girlfriend, a young New York songbird, isn't here tonight—back East doing some gigs, he explains. So he's here instead with a musician friend I don't know, who is leering slightly at Erin.

"So your mom says you're going to law school," says Stephan, looking down from his tall angular frame and square into her eyes. "I remember those photos of you on the picket line with your mom, and her stories of your going to logging protests and shit. I think this makes total sense."

Stephan has his flaws but he is uncanny at seeing inside people. He also loves young people and is dying to be a dad himself so he can spread his advice around.

Phil interjects, "Your mom also says you're having second thoughts about becoming a lawyer!"

She groans and gives me a look, clearly uncomfortable at suddenly being the center of attention. "My mother is always very free with information on my private life," she says pointedly. "And it's no big deal, I'm just a little confused about my future, about whether the legal profession is for someone like me."

"I think," says Stephan's clearly intoxicated friend, sidling over next to Erin and standing uncomfortably close, "you should forget about law school and become a model. You're beautiful enough to do it, you know."

"Back off," Stephan tells his friend unexpectedly, moving between him and the embarrassed Erin. He's smiling but means business. "Leave Erin alone. She's not like us. I'm pretty sure she's supposed to save the world."

She manages a demure "thanks," and turns her gaze to meet mine. We both smile. Maybe she just needed to hear someone else say what I've been telling her for twenty years.

Erin leaves the party after another half-hour of fielding conversations with my friends; a more age-appropriate party is happening across town. Phil is ready to go, too, but I make him stay awhile longer. I'm having a good time and I know it's good for him to be out and about, even if women are hitting on him right and left. Several times he comes to my side and sticks to it, hoping that sends a message of discouragement. And I link my arm through his to help.

"You're lucky I no longer have any self-esteem," I tell him as we're putting on our coats to leave. "Because if I did, I'd be pissed that this entire evening was about my batting women away for you—and you didn't have to do anything for me all night. Such is the difference between aging men and women."

He squeezes my arm affectionately. "Someone should be so lucky to have you."

Just arriving, fashionably late as we leave unfashionably early, are Marco and Elsa, whom I have not seen since they became "boyfriend and girlfriend," or in lurv, as Woody Allen coined. I'd like to avoid them, but as quickly as I utter an "oh, shit" they are upon us with hugs and kisses.

Phil, sensing my unease, quickly comes in close and puts his arm around my shoulder as we move toward the valet stand. Marco winks conspiratorially as he and the beautiful Elsa head into the party.

"Okay," I sigh, resting my head on Phil's brawny shoulder. "I guess I did need your services after all."

Have Yourself a Merry Little Gentile Holiday

"Wait, are you kidding? I'm in what and they say what?"

"You're in the local society newspaper with Phil," says Rosalind, who is the only person I know who reads such things. "The two of you are going into the Getty party and looking quite chummy. He has his arm through yours."

Why can't anyone I know ever wait until after nine a.m. to call with these little rotten-egg bombs?

"Kee-rist," I sputter, sipping my java, "this is not what I need. What else does it say?"

"Oh, nothing really," she demurs.

"Tell me *everything*."

"Well, it talks about how you're the new singles columnist at the paper, and there's just a hint of a question wondering if you two are an item," she says, sheepishly.

"Fucking great. This would be hilarious except that it's not. Merry Christmas to me!"

"Don't worry about it!" Rosalind says, feigning confidence. "And don't forget, we're trying to raise your profile these days!"

Right, the fame-o-meter rises with scandal. However, at this juncture in my fledgling career as a columnist, I think I'd rather emulate Molly Ivins than Helen Fielding. Or at least be known for the things I *do,* rather than things I *don't do*—like date Phil. I guess I'd better call him—as if he doesn't have enough to deal with these days.

"Yeah, I saw it," he says coolly. "It sucks, and I've already called the paper for a correction. But don't get too worked up. No one reads that rag anyway.

"Besides," he adds, "I have a feeling that what ends up in the national tabloids when the divorce gets going will be more offensive—and much more fictitious."

"Well, just as long as your wife understands that it *is* fiction and doesn't name me in a suit," I joke, but he doesn't laugh. "Hey, what about Christmas next week? Or Hanukkah, whatever. Are you going to be okay or do you need company?"

"Thanks, we've decided to have the holidays together for the sake of the kid," he says. "But I'll be glad—very glad—to see you and everyone at the salon the next day."

Ah, the salon: aka the extended family for whom you never have to stuff a stocking, and upon whom you can pass off your undesired crap. Every year we meet between Christmas and New Year's and exchange white elephant gifts. "Bring the weirdest present you get for Christmas and think no one in their right mind would want," I write in my monthly e-group invitation. "Because certainly there are several people at the salon who are not in their right minds and they might just take it off your hands."

Determined not to the let the society paper's faux pas ruin my holiday mood—and glad that I have the next two weeks off (after I write my Christmas column) and don't have to endure the suspicious glances at work—Erin and I march forward with our annual orgy of holiday indulgences.

For almost twenty years, the list has included going to see *The Nutcracker* at San Francisco Ballet. It's one we can practically dance along to, we've seen it so much. In fact, when Erin took classes at the prestigious school there in her preteen years, she was part of the children's corps on stage at the Opera House—one of a dozen or so angels who trotted out on stage at the beginning of Act 2. Everyone said *awwwwww*, Erin got a few bucks for each of her four or five performances and head lice from the wigs they wore.

We also do high tea at the St. Francis with Anne and Barbara and Julie, shop Union Square so we can see the tree at Neiman's, go find the perfect noble fir Christmas tree, drag out the ornaments, and make a Very Big Deal out of the tree decoration—with wine and candles and music. But in recent years, I must admit, my ornaments are no longer . . . satisfying. And yet I never buy new ones.

That is, until just this week, when Anne and Barbara dragged me to Filoli, the country estate in Woodside that was the setting for the TV series *Dynasty* and the film *Heaven Can Wait*, for some holiday shopping. After a sweetly transformative purchase, I'm inspired to use it as fodder for my Christmas column.

The second half of my life so far has been largely devoted to the pursuit of becoming My Own Woman as opposed to just the female sandwiched between a strong mother and a hardheaded daughter. I have striven to be someone who makes (and breaks) her own holiday traditions, rather than usurping those of her mother; someone who learns to live for herself as much as she does for her offspring.

It's not a simple task, becoming my own woman, but I'm making pretty decent progress. Or so I think, and then Christmas rolls around every damn year, and I'm reminded that I have a long way to go. As always, I take out my boxes and boxes of tree ornaments and assorted table goodies—and feel a vague sense of irritation. You see, none of these things are mine.

Well, OK, they are mine*—as in they take up space in my garage. But I didn't choose a single one. Most of them came from my mother, and some were bought, by my mom and by me, for my daughter. As a result, I have an eclectic mix of '50s-era painted wood storybook characters, some miscellaneous '60s-looking God's eyes, and Erin's kittens-in-a-basket ornaments and Swedish Santa Lucia table ornaments.*

Where, oh where, is my own style? My own tradition? My own ornaments?

I never lacked those; my mother was a Christmas-aholic who every year shopped the sale at the Filoli estate, where she volunteered, and managed to find some new tchotchke to build a centerpiece around and/or a new ornament that was indicative of the style of the times. She'd either buy one for me, or slough off some oldies but goodies on me—which is probably why I have far more than I can ever use.

Some of them I have sweet memories of—the ones Erin made, for example—but most of them are falling apart, and I can hardly remember where they came from. Every year I think it would be gorgeous to go out and get a treeful of new, extravagantly whimsical, artistic junk to hang, but every year, economics brings me back down to earth. You already have boxes full of stuff! I lecture myself. That would be expensive!

So it is with little enthusiasm that I agree to go to the annual Filoli sale with my sister and friends. I've been there before; it's a mob scene of children and adults roving in packs, listening to carolers, having spiced cider, perusing the acres and acres of decorations for sale. Why am I here? I pouted. I never buy anything new.

And then in the last room I found decorations by the children's book illustrator Patience Brewster. A sea foam–green tree was staring me in the face. About a foot tall, it was shaped like a metal cone wearing a ruffled skirt, with skinny legs wrapped in red-and-white stripes and curly-toed elf shoes protruding beneath. It had stick arms raised skyward, and from its hands shot stars. And in the middle of the tree, a face: Victorian, pouty-lipped, smiling.

I was enchanted. "Wow," I said. "This is so whimsical, so weird, so . . ."

"So you?" my sister finished.

I sighed at the discovery. "Yes, so me."

That day, I was the only one of the group to actually buy something. And what a strange difference it's made! Suddenly I was ready for cheesy carols and eggnog. I could not wait to put my new treasure in a place of honor on my table, surrounded with greens and white votives, where it awaits the enjoyment of Erin.

But first, I had to call and tell her about it, with such unbridled glee that she laughed.

"Mom, you really need to get a life!"

She doesn't realize that's what I'm doing, one Christmas decoration at a time.

When Erin arrives with bag packed for a couple days at home, starting with Christmas Eve tonight, she admires my strange tree/angel with striped socks enthusiastically. "Oh, Mom, this really is so cute! Why didn't you get me one?"

"Because . . . why do we need two? You're going to always have Christmas here!" I tease. "Even when you're sixty and I'm eighty-five! We'll be the two little spinster ladies together. No need to buy any Christmas stuff of your own!"

She laughs . . . fortunately. My smothering hasn't yet snuffed her sense of humor.

"What's all that?" I ask about a pile of paperwork she drops on the kitchen table.

"Applications for Oregon, Hawaii, Vermont, Tulane—and Davis. I'm not sure I have the test scores, but I might as well try, right?" She smiles.

I heave a private sigh. Career crisis averted.

"Yes, honey, might as well try." I smile. "You owe it to the world. And right now, we owe some holiday cookies for tomorrow's festivities! So we'd better get them made before we head over the hill for church tonight."

"Any word from the butthead musican?" she asks, pulling the tubes of cookie dough out of the refrigerator and turning on the oven. She looks up at me with a pained expression, as if fearing that the answer might cause me to crack like Christmas peanut brittle under a hammer.

"No, and it's been almost a month. I'll probably get a joke-y 'Happy Gentile Holiday' e-mail from him like I have the last few years, but I think I'm wasting my time if I think I might get more than that. I think I screwed up big-time by telling him I was thrilled that it seemed we were moving forward. Wrong! Wrong! Wrong! So I'm just trying to let it go."

"Mom," she sighs, "if that's the case, if that's all it takes for him to be put off, then he's so not worthy of you, and you ought to put him out of your mind.

"Maybe," she adds thoughtfully, "he's distracted by getting a Grammy nomination."

I almost spit my eggnog. "What? Are you kidding?"

"Yeah, for best jazz instrumental or something. Pretty cool, huh?"

"Cool . . . yes . . ." I get a rush of emotion I can't explain and feel near tears. When we first met, he was not even on the radar of the Grammys. I told him then it was only a matter of time, but he didn't believe me, having struggled for acknowledgment for decades. This is huge for him, and it would have been nice to share this milestone.

"You know what?" I tell her. "It's Christmas, and why spoil it with unworthy topics and unworthy men?"

She clinks her eggnog glass against mine, and smiles in agreement.

The cookies turn out great—frosted green and red, with silver sparkles—though Erin seems to have eaten half of them before we take off for evening services in Woodside. The night air is freezing and the church is beautiful—a huge wreath with the four candles of Lent illuminated above the front door—when we arrive. Anne is home, and singing a guest solo with the choir, so she is upstairs with Dad and Barbara. We tiptoe upstairs and slide into a dark corner of the choir loft, where we can take in the pageant.

I can feel my mother here tonight, as I often do. The only other place I've felt her presence as surely was in the woods, right after she died. All her Southern relatives flew out for a memorial, so we decided we'd have a big picnic in the redwoods on that Sunday. It was also, God love her, Erin's eighteenth birthday. I went ahead that morning to scout a location big enough for our group of maybe thirty people.

I was alone in the redwoods and stood there feeling heavy and numb with grief in the cool March air, studying the map of picnic sites. An unexpectedly warm breeze whooshed through the redwood trees, carrying a scent of my mother's perfume: Estee Lauder's Youth Dew. I got goose bumps. "Are you there, Mom?" I said, choking on tears. But I knew, beyond anything I'd known in my life, that she was. And she was happy, to be done with her failing body and free at last.

I also cling to a story about Lisa's death as evidence of something beyond this life. After she died at home, and Theo was just a little guy—just seven—Terry brought him into the room where the hospital had put her body. Theo touched her still hand, and then looked up at his dad with a dazzling grin. "She's having a really good time with Grandma right now!" he said, sure of every word he spoke.

I hope to join their party someday. But not too soon. I look down at the order of service and scan the list of donors of poinsettias, which adorn the sanctuary gorgeously. I see my dad has bought two "for Lisa and Betty, from the Buelteman family," it says. I point it out silently to Erin. "We better give Grandpa some money," she whispers.

When it comes time to ask for prayers for those we're concerned about, I muster my bravery and call out "For the hungry and the homeless"—not because I'm Mother Teresa but because Mom always did, and it's Christmas. Erin looks at me knowingly, as do Dad and Anne, and they all smile in loving understanding. And that alone is like religion to me.

As holidays go, Christmas is hardest on my singlest of single friends. The ones like Peter and Claudia who are estranged from their families. Or those undergoing a breakup like Phil. But I have no complaints. Even though I feel wistful about Lenny, I am cocooned by family. I get Erin this year! And this is the one morning of the year she wakes up grinning.

As always, this Christmas Day, which begins with mimosas in our living room with fire blazing, is a green-and-red orgy of affection. Erin surprises me by giving me a DVD of one of my favorite movies *(A Fish Called Wanda)*.

"But honey"—I smile, puzzled—"I don't have a DVD player!"

She grins excitedly and pulls a large box out from behind the tree. "Now you do!"

I protest the expense, but she waves it away. "Mom, this year I made almost as much as you, and I know that a year from now, when I'm back to being a student, I'll be poor again. So just let me! Please?"

Dinner at Rob and Julie's is also an alcohol-fueled celebration of the ties that bind. I'm compelled to take Robbie and Skyler into a separate room and play them some hilariously obscene songs from the new

South Park Christmas CD; soon they're covering their mouths with their hands and engulfed in guilty teenage glee.

It reminds me of when we were kids, opening our gifts with the fire blazing and cinnamon rolls cooking and music playing from Dad's cheesy "Mighty Wurlitzer" record, which we gave him grief about year after year: the reckless joy and comfort of being with people with whom you are truly at home, anywhere in the world that happens to be. Christmas looks a little different every year I get older, but these are the things that remain the same.

This is true, too, of the salon group. Christmas isn't complete without them anymore. For our holiday salon the following night we have a more modest-size group than usual—just twenty-two—since so many are traveling for the holidays. But we are avid revelers. I bring a decorated box, into which gifts are dropped and then selected again by recipients who exclaim their extreme pleasure at now owning a paint-by-numbers kit, an orange sweater, a Homer Simpson bottle opener that says *Mmm, beeeeer!* when you pop a cap.

Phil is clearly in the Dumpster, but is cheered by the D's and Po and Michele, who surround him for a pep talk and remind him that perhaps he hasn't yet met Ms. Right and that he just needs to keep his eyes open in case she walks in the door. (I want to interject that this philosophy has not, thus far, worked well for me, but now's not the time for reality.) And Peter takes me aside at one point to say, sotto voce, "I know what you did on Christmas and there are not big enough words to thank you. You take good care of me."

He's referring to the fact that I knew he was alone and made a call to Rosalind and Dieter, who were having "orphan" friends over. They were more than happy to include his sunny presence in the circle.

"Please," I say, squeezing his arm. "You've done way more for me than I could ever pay back in one lifetime. I only want as many good things for you as you do for me."

We toast a variety of recent successes, including the launch of Po's book. But the sweetest part, as always, is the outpouring of quiet "love yous" expressed when good-byes are hugged—a bit earlier than usual this month. But it only makes sense; we have to rest up for New Year's Eve just a week away at the D's, which already promises to be a killer party.

Walking in my door, I am taken by the sight of my new little fantasy tree—grinning and shooting stars from its hands—surrounded by a pine wreath on the marble coffee table. And the big tree, gorgeous in its illumination, the cats sleeping on the displayed presents beneath. I pause a moment before turning on the overhead light and feel a rush of gratitude: this Christmas was really quite wonderful. I got everything I wanted—everyone's healthy, and I'm loved.

Despite, or perhaps *because of*, a lack of male complications.

Let this be a lesson.

Exhausted, I turn on my computer and check e-mail. What do you know—there's one from Lenny. I debate whether to read it at the risk of it ruining my excellent frame of mind. Holding my breath, I click it open.

"Hello and Merry Gentile Holiday to you. My humble apologies for dropping out of sight again," he writes. "It was terrific to see you last month as always. I can't believe the things I do when we're together—you bring out the animal in me."

I'm not smiling. Get to the point.

"Since I got the Grammy nomination, things have gone a little nuts. My manager wants me to line up a tour right now to cash in on it. I'll let you know if it takes me out your way. This time, maybe we'll even splurge on a hotel room. Hope your holiday was grand."

He signs off, "Jew Boy Lenny." No Xs or Os.

I sigh. Yes, it was a grand holiday. And if I didn't get all the love I want, I got all the love I need.

Resolution One: No Underwear

Battling holiday burn-out after being out almost every night for a month (*must make just . . . one . . . more . . . party!*), and a blue mood thanks to Lenny's nonchalant approach to our don't-call-it-a-relationship, I sit in my bathrobe, Noodge curled in my lap, and stare at a blank Word document on my home computer, wondering what to write for the all-important first anniversary column of "Single-Minded."

Of course it's tempting to weigh in with a set of resolutions that might supply my anxious readers with a cup of inspiration—resolutions I have no hope of keeping. They might also be expecting me to pontificate on the phenomenon of New Year's Eve: the joys and wonders thereof, or the difficulties of going it alone on the biggest date night of the year next to Valentine's Day. Unfortunately, I'm not at all enthused about the topic.

Or they might hope I'll tell them to buck up and what's the big deal anyway and don't buy into the socially imposed bullshit that you need a man when you're really just fine on your own! If only I felt that strongly about it.

I'm kind of sick of the soapbox, sick of the male-female tango. Clearly, I have a case of opinion fatigue, something I never imagined would happen. But I have a deadline of five p.m. today and a need to fill a cavity in the Living section. So I decide to just plow ahead with what I'm thinking right this minute and let honesty be my guide.

Hmmm, the invitation to my friends' New Year's Eve party says not to wear underwear but doesn't really say what to wear as, you know, outerwear.

No, no, these are not cheesy swingers; it's my friends' way of adding a little whimsy, a needed jolt, to the tired annual ritual. But how will they know if we follow directions? Will they check? Maybe frisk us for VPLs at the door?

I stare unhappily at the options in my closet; nothing seems right. This would make me look like a teeny-bopper. That would make me look fat. Maybe the internal debate about attire is merely a cover-up for the nagging little voice that keeps hissing at me: "It's New Year's Eve and you don't have a date? What kind of a loser are you?"

I shake it off. After all, this has been a banner year, and things are percolating right along. My life in the best city in the world is excellent. There is so much to do every week that I have to commit to staying in occasionally to catch up on my video-viewing, cat-brushing, laundry—sleep. Everyone in my family is healthy, my daughter did fine on her LSATs, and she still likes me even though I drive her crazy sometimes.

I have good friends—of both sexes—who indulge my need for rock 'n' roll, incessant talk about relationships, sushi. Friends who buck me up when this aging burden gets too unwieldy to carry alone. Friends who try to set me up sometimes and tell me, however disingenuously, that they can't understand why I need to be set up.

Still, if I just had the magic outfit to this New Year's Eve soiree, mightn't it fill that nagging void inside . . . ?

Who am I kidding? No matter how glorious it is being single—most of the time—I do believe that human beings are genetically programmed to want to pair up. Our quest for bonding makes us do stupid, inappropriate things, alter our standards, backslide on our beliefs.

Especially at the holidays, when we're bombarded with ads (shoot me if I see one more!) featuring happy and loving couples giving each other everything from diamonds to cars. (Now there's something your average Jane and Joe Schmo can identify with.)

Anyway, I'm not alone in having thrown myself into a no-cheese-at-the-end-of-the-maze situation. I think more inappropriate bonding goes on during the holidays than any other time. And New Year's Eve? Lord, the mother of all have-to-have-a-date holidays. The temptation for single people is just to reach out and grab someone and drag them along so you won't be the only person not making out at midnight. But I'll refrain and enjoy my friends instead.

And I'll resolve to make 2003 the year I work on my own dating hang-ups so that next year I'll at least have the option of making out at midnight.

I seem to have also written myself in the direction of making some resolutions after all. So be it! Maybe if I put these out in the universe, I might feel more compelled to abide by them. So here goes:

- *I shall stop recycling exes. Except for once in a while.*
- *I shall not disqualify men as dates for clothing faux pas: ironed jeans, tasseled loafers, blazers with patched elbows, skin covered with tattoos.*

- *I shall be less shy at parties about walking up to people to whom I'm attracted.*
- *I shall not allow my self-esteem to suffer when such attempts fail disastrously.*
- *I shall not feel bad about the fact that my friends seem to be all pairing up with fabulous men. (Except maybe the one who is now dating my ex. I deserve to feel crummy about that one.)*

Hmmm, I wonder if that's not a little mean, taking a swipe at Elsa. Oh well, she never mentions the column to me so she probably doesn't read it, and I'm trying to be brutally honest here.

- *I shall stop worrying so much about clothes and realize that love can bloom only when you are beautiful from the inside out.*

Okay, maybe I'll take my own advice after the New Year's Eve party. In the meantime, damn it, what am I going to wear?

Satisfied and smiling, I e-mail it in. This was a good exercise; I feel bolstered and hopeful that things can change. I'll go to the party and hold my head high and at least pretend that I think I'm hot, which is sometimes half the battle. I won't act like I'm turning fifty in a few months. I think the watchword, not just for the party but for the next year, is *dignity*. I need to cultivate my own sense of it, and teach it in my writing to my readers.

At the very least, I should refrain from ever again fucking in the backseat of a car.

"Okay, are you guys checking or what? Do I need to drop trou?" I laugh as I hug Dan and Dayna at the top of their stairway. Their beautiful two-level Victorian flat is already filling with revelers, and I can hear the crisp pop of Champagne corks in the dining room.

"I'm too much of a gentleman to frisk!" Dan winks, looking sigh-worthy in a vintage tux shirt. And Dayna laughs: "Oh, you know us, we're just trying to get people to be creative!" She looks stunning as always in her eclectic outfit of bargain-basement couture clothes found on eBay. One of these days she and Dan will get nominated for an Oscar and she will outshine them all.

They work on this party for a week and invite a hundred of their closest friends: artists, dancers, authors, filmmakers. It's like a very posh salon but three times the size. The dining room table is so full of food it's like a traffic jam of turkey, ham, and cracked crab. Dozens of candles burn throughout the house and Charlie Parker is on the stereo. From their windows, the downtown skyline looks like the Milky Way lying sideways across the horizon. God, I love this city.

Po and Michele arrive with an old friend of ours, whom I have not seen in a couple years since he defected from The City to Iowa. Hailed as the great national hope of fiction-writing, and the handsomest author next to Po there's ever been, he wraps me in his big-bodied embrace. "Congrats on the column! Po pointed it out to me Sunday and I thought it was excellent. I think it really suits you!"

Before I can express how enormously flattered I am, he adds nosily, "So who's your date tonight?"

"Uh . . . no date, which is the story of my life these days." I smile, and am happy that he looks incredulous.

"Jane has just gotten very, very picky," Po teases. "She used to go out with anyone, now she has a laundry list of requirements down to here."

I flash him a gimme-a-break glare. "Right! It's not so long, really. Just be warm, breathing, and sexy—those are my requirements."

"I'm with you there," interjects Craig, sidling up and awkwardly holding a cracker topped with cheese that's about to plummet over the side. "Since Julia Roberts hasn't called me, I think it might be time to consider normal women."

Poor Craig. Compared to him I feel like a sex goddess; I don't think I've ever seen him on a real date, at least one in which romantic fondling was involved. I put my arm around his shoulder. "Baby, we'll find you someone. If not tonight, then soon."

He rolls his eyes and sighs.

"Talking to the enemy, I see?" Phil makes his usual dramatic entrance and shakes Craig's hand. Phil sees Craig's Web site as a threat to his newspaper.

"Phil, does this man look like my enemy?" I say, not removing my arm from Craig's shoulder.

"It's all right, I can handle him," jokes Craig, who only comes up to Phil's chin. "But not tonight, it's New Year's Eve!" And he's off to the bar.

"My dear, that's not the nicest way to say seasons' greetings!" I chide Phil, giving him a hug and kiss.

"I know, sorry. Maybe I shouldn't have come. I'm not really in the mood, but I just had to get out of the house. Crazy-angry phone calls every ten minutes."

"Hey, you two, should you be standing this close together since there might be paparazzi nearby?" teases Claudia, looking gorgeous as always. She kisses Phil and he smiles broadly, momentarily happy.

But almost on cue, his phone vibrates in his jeans pocket, and he is off to the patio to answer it. We won't see him again tonight.

"Bad stuff, huh?" she says. "Goddamn, when I hear about some of these nasty divorces it's almost enough to convince me not to marry again. I mean, almost. Speaking of marriages-to-be, are Rosalind and Dieter coming tonight?"

"No, it seems he has whisked her away to the Sonoma Mission Inn as a post-Christmas gift, to spend New Year's Eve wining and dining and getting massages and mudbaths," I sigh. "Is it possible for him to be any more romantic? Could he maybe teach a course in how to woo a woman?"

Claudia rolls her eyes. "Shit, I'm still looking for a real boyfriend, one who will bring me flowers once in a while. I don't even care if he marries me at this point. In the meantime . . ." She looks off toward the front door, and spies Frederick coming in, a young African-American hunk and artist with whom she's had a dalliance from time to time. "There's always those men for when we are *in need*."

She grins wickedly and is off like a shot in his direction.

Claudia is still able to carry on the no-strings routine with relative aplomb, but I'm so over it. I hope 2003 sends me someone brilliant and kind and like Lenny, but who loves me. Okay, maybe my laundry list does require more than a warm-and-sexy bod after all.

I'm surprised to see Peter come in the door, since he is not one for big parties. Especially since he wears the same clothes to everything; the concept of party attire is lost on my grassroots friend.

"What brings you, darling one?" I ask, wrapping my arm through his.

"I just felt . . . enthused." He smiles. "Something about the new year and the opportunity to infuse new life into one's routine, let go of old habits. It's a paradox I embrace."

There's never small talk with Peter.

"So, did you make resolutions?" I ask, sipping Champagne. "Or are you perfect just the way you are?"

"You joke." He blushes. "But yes, I would say I could use a little work. How about you? You're on such a roll—you're tapping into such a nerve. I see it every week in the letters to the editor. You are becoming a spokeswoman for an entire sociopolitical class of women: the single woman of a certain age. This year could be big for you."

"Do you think so? That would be nice! Although sometimes I feel so conflicted. I want to make a difference and be a spokeswoman and raise the flag of independence; then other days I want to say fuck it, just give me a boyfriend!"

He studies my face. "Yes, it's the eternal quandary. It's what women your age were raised to think they deserved. Maybe even what they needed. But . . . how shall I say . . . I think you need to embrace what could be a higher calling. If you do, the men will come."

I want to make a joke about men *coming* to diffuse the intensity of the moment, but Peter would be offended.

"Oh dear," I say, looking over his shoulder and down the hallway. "Marco and Elsa are here, speaking of male frustrations. I never quite know what to say."

They approach us to say hello, and Elsa shyly takes me aside while Peter and Marco talk. "I just want you to know how much I appreciate your kindness regarding Marco and me; I know it's probably been a little awkward for you."

"Well"—I smile, hoping I sound convincing—"we're all grown-ups, and it doesn't hurt me to try to act like one!"

Oh Christ, I just remembered writing that little whiny aside about her and Marco in my column. Mental note: see if I can edit that out before Sunday.

I decide it's time to switch to water since I've been overserved in the Champagne department. And this year I didn't get a hotel room in The City like I have on other New Year's Eves. I head for the kitchen and pull a Calistoga out of the fridge, and when I turn around I run smack into a handsome man—oof! Straight into his broad chest. He looks familiar.

"Jane!" he says, smiling and holding out his arms for an embrace. I decide to play along because, hey, free hug with handsome guy. "How are you?" I say, embracing him and then standing back and studying his face for clues. He stares back at me intently. "It's . . . Ken," he says, realizing I can't recall his name. "I was a lobbyist for various environmental organizations when you were at city hall—Rainforest Action Network? Greenpeace?"

"Oh, right!" I say, remembering a hunky outdoorsman with more facial fair. "Didn't you used to have a beard?"

"Now you remember! I had to have it then; it was part of the uniform. Nowadays with the Bushies in power it pays to be a little more clean-cut if you want to influence anyone."

He smiles dreamily. "You know, you look . . . really fantastic . . ."

My impulse is to look down at myself and say, Are you serious? But instead I smile and flirt back. "Well, so do you! What have you been up to these last, oh, five or six years?"

He tells me, grinning constantly and speaking slowly (which would be disconcerting if he weren't so attractive), that his personal life went to hell in recent years when he started making more trips to D.C. to lobby on the national level. Now he's getting divorced and they're fighting over their five-year-old son. "But," he adds, "I'm still determined to get back into life—get out more and do more things."

Ken pauses. "Know of any good tour guides?"

I smile. "Honey, you just met the conductor on this train."

"That's what I figured from reading your column—you seem so busy all the time doing such cool things. I'm a big fan. I read it every Sunday, seeking insights into the female brain."

He laughs unexpectedly, and loudly.

Dan walks through the crowded kitchen area, crowing that it's a quarter to twelve and to gather upstairs by the TV for the countdown. It's fish or cut bait time. I look at Ken. Think I'll fish.

"Let's go upstairs," I tell him. "Where the music is."

They've done the annual switch from background jazz to disco, and the hardwood floor is starting to vibrate with feet stomping to "Brick House" by the Commodores. Ken takes my hand and pulls me into the dancing crowd, and soon we're doing the bump and grind and I'm getting lost in the joy of the tribal mating dance. Here and there he goes off on his own and waves his arms around like he's the only person in the room. Which is cute but a little weird.

Ten . . . nine . . . eight . . . seven . . . the countdown starts, and Ken suddenly focuses all his attention on me, and pulls me in close with a fixing stare. And at the call of Happy New Year, he lunges at me for a kiss, tongue and all, and his hands move quickly down my back and squeeze my backside. Okay, he's lost me here.

"Dude!" is all I can sputter, as I pull back, laughing. I catch the wide eyes of both Peter and Claudia watching us. Dignity, where have you gone?

He looks chastened. "Oh, I'm sorry, I'm just a little . . ."

"Carried away? High?"

"Definitely both," he says, smiling and pulling me back into him and spinning me around. "I took a tab of ecstasy about two hours ago and I'm kind of peaking."

Jesus. Well, this explains the behavior. But the mystery is why a man my age, or maybe even older, would be ingesting a cheesy dance-hall drug? It takes the wind out of my sails more than somewhat. I'd prefer a man to be attracted to me when he wasn't thinking *everything* is beautiful, even the coffee table.

"Yeah? Hmmm . . . Well, I'm not really on your planet here," I say, slowing him down and trying to extricate myself from his hyperkinetic grasp. "And I should probably take off. Happy New Year!"

He looks slightly crestfallen as I back away. "Can I call you?"

"How about e-mail?" I smile, not wanting to be overly discouraging but knowing I'm ready to say my good-byes. "If you read my column, you know my e-mail address is always at the bottom."

I kiss the tips of my right fingers, wiggle them at him, and turn to go. *Evacuate! Evacuate! Oh Lord, this was a weird one.*

"Jane!" I hear Ken's voice calling out behind me, and turn around.

"I'm a Leo!" he shouts, and winks.

Boobs, Female and Male

The first e-mail I get in response to my New Year's column is from Elsa: "Jane, if you were 'feeling bad' about me and Marco, why didn't you just say so rather than putting it in your column for everyone to see? I thought we were better friends than this."

I recoil, mortified. My mental note was made on a mental notepad soaked with Champagne, and it was promptly forgotten.

"Oh Elsa, I'm so sorry!" I write frantically. "I don't know why I put that in there. I was aiming for brutal honesty, I guess."

She responds: "It's okay, but you might want to consider who you hurt next time you decide to spill your guts."

Oh shit, she's right. I've lucked out so far in that no one I sniped at took umbrage—probably because they all had it coming. But Elsa is an innocent bystander, and a friend. Ugh, perhaps I've gotten so high on my columnist horse that my sensitivity has gone by the wayside. And I suspect my other friends who read the column are completely aware I was referring to her and also think I'm a sour-grapes-eating jerk.

"We can't run a correction like this." My editor David chuckles.

"We can't say 'Jane Ganahl had a lapse of sensitivity and hurt her good friend and apologizes.' It's just not done! Have you considered flowers?"

Flowers! No, I don't want to do the Guy Thing and send them to right a wrong. I'll see if I can take her to lunch and convince her I really am happy for them (even if I'm not, quite) and restore a healthy sheen to our friendship.

Meanwhile, I mitigate the self-loathing by reading the outpouring of attagirl e-mails in response to my New Year's resolutions; it seems many women also struggle with issues of self-acceptance. And what do you know? Here's an e-mail from Ken, aka Mr. Ecstasy.

"Jane, I owe you an apology for coming on so strong and groping you the other night. I wasn't quite in my right mind, although your charm is also to blame! If you'll give me another chance, could I at least buy you dinner?"

I smile, and e-mail back quickly: "And if I did, how could I be sure you won't slip a tab in my drink?"

There is a pause. "I guess you can't be sure! But one thing that IS sure is that you'd find your mind opened in ways you can't imagine!"

OK, I really don't have time to call Nancy Reagan and ask her for some "just say no" materials to pass to my new suitor. Dignity . . . wasn't that my new watchword? I'm pretty sure Leo isn't a druggie. Still, Ken is awfully attractive, and I'm a sucker for a man with a cause.

One of my chief New Year's resolutions (not made in print) is to take better care of myself, so off I go to my annual OB/GYN visit, which I dread more as I get older. The potential for bad news increases with each passing year. I adore my doc, whom I've been seeing for a decade and a half now and who has seen me through several bouts of what he called "honeymoon-itis," a minor infection caused by so much sex that my body's circuits would fry and I'd get sick.

Those were the days.

But on this day I find myself sitting in my paper gown, cringing at being weighed, and answering personal questions. "Wow, almost fifty now!" he says, reading my chart. "Have you noticed any hormonal imbalances?"

"Well, I am kind of emotional these days," I tell him. "But I'm under a lot of stress with the column, too."

"So how often would you say you cried, got tearful?" he asks, jotting it down.

"Oh, not that often. No more than once . . . a . . . *day*?"

My doctor stops writing and smiles.

And it hits me: "Wow, I guess that's kind of often!"

"Yes, you could say so!" he quips. "We should run some tests, find out if you're in menopause. And you're also due for a mammogram."

"Well, something's *paused* in recent years for sure," I say bitterly. "And I'm pretty sure it's *men*."

He winks. "I know. I read your column every week!"

Okay, it's one thing to have anonymous fans, it's another thing to have one whose job it is to stick metal objects where the sun don't shine.

He sends me down the hall for a blood test and down the street for a mammogram, which is truly one of the least fun things a woman can do, especially one with small boobs. *Any breast cancer in the family?* I am asked, as nurses wedge my tissue between the plates. No. This is not a concern. I am more wigged about the menopause potential. I haven't done a shred of reading on it—haven't felt the need. Guess it's time.

"Hey, when did your mom go through The Change?" I find Rosalind at her desk to ask about her mother, who is a very young sixty-ish.

"Oh, she was late—a little after fifty. Why?"

"My doctor thinks I might be hitting the change. And I can't ask my mom for information now that she's gone. I've done some reading and the good news is that it might account for some of this mysterious weight gain in recent years. But I'm also not keen on taking hormones."

"Well, my mom did and she did great with them. Speaking of hormones, I had another conversation with Dieter about children. At least he's not adverse to them—or so he says! Which is good because with forty looming, I'm more worried about becoming a mom than I am about getting married. And I know Dieter would make a great dad.

"Then again," she adds, furrowing her brow and sinking lower in her desk chair, "I think Dieter always knows when I am about to hang it up, and then he'll throw me a lifeline—like the kids discussion."

"I'm so sorry this has become such a drag for you!" I tell her. "I'm always amazed when someone says that women are the more complicated sex, when men are so seriously fucked up in their own way!"

I tell her about my mind-expanding new suitor and she laughs out loud. "Oh my God, how do you *find* these crazy guys? Still, he sounds promising. Washington lobbyists make decent money!"

"Well, I love that he's a do-gooder, but this ecstasy thing is a buzzkill for sure. I'm still debating. I'd like to find someone to date, but not if it'd be like going back to college."

The good news is that, unlike Rosalind, I'm way past caring about whether someone would make a good dad. Which is good because Ken seems like the kind who'd be more interested in instructing his kid on the art of joint-rolling than playing catch.

Opening the mail a few days later, there is a letter from the Breast Health Center, saying they need to see me again right away for a rescreening. Some "irregularities" were detected in my mammogram. Confused, I call them, and am told that this is routine, that there is something unidentifiable, perhaps merely a flaw, in the film. My mouth dry, I make an appointment for a retest tomorrow. And try to put it out of my mind until then.

I'm a quavering mess by the time the retest of my right breast is done, despite the medical assistants who are cheerful and reassuring. Standard practice, happens often, they say. Get dressed, they tell me, and the doctor will review the films and talk to you shortly.

But when the doctor comes in, holding my films, I know by the look on his face that he's not here to tell me to go home, everything's fine.

He holds the film up to the light and points out a cluster of tiny dots near the center of my breast. Words like biopsy and abnormality and out-patient surgery are coming out of his mouth, but I have checked out, watching his lips move but feeling like I'm sleepwalking through a bad dream. He is sounding cheerful and upbeat about whatever the hell it is he's saying, but I'm pretty sure the gist is *Put your affairs in order, you're going to die soon.*

"We should schedule you for a biopsy as soon as possible," he says, and I snap back to attention: there's something for me to do here. "Here's the number of a surgeon with your health plan. You need to call him to set up an appointment."

"Oh God . . ." I suddenly can't move, and put my face in my hands. He pats my shoulder, as I'm sure he's done for countless women like me with fucked-up mammograms. "It's just that . . ." I say, fighting hysteria, "my mom and sister died of cancer not too long ago."

And much as I'd like to see them again, I was hoping it wouldn't be for a few more years.

"Well, your chart says no breast cancer in your family, right? So that's good, that means it's quite possibly something else." He smiles, looks me in the eye to make sure I'm hearing him, and sends me on my wobbly way.

I go immediately to the surgeon's office and introduce myself—undoubtedly looking like a fruitbat with my wild red eyes—and say I want an appointment as soon as possible; they are able to accommodate me in three days. They explain it will be an outpatient situation, so I'll be in the hospital for half a day, and will need to be driven home.

Driven home! Shit, I can't tell Erin about this. She'll freak out. Nor Dad, who just left on his walkabout and is probably halfway to Arizona. Nor Rob and Julie, who are in a crisis of their own dealing with Julie's aunt being near death in a nursing home. Nor even Anne, with whom I have a good-humored plan for mutual geriatric care, who's in Cincinnati or God-knows-where.

It's time to circle the friend-wagons. Rosalind offers to drop me off and pick me up; her apartment is close to the hospital and I can stay there all afternoon until I feel fit to drive home to the coast. I have offers from Claudia and Phil and Po and Michele to help if I need it after I get home, but I don't think I shall. I'm told I'll be right perky when the medication wears off.

And I'm not afraid to go under the knife; it's the *pre*surgical time that has my nerves shredded. Erin leaves me a message asking why I haven't called her in a couple of days. She always seems to know something bad is up. And I don't want to call her back for fear I'll blurt out my anxieties and she, like the symbiotic, psychic twin that she is, will suffer as I am. Can't allow that.

I'm almost relieved when the day arrives and Rosalind drives me from her house to the hospital. "Don't worry," she says. "I know you're going to be fine." I wish I shared her enthusiasm.

When I check in for the surgery, the gray-haired nurse asks my age.

"Fifty," I surprise myself by saying. "I mean almost fifty! Not for another few months."

She smiles at me understandingly; we are in the same sorority, sister. I pledge to try not to die young.

They have me leave my things in a locker next to a recovery bed; my purse contains my notepad so that I can record what I'm thinking and feeling. But after I pop the Valium they give me I don't care about writing anything down. Besides, if I were to write about this it'd be like opening a vein on the page. In the operating room I am put in a "waking sleep" situation while a curtain is placed below my chin, presumably so I can't see them sticking needles in my breast to aspirate the tiny lumps. But I am so completely out of it that when I'm wheeled back to recover I don't remember a single image from the time the drugs took hold.

In the recovery room, the surgeon tells me it will take a few days before the results of the biopsy are known, and that I should just take it easy, put a sports bra on for support and ice on my breast for the pain. "We really had to dig around in there," he says, which sounds so grim I don't ask for more information. Rosalind picks me up and ushers me into her Victorian flat and to her fluffy bed, where I sleep the afternoon away with Oliver, her snoring pug, while she returns to work.

When I wake up and feel alert enough to drive, the sun is setting. And I feel dreadfully alone. My boob hurts under the bandaging but I need to get home before I can take a codeine pill.

And suddenly I'm filled with anger. All this yakking I've done about how great it is to be single. Well, how do you like this, spokeswoman? So you're getting raises and speaking engagements, but there's no one to hold you when you're freaked out and in pain. Just a week ago my biggest worry was what to wear to the New Year's Eve party and now I'm scared that it might have been my last. That I won't get to live to be a grandma.

I feel myself losing it again, a flush of anxiety rushing to my throat. *Okay, just stop it,* I lecture myself. *Ain't no way God is going to zap your family three times. Just relax.*

Erin calls me that night when I'm in a stupor in front of the TV, congested from weeping and woozy from pain killers (the bag of peas on my swollen breast not fixing the situation) and is alarmed at my tone. "Are you okay?" she says. "You don't sound okay!"

"I think I'm coming down with a cold," I lie.

Oh, and maybe cancer, too.

"And this glass of wine I had went right to my head."

"Well, I hope you're not driving anywhere tonight," she says, donning her matronly tone.

"Honey . . ." I say, desperate to tell her, but knowing I can't. "I just love you."

"Mom!" She laughs. "Go to bed—you are hammered! And I love you, too."

Before I head upstairs, I pause at the computer, sweetly pleased to see e-mails of concern from my few friends who know what happened today. But there's one who doesn't. Woozily, and with my better judgment mechanism in the "off" position, I e-mail Lenny: "Call me, I had to have a biopsy. I wish I could talk to you." And off it goes—an SOS via DSL.

When I wake up, I immediately regret sending the less-than-coherent e-mail (*biopsy? what?*), and also realize with every passing day that I *don't* hear from him I'll get more peevish. Then again, I have more important things to worry about, like my future. The good news is, that despite a right boob that is swollen and Frankenstein-like with several incision marks, I am back on my feet physically fairly quickly. Emotionally is another matter. The thunderstorms of tears are still coming regularly, anxiety preventing me from working or doing anything constructive.

But at a certain point, every human being under duress must get tired of wailing and worrying, and start thinking realistically about things. I have a fat life insurance policy so Erin would be more than taken care of. I don't have a will but I can make one. Maybe I could buy a do-it-yourself book? I do worry about my dad surviving the death of another child. I think about calling Lisa in Vancouver and asking for her input, but decide I should wait until I know for sure what I'm dealing with.

I try not to think about the events surrounding my mother's and sister's diagnoses. The Chinese brain surgeon who met us in the hospital waiting room after Mom's head-opening operation, who told us that, at this point, "we should not so much talk about *quantity* of life but *quality*." And Lisa's phone call telling me: "It's what I feared. It's cancer. But no matter what happens, you have to be strong."

Well, I'm not strong. Not like she was.

My friends are like personal trainers in fortitude. I get flowers from both Phil and Stephan, of all people, whom Rosalind ran into in the gym and told the news. "Fight like a banshee!" is his message, which makes me smile; I recall that Stephan's mother is a breast cancer survivor. Claudia makes the drive down from the city to bring me vegetarian soup. Peter gives me daily telephone pep talks, and Rosalind seems to call every few hours. Phil asks if I want him to come down and play me some guitar—he knows how I love his blues guitar playing. I demur, since I know he's up to his neck in crises of his own, but thank him for the offer.

"I think I've discovered why the blues are so big with people our age," I tell him. "And why most of the blues masters are older. It's because we're all starting to fall apart! It's like the backstory is: I've been around, I'm full of sensual fun, but goddamn, my feet hurt."

He chuckles. "I'm glad you haven't lost your sense of humor. You're a lot stronger than you think."

I'm not so sure, but I keep his words in my hip pocket for the times when I start to falter.

When Po calls four days after my surgery, I'm padding around my kitchen making oatmeal. "I think I'll go back to work tomorrow," I tell him. "I'm feeling pretty okay, and too much alone time is bad for the brain. Work is a great distraction."

"What do you hear from Lenny?" he asks, tentatively.

"Well, like a dope I sent him an e-mail when I was at my lowest ebb, asking him to please call me—and he hasn't," I sigh. "But oddly enough, in light of other things in the balance, it hasn't seemed so important."

"You're really handling this well," he says. "If it were Michele who might have cancer, I think they'd have to tranquilize me."

"Which is why it's good that you married Michele—she is much tougher than you," I joke. "I suspect if she were in my shoes, she'd be doing fine."

I get a beep and put Po on hold. It's my surgeon on the other line.

"I just wanted to let you know we got the results back and you're fine. The spots in your breast are calcifications, not cancer."

"What?" I am breathless. "Calcifi-what? I'm okay?"

"Yes." He laughs. "You're fine. Call my office if you want more information."

I get back on the line with Po, and burst into tears.

"Oh no!" he's alarmed. "What happened?"

"Po, I'm okay!" I say between sobs. "There's nothing wrong with me! It's not cancer, it's something called calcifications."

"Fantastic!" His voice quavers slightly. "I'll let folks know!"

Euphoric, I call Erin with the news. There is a long silence on the other end. "*Are you kidding me? You kept this from me?*" She is sounding angry—a rarity for her. Then I hear tears. "How could you not tell me?"

"Honey, I didn't want you to worry. I thought if it turned out to be nothing, you'd have freaked out for no reason!"

"I understand that," she says, sniffling. "But for God's sake, I am an adult now, Mom! I could have stayed at home for a few days and taken care of you! When you treat me like I'm still a child you rob yourself of support, and you rob me of being able to help you. You've taken care of me my whole life; the least you can do is let me return the favor!"

Oh dear, she is right—again.

"I know, sweetie, but I lined up support just fine! My friends were really great. In fact, it was a reminder that even if I'm single forever, and don't live anywhere near you, neither one of us will have to worry that I'll die alone and unloved!"

She manages a little laugh. "Okay, but promise you won't do that again!"

"I don't need to promise anything because this will never happen again!" I laugh. "It's only perfect health for me from now on."

I tell Anne and Rob, who are similarly unhappy with my silence, even though I tell them the same things I told Erin. The only one who really understands how I handled it is Dad.

"Oh, honey, you did the right thing," he says, from his Motel 6 room in Moab. "I just feel bad that you had to carry that burden alone. And I recall that this has happened before. Didn't Lisa tell you first that she might be sick, and asked you not to tell the family until she knew for sure?"

"Yeah, Dad, you're right. She had to tell someone, and I was visiting her in L.A. I had to keep quiet for something like two weeks until her biopsy came back. It was pretty terrible living with that possibility."

And unlike my own, Lisa's results were catastrophic.

"Should I come home?" he asks. "Do you need me there?"

"Dad," I say gently. "Thanks, but I'm fine! No need to do anything but have yourself a fabulous drive! I assume you've ruled out Michigan?"

He chuckles. "Yeah, Barbara was fairly insistent that it would not be a smart move. So I'll head due north tomorrow and then west on I-70 . . ."

He goes on to cheerfully describe his route to Idaho in great detail; Captain Bob in command of his clipper ship Cadillac. What a great, long life he's had. I suddenly feel a greater empathy.

Fully a week after I e-mailed Lenny, I get an electronic response as I'm going to bed. "Biopsy? God, what's happened? I want to call you but I'm afraid of what you might tell me! I'm sorry it took so long to answer, but I've been really busy. . . ."

Busy? If the situations were reversed, I'd have been on a plane. But that is me, not he. I can't think of what to say—am I pissed? do I give a shit?—so I don't answer right away.

The next morning I get my first flowers from Lenny. Roses—the very thing he said he never promised me. And I'm not even dying. I can't decide whether to laugh or cry. "Lenny, you fucking *boob*," I mutter, putting the flowers on my coffee table.

"Boob!" I laugh out loud at my word choice. And I am off to the freezer for another bag of frozen peas for my almost recovered mammary. It will be fine and so shall I.

Hell, maybe my best times are still ahead! Maybe it's also time to quit playing it so safe. Life, as I've learned in living color, might just be a lot shorter than one plans.

I sit down at the computer, bag of peas in my camisole, to write. But before I answer Lenny's e-mail, wrestling with my conflicted feelings and telling him *Thank you, it's OK, calm down, I'm fine,* I look up Ken's e-mail address. Time to finally take him up on his invitation.

The Ecstasy of Altruism

I feel like Dr. Frankenstein running around the lab shrieking, It's alive! It's alive! But the monster in question is *me*, and despite stitches in my breast, I'm in a far superior mood than the dude who woke up with bolts in his neck.

And I've made a date with a hot environmentalist and recreational drug advocate. And I can't wait.

It's a cliché but it's also true: when you brush up against your own mortality, it can give you a new lease on life. I feel like kissing strangers, going to church on nonspecial occasions or taking up Buddhism, washing my car, giving the kitties an extra helping of food, and giving everyone, even the president, the benefit of the doubt. I've told my friends and family I love them several times, to the point that they're telling me to shut up already.

It's an impulse born of utter relief. And it happened to me only once before in my life: a few years ago when I was driving home from reviewing a rock show in The City—Son Volt, I think it was—when I hit the freeway at two a.m., two cars filled with apparent gang members sped up close to me and started shooting at each other. On either side of me. I was stuck in the middle of these two careening cars, and could hear the *pop pop pop* of their guns as I ducked my head and somehow managed to avoid crashing. As they passed, I slowed down until they were out of sight.

I was severely rattled by it; especially after Phil looked at my windshield and found several small-caliber bullet pockmarks in the vicinity of my head. But not so rattled that I didn't go on a pretty hearty bender for a week or so with my young lover du jour—drinking, going to music venues, screwing until all hours, and generally celebrating life until I almost died of more natural causes.

How very cautious I've become in contrast! And I'm tired of playing it safe and sticking to my tired formula for living! Okay, I know I said no more casual sex, but maybe I spoke prematurely. It certainly has provided me with memorable experiences—the likes of which I'm craving now. The likes of which I'm hoping Ken can provide.

I'm ready to have my world rocked, but in small doses, as befitting a woman turning fifty in just a couple of months. I feel like taking a walk on the wild side—as long as I get my seven hours of sleep afterward.

This is rebellion, midlife-style.

The only thing I don't feel like doing is writing a column about my health crisis. Phil encouraged me to do so, saying it could help women by reminding them to stay current on their mammograms. But I've been balking, perhaps fearful of reliving the scare by writing about it. It's true that I've been able to sort out my feelings about the various unfortunate events in my life this last year by turning them into column fodder. But this one was resolved so well that perhaps I don't want to tempt fate by writing about it.

And the only bad health news I've gotten since my biopsy came back is that I am definitely cruising toward fifty with my hormones in a tailspin. My OB/GYN has prescribed a low-dose HRT to "see if it might help with the mood swings," and even though I can think of various other commodities that might be better at smoothing out my moods—winning the lottery, getting Erin into a local law school, having a closet full of suitors who want to have sex all day—I grudgingly take his advice. When I show up at my local Medicine Shoppe to pick up my prescription, the pharmacist smiles at me as he rings me up.

"I read you every Sunday," he says shyly.

"Oh, wow, thanks!" I stammer. "I'm glad I'm not here for anything grosser than a hormone deficiency! Like . . . a nasty infection of some kind!"

I really need to develop a more gracious response to situations like this.

Meanwhile, I continue to disabuse the world of the rumor that I am dying. I told very few people about my scare, but rumors in our little community travel by Pony Express sometimes, and every day I get another e-mail of concern. So I've written an e-mail that I just keep sending out as needed: "thanks for asking but i'm actually okay! the biopsy came back negative and i'm fine . . . the procedure itself was a bit of an ordeal and i'm still in pain from scalpels attacking my cupcake, but i am personally ELATED that the buck stops here in terms of family cancer catastrophes. . . ."

I've also disabused Ken, with whom I'm dining tomorrow night, of the notion that I'll do ecstasy with him, and he says he's cool with that. I mean, I *am* up for new experiences, but drugs, based on some bad experiences in my youth, most notably with Vince, scare the shit out of me. I told him this and he has not tried to talk me into anything. In fact, he dropped the subject right away. The longer we've e-mailed, the more I've switched from apprehensive to excited; turns out he's funny, sweet, and not as big a freak as I might have thought. And he's been reading my column regularly and doesn't think *I'm* a freak either, so that's always a plus.

It's true that his life is in total chaos, with his wife hanging him out to dry on their divorce and keeping their son from him, and he's been couch-surfing at various friends' homes for the last year. But hey! He's an altruist! His do-gooder résumé is as long as my arm, which is always a strong selling point. With each rung he's climbed on the nonprofit ladder he gets closer to heavenly.

Erin and I have never had the same taste in men in terms of their looks, but this is one area in which we enthusiastically agree: do-gooders are hot. And it turns out she's eyeing one of her own.

"Mom, you won't believe this guy I met the other night," she says, settling into the couch to watch a Jane Austen film with me. (She's been spending a lot of time at the house since learning of my biopsy; I think it's made her appreciate me more, if that's possible.) "He's a med student, going into his third year, and he's going to spend the summer in Ethiopia working with UNICEF. And when he graduates, he plans to work in a public health clinic instead of a fancy doctor's office—can you imagine?"

"Yes, I can imagine," I tell her. "This guy I'm seeing tomorrow night is cut from the same cloth. Probably made of hemp."

"Yeah, you mentioned him," she says, munching popcorn. "But you've gone out with other guys like him. I can recall a few. . . ."

"Yes, you met the surfing lawyer. And the head of the Greenies I dated at city hall. And you know, I think that kind of altruism is one thing that's always kept my heart open to Lenny," I say. "He can be self-absorbed, but he also teaches young people every summer for free."

"Yeah, well, I'm hoping this new guy is so awesome he makes you forget about old what's-his-name," Erin says. "You need someone who'll take better care of you!"

"Honey, I don't need to be taken care of. I'm doing pretty good on my own!" I protest, although in light of my health scare, I can see why she would want such a thing. "But you know, Valentine's Day is coming up in a couple of weeks and wouldn't it be swell if we *both* had dates for a change? Hell, I might yet get one to my birthday party!"

She smiles. "Oooo, Valentine's Day! Hadn't even thought of it!"

"Well, *I* have, because I have to cough up a column and I'm not sure what to write."

"I have a feeling," she says, tossing a piece of popcorn at me and grinning, "that the column will write itself."

"Tonight is your *third date* with this guy? And you've been out in public no less? You must really like him!" Rosalind teases me at work a week later. "I never did get to meet Andrew, since you kept him out of public view."

"I do really like this guy." I smile. "The first two dates were darn close to magical. He's fun, I totally admire him as a human being. . . ."

"But?"

"But nothing, really. It's just his life is a little chaotic and I have misgivings about his use of recreational drugs. But I'm trying to be open-minded, in keeping with my new commitment to embrace life and all its experiences."

"Speaking of which, have you had sex yet?"

"You know I'd tell you if we had!" I laugh. "We've kissed good night—he's a fabulous kisser. But he's being a gentleman and not pressuring me. Besides, he knows my breast has been a little too tender for body-slamming purposes. But tonight might be it, though. He's coming down to have dinner at my house. I'm actually cooking! Which is sort of a trial by fire—if he still likes me afterward, he must really like me."

"Well, this bodes very well for V-Day next week! Very well indeed!" She is as gleeful as if the hot new romance were hers and not mine.

"What are you and Dieter going to do for the big day?" I ask, hoping the news is good since my fingers are still so crossed for these two.

"We're, uh . . . going to Paris!" she says, eyes wide. "He gave me an early Valentine's Day card with our reservations for next week! We're staying at the Ritz, and flying first class. Jane, I think this really might be it! I think he's really going to set a date when we're there."

Paris! Didn't I used to say that's where I wanted to go for my fiftieth? Where did that dream go?

"That sounds amazing. And I hope this is it! I've been counting on being a bridesmaid for two years now! I will personally kill him if he doesn't pull the trigger this time."

"You won't have to," Rosalind says coolly. "Because I'll do it myself. No kidding. This is it or it's over. But you! You go and have a fabulous evening and report back to me. And like I always say, be open-minded!"

He is so goddamn beautiful, looking at me over the top of his wineglass. Well, handsome. No, beautiful. His eyes are killing me. We've had more than a bottle between us, and laughed and talked for hours already. I am kite-high on him, on life, and on all its possibilities. He keeps touching my jeans-clad knee under the table and I know it's going to happen tonight. And I don't care about the extra pounds I'm carrying or the fact that I'm almost fifty, because he's the same age and holy shit, this fabulous man wants me. We're listening to Pink Martini and he pulls me out of my dining table chair and starts to dance with me. I mean, really dance compared to New Year's Eve.

"What do you think? Do you want to try some?" he smiles down into my face.

"What, you mean X?" I sigh, my defenses effacing. "You have some with you?"

He pulls a plastic bag out of his pocket and holds it up. "I swear to God you'll love it." And then he kisses me, erasing any doubt.

I give in. "Okay, then . . ." I hear myself saying. "Let's do it—together."

In a trice he's preparing the drug in a glass of water as I watch in tipsy fascination. I drink my share, and we go downstairs to the living room to make a fire and put on some music he's brought with him: a Café del Mar compilation, which immediately fills the room up to its high ceilings with sensual sounds. Right away he is feeling the effects—perhaps because he does it so often it never quite leaves his body completely. We lay on the couch, with only the fire to illuminate the room, and it's heavenly, and he is taking his time making love to me, kissing my neck and face slowly.

"Mind the boob," I say to him softly when things begin to advance. He looks deeply into my eyes and touches me there . . . carefully, sweetly . . .

And suddenly it feels like my hair is on fire—and sticking straight up like it's being blowtorched. But in a nice way, if that's possible.

"Oh my gawwwwwd," I say in wonderment, feeling like I'm taking off into space.

"Didn't I tell you?" he breathes. And then we are having sex, and I'm pretty sure it's fabulous, but for the next couple of hours I'm not really sure about anything. All I know is that I end up naked on the carpet on top of a throw blanket and it's either very late at night or early in the morning. I am exhausted but still buzzing. Where is Ken? He is dancing. Naked. And twirling around my living room. My cats are nowhere to be found—probably hiding in fear. I need to collect myself.

Sitting up and looking around, this is indeed my living room, in my house. My arched windows looking out at . . . oh, the moon! It's never been so close to the earth before! Its beams are shining down like a searchlight. Maybe it *is* a searchlight!

"Can you see?" I say to Ken, gesturing happily to the window and pulling the throw blanket around me. He doesn't say a word, but just smiles and keeps on dancing.

I have to see for myself, so I walk out the front door and pull the blanket with me. Which shuts the front door behind me. Which locks the front door. I stare at the moon for a glorious moment, but then, realizing it is, in fact, just the moon, and it's a freezing February night, I immediately see the folly of my adventure. I am locked out, naked but for a blanket, and Ken is inside with the music cranked up and dancing around incoherently.

I start knocking on the door, but he doesn't answer. I knock harder. My neighbor's light comes on. Then I flash on a sweet word: *hide-a-key!* I fumble around in the potted plant by the front door, dislodging two snails in the process, until I find it. I let myself back in, and Ken is still dancing, oblivious to my moment of crisis.

I try to engage him by dancing coyly next to him but it's hopeless; he is off on a planet I haven't got a visa to visit. I'm suddenly tired of this little experiment and just want to get some sleep. I take his arms and stop his twirling for a moment to kiss his lips, and I mumble: "I'm going upstairs to bed now. I'm going to be fifty years old soon."

And when I get up to my room, I plant face-first in the bed and am gone. Sometime later I am aware of his body climbing into the bed and lying close to mine and it feels sweet. He puts his arms around me and pulls me close.

I could swear I hear him say: "I love you."

When I wake up and look blearily at the clock, I see it's almost ten a.m. Since I have no idea what time I actually went to bed, I have no idea how much sleep I got. But right now it feels like about twenty minutes.

"Mmmm," Ken says next to me. He looks sweet sleeping, handsome, too.

Oh God, *did he say he loved me*? Was this some kind of X-inspired hallucination? I feel suddenly awkward, like the balance of the universe is off. Or maybe it's just that I electrocuted half my brain cells last night. Jesus, I feel like crap. I delicately extricate myself from the bed and stumble into the shower.

When I get out, Ken is putting on his clothes. This makes me very, very happy. "Hey, you OK?" he asks, smiling.

"I don't feel so good," I tell him, pulling my robe around me and leaning on my bathroom counter. "Massively hungover, or something."

"That's normal the first time. It gets better!"

"Yeah, well . . ." I say, rubbing my bloodshot eyes. "Just so you understand, this was kind of a one-shot thing for me. It was fun, in its own weird way, but I don't think I need to do this again."

He is clearly disappointed. "OK, we can talk about it," he says cheerfully. We? He is thinking in the "we" context?

He comes over and embraces me warmly. We kiss, and he whispers in my ear. "I meant what I said last night—I really think I'm in love with you. I hope that doesn't freak you out."

My stomach drops. "I thought maybe you were just high!" I laugh softly. And I look him square in the eye, feeling the nagging need for a reality check. "But how can you think you love me after three dates? I can't imagine the sex was even all that good—at least *I* don't remember it!"

He laughs heartily. "You're so funny. It's another reason I love you."

Right now, I just want coffee and to sort out my thoughts—one pile for the exciting, another for the too-weird-to-consider.

"Can we talk about this when we're both . . . I dunno . . . more *normal*?" I ask.

"Of course, and you're going to be my date for Valentine's Day, right? Let's go somewhere fabulous. My treat."

"Now you're talking," I say, smiling as I continue steering him toward the front door.

He kisses me as he takes his leave. "You know how I feel," he says tenderly. "Just think about it."

I am reeling; here is what I would consider a fantasy man—well, except maybe for that little drug issue—and I'm not sure how I feel. I really want to get excited about his immediate expressions of affection; I mean, haven't I been complaining for ages that even if marriage isn't part of the deal, that love is the endgame? The goal?

And what the hell is love about, anyway? I thought I was in love many times, only to find out it was just passion. Couldn't it happen in the reverse? Couldn't I think something is based on passion when in fact love is at the core?

I don't really think so. The plain fact is, I should be more excited—the way I'd be if Lenny suddenly told me he loved me. The thought puts the tear ducts to work.

I feel like slapping myself. Here I'm pondering a new man who says he loves me and yet Lenny is crowding him from my fantasy. This tells me something important.

"Ken, you are lovely and wonderful," I e-mail the next day, after coming back to earth with a dull thud. "But I feel like we're on different levels in our feelings. I am not in love with you, and I'm sorry. It might have something to do with someone in my life who continues to linger in the background. But I also question whether your feelings are real or whether they're just born of neediness; you've been through so much lately. Perhaps if you took more time for yourself, things would become clearer? I'm not entirely sure the clarity you need can be found in a dance-hall drug. I hope you understand. XO Jane."

I hope he does, because I'm not entirely sure I do. All I know right now is that I'd rather see friends who love me on Valentine's Day than try to talk myself into loving someone wrong for me, just so I can say I have a date on the Big Day.

I've also been thinking a lot about my sister, who died the day after Valentine's Day. "There will always be guys after you, but you have to be careful with your heart," Lisa told me, when I was in a weepy state over yet another fucked-up affair. "I worry that you give love away too easily. Try holding out for when it feels exactly right. And value yourself more."

Just in time for Valentine's Day—a reminder about self-love.

Erin told me the column would write itself and so it has:

It goes without saying that we singletons have our own burdens to bear on Valentine's Day. The nonstop assault of advertising (most especially the jewelry juggernaut), TV programming, and movies selected for maximum romance potential all conspire to send us down that dark rabbit hole of self-loathing. Another Valentine's Day and I'm alone. No roses, no chocolate, no boyfriend. I'd better just hang it up and accept my fate: to die alone and unloved by anyone but my cats.

To hell with that thinking.

First of all, think of the other no's: no arguments over mismatched Valentine's Day expectations, no disappointments over lack of gifts, no having to sputter a thank-you for said Gothic bustier, no wondering why you wanted a relationship this badly in the first place.

I'd like to suggest a radical solution to all of this catharsis-forcing holiday hoo-ha. And I don't mean sitting home alone and crank-calling the happy couples you know. My idea is simple: love yourself. Whether you're in a couple or alone. Spend the day appreciating the fabulousness of you.

Stop twitching—I'm not going New Age on you. I'm talking about spending some quiet moments in which you add up all the great things about you. You work your butt off. You're good to people you know. If you're a parent, think of the laundry you've done and meals you've cooked and the unconditional love you've dished out by the truckload. People are better for knowing you.

Got it? OK, now treat yourself this V-Day. Think of what makes you happy, and seek it out. Chocolate, a good meal, chocolate, a movie, chocolate, roses, chocolate.

Better yet: if you really want a Valentine's Day experience that will stick to your ribs for longer than a day, do something nice for somebody else that day. Have dinner with a lonely relative. Volunteer. Take flowers to an old folks' home, donate blood, work a shift at a soup kitchen, go to an animal shelter and take a new friend home with you.

The truth is, all the men I've known in my life have not taught me what love is. The only valentine parked permanently in my display case at home came not from a lover but from my daughter: a hand-sewn stuffed butterfly made from three little hearts that she'd painstakingly constructed when she was very little. She made it to cheer up her mom soon after she and I became a two-person family.

That's what love is.

I have lunch on Valentine's Day with the ladies—Rosalind, Claudia, Michele, Dayna. I bring chocolates for everyone but Claudia—she gets flowers.

When I get home there are two e-mails from the two men most recently in my orbit. One is from Lenny, sending Valentine's greetings, which are, of course, without even a shred of sentimentality. "Jane, glad to hear you're going to be okay. Again, I'm sorry it took so long to contact you. It's called making hay while the sun shines and before these fuckers wise up."

Lenny, always on about his career. Glad you're not dying but have I mentioned my recent career peak?

"Off to the Grammys, wish me luck."

"Luck, Lenny," I respond, sighing. It's almost as good as love.

And from Ken: "Jane, I understand and I'm sorry if I somehow pushed you away. I'll admit to my emotions being a little on the raw—possibly needy—side since my divorce. You are probably wise to tell me to cool my jets. But can I reserve the right to call on you in the future, when stability is a little more at my disposal?"

I smile when I write him back and say, "Absolutely—and thanks for the . . . uh . . . interesting evening."

I call Erin on Lisa Day—February 15—feeling like balance has been restored to the universe, even though it means I'm alone again.

"This is your post–V-Day nosey-mother call," I tell her. "Tell me everything and make it cheerful!"

I do not tell her of my X-rated adventure. Dignity, what's left of it, must be maintained.

Wings Clipped and Unfurled

"Dad's had an accident," says my brother on the phone, the evenness of his voice keeping me from hyperventilating. "He's OK, just bruised and shaken up. But his car is totaled and he's stuck in Utah somewhere."

"How . . . ?"

"He swerved to avoid a deer on the road to Park City, went down an embankment, and tore out the undercarriage from his car. His cell phone didn't work there, so he was lucky to flag down a passing highway cop. He just called me from his hotel room."

I ask him anxiously for the number, but he cautions me. "Let's all give him a break and not remind him that we've all worried that this might happen. I can tell he's pretty upset about it, and you know how much these road trips mean to him."

My dad is sounding sad and humbled when I reach him. "Maybe you kids were right to worry about me." I assure him it could have happened to anyone, just as he said to me after my first fender-bender in my teens.

"Dad, this was a fluke. Really. Don't take it so hard." I try to keep my own voice from quavering.

"Maybe," he says. "But maybe my days of taking road trips are over." He might as well be saying he might be done with breathing. Captain Bob quit traveling? Have his clipper wings clipped? Inconceivable.

After Dad is checked out by a doctor and found to be fine except for some bruises, we all talk on the phone—Rob, Barbara, Anne, me, and a very upset Erin—and agree that he's OK enough to drive himself home. And he's decided to buy a new car, since he needs one now anyway, to finish the trip. Thank God there's a Buick dealership in a nearby town; having to buy foreign would have rubbed salt in the wound. The difficult talk about his limitations will wait until he gets back. I have always left it up to him to call his own shots in the aging department, but it's become clear that we might need to butt in for the first time.

But if the world is closing in a bit on Dad, others in my sphere have been busting out and spreading their wings.

Lenny didn't win the Grammy, but I had to watch the show anyway, looking for glimpses of him in the audience. I only saw him once, when they flashed on him before the award was announced; he smiled warmly and applauded when his competition won out. And, I happily noted, he was sitting with his mom in the audience. I sent him a better-luck-next-time e-mail, and got a sweet one back today: "It wasn't all for nothing. My record label is now giving me a shitload of money for the next album. They might even let me come out to California and record it at The Plant in Sausalito. In fact I might be out there in April to check it out. Are you up for more sex in the backseat?"

Of course, April is also my birthday—my fiftieth—which he didn't mention.

"Maybe," I respond. "Let me know what dates you're talking about and I'll see if I can squeeze you into my busy car . . . I mean, schedule. I have a lot going on in April, so let me know as soon as you can!"

Maybe I should have spelled it out for him: A-P-R-I-L . . . E-I-G-H-T-H. But self-restraint and dignity—my watchword of the year—force me not to. And now I have to hope he remembers. But after all this time and worry, how ironic would it be to have Lenny be my birthday date? I suppose it's possible that one of my friends might throw drinks on him for how unwell he's treated me. But to walk into my party with him? Well, it'd be worth any amount of chaos.

"This is a weird thing," Peter says cautiously, during a check-in phone call, the likes of which have been more frequent since my health scare. "But those early nibbles of interest in turning my book into a film seem to be paying off; I'm going to England to meet with the producers."

"Oh, you're kidding! That's so fantastic!"

"Well, it's just early in the process, but they might even be interested in having me write the script! Me, a scriptwriter? I'm not sure I can!" He chuckles.

Peter taught himself to write on a discarded typewriter while squatting in an abandoned building; I imagine screenwriting courses were not part of the curriculum.

"Peter, this is going to take you to a whole new level!"

"From your mouth to God's ear, honey-bunny. I'm so tired of being poor I could shit."

I also get a call from Po on the same happy morning. "Are you continuing to mend?" he asks. "How did the Commonwealth Club thing go? I'm sorry we couldn't make it but Luke was sick."

"Yes, I'm doing fine, thank you! Very little pain at this point. And the Commonwealth Club thing was great, really fun. Sold out, lots of single people there, Craig did great on the panel, I got some laughs . . .

and some groupies! There were some guys there specifically to meet me, because of the column."

"All right!" He laughs. "Way to go! Anyone you'd want to take home with you, now that you jettisoned the enviro guy?"

"Alas not. They were mostly sad-and-lonely types. But what's up with you? You sound mighty chipper today."

"We're pregnant again," he blurts out. "After a couple close calls, we really are. We're over the moon!"

"Oh, sweetie, fantastic news! Do you know the sex yet? What does this mean for your house hunt?"

"No, she's just barely pregnant. We won't know the sex for a couple of months. But I have a feeling it's a girl, which would be just great! And this means we need to speed it up on the house hunt! Or do some serious remodeling to the one we're in. One bathroom will not do for two adults and two kids."

The fact that Po's book is a bona fide bestseller probably means they can afford something fairly lavish. Well, good for them. Note to self: consider dating men in future who don't have to struggle for their rent. Do-gooders or otherwise.

Rosalind, on the other hand, has mastered the art of finding unstruggling men. She's returned from her whirlwind in Paris with Dieter exhilarated, if not completely satisfied with the result. "Well, he didn't set a specific *date*," she says, not looking me in the eye as we wait in line at the *Chronicle* coffee stand. "But he did say let's talk to a Realtor about buying a house together. And we did settle that he's okay with having kids! Not excited about it, but . . . as long as he doesn't object, I'll do the work!" She smiles. "So we're one step closer."

"God, I hope so. I've been thinking a lot about you guys—how you are together, how he looks at you. You are crazy in love! So it makes *me* crazy that his commitment phobia is the hang-up here. Just don't go so long that you start to sacrifice your self-esteem in the process!"

"How's your dad?" she asks, furrowing her brow. "That must have really scared you, huh?"

"I think it scared him worse than it scared us," I sigh. "He's on his way home now, although the bruises he got in the crash make it so he's only comfortable enough to drive a few hours at a time. I'm afraid at age eighty he's finding he might need to start confining his travel. God, only thirty more years for me before I go on house lock-down?"

"That's right! The big five-oh is only a couple months away now!" she says cheerfully, dipping her tea bag into her to-go paper cup. "What shall we do for Miss Jane, the social diva?"

"God, I don't know," I groan, sipping my vanilla latte. "Part of me wants to do it up big—have a big party for the salon group with fifty or so people. The other part of me wants to just avoid the entire goddamn thing. In my dream universe I'd go to Paris. But Erin can't go because she'll be in court on a big case, and I clearly won't have a boyfriend by then, and I can't go *alone*. . . ."

"Why not? Why can't you go alone? Women travel on their own all the time now!"

"I know—my sister has taken boats down both the Nile and the Yangtze by herself. It's just that I never have! Boyfriends, husbands, Erin—someone was always with me."

She purses her perfect lips. "Well, I think because you're the new spokesperson for single women of a certain age, you need to get with it! Really think about treating yourself and going for your fiftieth! But not on your birthday itself—after! I just decided that I'm going to throw a party."

Oh good—I was hoping someone would so I wouldn't have to do it myself.

We go by Phil's office windows and wave, and he gestures for us to come in.

"What was this you forwarded to me today?" he says, squinting at his computer screen.

"It's a press release," I tell him, "about the concept of a 'wing-woman' and how she can help a bashful guy get dates! She goes out with him to bars and helps him meet women. And when I saw it, I thought of you! You've been such a Grumpy Gus lately, I thought maybe it would cheer you up to go out! I might even want to try this as an experiment for the column."

He rolls his eyes. "Okay, first of all, I don't recall saying I was looking to get dates. And second . . . you want me to be your guinea pig for this?"

"Yes! And Rosalind would go with us! Come on, you need to break out. You've been miserable lately and you know it. Maybe the attentions of some pretty women will make you forget all your troubles?"

Rosalind laughs. "Jane has gotten a new lease on life by cheating death, and now she wants to fix everything for everyone."

He chuckles. "So what else is new? Okay, I'm game. But you can't say who I am. I already feel pathetic, I don't want to look it in print."

We set a date for Thursday night, because Thursday is the new Friday, right? On my way into The City, I call my dad's cell phone, not sure if he'll be in range. In fact, he answers, and is just outside of Reno for the night—just one more driving day and he's home.

"I don't think I've ever been so glad to be getting home. Usually I'm sorry when a trip is over," he says. When I ask how he's feeling, he chuckles. "Nothing is wounded but my pride."

"Well, let's have dinner this weekend and debrief," I tell him. "I promise I won't give you any grief. As far as I'm concerned, you should keep on driving until they take away your license."

"Which might not be too far in the future," he says grimly. "Will Erin join us? Has she heard from Davis or the other schools?"

Of course El Cheap-o father is holding out for El Cheap-o school.

"Not yet, Dad, but any day now!"

In the horse race of aging, there comes a time when you pull up neck-and-neck with your parents, when you are dead equals. When you can speak to each other like human beings rather than playing the parent or child card. I hope we're there; I may need to ask him for money if Erin has to go out of state. And I'd much rather take it from a friend than a parent.

I meet up with Phil and Rosalind in the Redwood Room of the Clift Hotel. The bar has a rocking reputation for attracting hip sophisticates. Or so I thought. Tonight the clientele seems to have shopped at The Gap and been groomed at Supercuts. "Oh man, everyone here is in their twenties," I groan. "Which might not be bad for Phil . . ."

"I'm not interested in dating someone that much younger," he says quickly. "You run out of things to talk about too quickly."

Rosalind and I both roll our eyes. We know he's had several dalliances with women as young as Erin. But it's testament to his fiber that he at least pretends to want older women.

It occurs to us that even if Phil saw someone he wanted to meet, we're sitting off in a corner booth, which is the wrong place to be. Short of shanghaiing someone at the bar and dragging them back to our table, it would be hard to make a casual conversation look . . . casual.

I have a notepad in my little purse, onto which I'm making notes.

I discover I've made one Wingwoman Mistake: When looking for women to introduce your male friend to, don't sit down at a table.

It makes it impossible to casually approach someone. Stand up, preferably near the bar, so if you jostle someone, it will seem like more of an accident than a creepy come-on.

I've already rehearsed what I would say to a possible quarry, based on what I've read that authentic wingwomen say. "What a great blouse! Where did you get it?" "Have you tried the cocktails here? I'm wondering about this really exotic one, with orange liqueur, tobacco, and garlic?" "Would you like to meet my friend? He's smart, kisses well, and dances even better."

I run this idea by Phil and he almost turns green. "Please, I'm begging you. Just be subtle—that is, if we ever do meet someone. I'm not at all sure this is the place to meet my kind of woman."

It becomes clear that I've made another Wingwoman Mistake: I didn't talk with my friend about what kind of woman he was interested in meeting tonight. Age-wise it doesn't really matter, my friend is in his 40s, but has been attracted to women of all ages. But he wants someone who reeks class: smart, intellectual, beautiful, well-dressed. Here, it seems, we will only be encountering mall babes, with badly frosted hair and micro-mini skirts.

"Hey, I'm going to say you're in your forties, okay?" I say, looking up from my notepad. "That will throw people off. But is it okay that I describe you as always wearing cowboy boots?"

He is not seeing the humor in this and seems too uptight to do a proper job of scoping, so Rosalind makes a suggestion: "Let's get out of here and find a better bar with people our age."

So we are off to a newish bar a few blocks away, and this appears to be more happening than the Clift. But on closer inspection, it's also happening with single people about twenty years our junior. If there are any unmarried women here, they were raised on Britney Spears, not on Phil's favorite, Etta James.

Another Wingwoman Mistake: Do your homework on a bar's profile.

But this time, we're determined to stick it out and try to make this experiment pay off. We're too tired of running around to try another bar, and we're all starving for some bar food. So we park at one corner of the bar and start to make observations of the scene around us—like horny junior sociologists.

There is a running dialogue: "How about her?" "She looks like she's with that guy." "No, that's not a guy, that's her boyish girlfriend." "Maybe she's gay?" "We all have lesbian friends." "Maybe she's a lesbian wingwoman?" And other such nonsense. It's getting pretty tiring, and we have yet to make a single introduction.

We finally spot a gaggle of gorgeous young women, clearly out on the town together—and for the first time tonight, Phil's interest is sparked. We ponder how to approach them; Rosalind likes one of their purses and is thinking of striking up a conversation based on a mutual love of handbags. But before we can make our move, three men who look to be in their sixties approach the three women—easily forty years younger than they—and even though we can't hear what they're saying, they're clearly flirting, in a fumbling, pathetic kind of way that makes me want to run over and rescue the girls. ("Come on, girls! The bus is waiting to take you back to the convent!")

The longer the men persist, the more foolish we feel, standing there as though we are in line at a candy counter, shifting from one foot to the other. Finally, Phil jerks his head toward the door. "Let's get out of here," he grumbles.

And so ends my sad career as wingwoman, a role I gladly relinquish.

What did we learn tonight? We discussed this on the way back to the car. That this kind of thing is best left to the young. That meeting people through "natural means"—or, God help us, even online—is far less torturous than hustling them in a bar. But what seemed especially clear, as my guy-friend noted in hugging us goodbye: "I think from now on I'd rather stick to evenings with friends like you. At least with that, you're always sure of a good time."

When Phil reads my column a few days later, he sends me an e-mail thanking me "for not making me look like a pathetic dweeb. I should probably hold off on any more setups, I'm just not sure I'm ready to take that step yet. Maybe I never will be. Maybe I should just join a monastery."

"Aw, honey," I write back, "you're just bruised by love gone bad. There will come a day when you look back on this misery and laugh about it. Really! Soon you'll be ready to fly."

As will my darling daughter.

Erin is unusually subdued when she comes over Sunday afternoon, to do laundry and go with me to a welcome-home dinner for Dad.

"Mom," she says cautiously, rightly fearing my implosion, "I didn't get into Davis. They said they got twice the usual number of applicants this year, and that normally I would have been a shoo-in."

I am speechless, worried about saying something idiotically angry, or falling down in needy despair.

"But," she continues, brightening, "Oregon says they can get me some scholarship money if I enroll. And Mom, it's so beautiful there—I still remember our last road trip up the Willamette Valley. And I looked it up online: there are rivers for kayaking and decent surfing on the coast, which is only forty-five minutes away. . . ."

I sit down at the kitchen table, feeling empty. "Well, you've clearly got it all worked out," I sigh. "And of course they want you—you're *overqualified* there."

"Mom." She sits down with me. "Their environmental law program is one of the best in the country. I also got accepted at Hawaii and Vermont, but isn't Oregon better in terms of location? A quick plane flight, a nine-hour drive."

"But what about cost? I recall that Oregon's out-of-state tuition is twice what UC's is. I realize the scholarship would defray that somewhat, but how will we manage this financially?"

Unlike my parents, I've always been brutally honest with Erin about my finances, looked at them as a "we" situation. You could call it teamwork, I call it hedging my bets that someday she'll make enough money to not have to worry as we have.

"I've got my savings from working these last couple years," she says. "And I'll look into student loans."

"Well, okay, but I was going to help you, too. I'm deeply committed to your not finishing law school with $100,000 in loans! I suppose I could talk to Grandpa, but you know how he is about money."

"Well," she says, smiling and taking my hand, "let's not worry too much yet, okay? I'm excited, Mom. I've really turned a corner on this and am eager to go. I'm ready for it."

She most definitely is. I most definitely am not; my throat is choked with sorrow. But I can't depend on her to be a buffer against loneliness forever.

"Besides," she adds, "your life is fantastic right now. Your job, your friends—and you have guys asking you out! Like that guy Ken—how come you gave him the pitch so quickly? He sounded like a good one."

"He was a 'good one' in some senses, but just not right for me. He was looking for me to be an anchor in his life, but I'm already keeping too many ships from ending up on the rocks."

She laughs. "Well, you've always been mine!"

She suddenly wells up with tears. "Don't forget, it will be hard for me to leave you, too! Who will talk to me every day and give me advice?"

It seems our horse race has also pulled neck-and-neck.

Someday My Prince Will Come . . . Not

Not wishing to tip over the welcome wagon, Erin and I decide to only tell my dad the *good* news—she was accepted to every law school she applied to but one (OK, the most important one)—and leave the bad money news out of it. This is his first dinner at home after his life-altering accident, and I don't want to turn the evening into a tableau of my fiscal woes. He is thrilled for Erin's probable move to Oregon; it's always been one of his favorite walkabout destinations. Plenty of Motel 6's up I-5.

"Although from now on," he says soberly, "it looks like I'll be flying."

"Yeah, well, I'll believe it when I see you hobbling onboard with your cane, ready to critique the takeoffs and landings," I tease him. "I can't see you giving up your road trips, Dad, even after this accident."

I've been hoping, despite everything I know about the old man, that his button-bursting pride in his only granddaughter might inspire him to offer help with tuition. But he hasn't, and I doubt he's even thought about it. The fact is, I've had no financial backstop whatsoever since Erin was three. And I have no one to blame, or perhaps credit, but myself and my pride.

I never believed in the concept of Prince Rich and Charming, or even in the notion that women ought to be rescued. I always wanted to stand on my own two feet. But goddamn, these are the times that try a single woman's soul.

I've always walked a microscopic tightrope between solvency and quite the opposite and it doesn't take much to tip the precarious balance. There is also a fine line between being proud of the fact that I've almost never asked for help, and wanting to kick myself for being such a haphazard spaz about finances. Most women pushing fifty have them a little better in hand; they know their IRAs from their HRTs. Sigh. I can see sometimes why my dad was hoping for someone to ride into my life on a white horse carrying either a bucket of money or a functioning calculator.

"I think you should just come out and ask your dad for some help," says Rosalind over lunch when I vent my frustrations.

"I know, it's just he and I are such equals these days, and asking him for money would make me feel like the irresponsible teenager again. And he's really got tough boundaries when it comes to money—his family came through the depression, you know."

"Well, so did my dad, and he always sent me money whenever I asked, which was often!" She smiles. "It's funny to me how people can have such different points of view about money. I mean, look at you, you and Erin are a team. You've never run a trip on her when she's needed help."

"Probably because she's so naturally good with money." I laugh. "I've never needed to remind her to be responsible! So she deserves my help, damn it. And I always told her I'd help with grad school, whatever it was."

"Have you thought any more about Paris for your fiftieth?" she asks, clearly trying to distract me. But the very thought only makes me feel worse.

"I can forget about Paris now! It would be ridiculously irresponsible to go. What would I do? Put it on my credit card?"

I need to chill; I don't share her values, or her ability to take money from men. Every woman has to make her choices, and I've paid for mine.

"What are you working on?" Erin asks when she sees me going through a pile of paperwork at home one Saturday afternoon.

"I'm looking at refinancing the condo and trying to figure out if I can get a better APR than I have now," I sigh, leaning heavily on one elbow. "Because I'm getting old and will soon be in the poorhouse or living in Dumpsters with cats walking all over me because I can't manage my finances and I'm always living hand to mouth!"

She furrows her brows. "So, how soon did you say those mood-stabilizing hormones were going to kick in?"

"Soon, I hope!" I sigh, looking at the stack of papers requiring my signature. "Hey, are you sure it's not too late for you to fall in love with a capitalist pig before law school?"

"Not likely! You know about me and men with money—I don't mix well. Besides, I want to stand on my own two feet!"

This is sounding horribly familiar.

"Well, and on your feet, too," she adds, grinning.

"Have you mentioned our money crunch to your dad?" I ask cautiously. "Any chance he might help?"

"Yes and no," she says with some embarrassment. "He's just changed jobs, you know, and his wife's health has been so bad since her transplant. . . ."

Bite your tongue, Jane, no sense in trying to compete with that.

"Okay, fine," I say, forcing a smile. "But how do you know you don't mix well with monied guys? The only one I recall you went out with was that guy in college!"

"Oh yeah, and *that* was a treat." She snorts. "He'd brag about his family's penthouse on Central Park and their place in the Hamptons, and then he'd go off on ski trips every weekend and invite me along and of course I couldn't afford to go. . . . That was big fun."

I feel a wave of sadness thinking of things she's had to give up. "Well, I wish I could have done everything for you, and I envy the parents who can hand life to their kids on a platter. Then again, I suppose a little struggle makes the good life seem sweeter, yes?"

"Yes!" she answers emphatically. "You have nothing to apologize for or be envious of."

"I know, it's just hard not to feel wistful sometimes when I see how great my friends are doing. You've seen Phil's house in Seacliff. Po gets thousands of dollars just for doing an appearance! And Dieter gave Rosalind a car for her birthday! Not to mention that honking engagement rock."

"Yes, but have those grand gestures gotten her a wedding date?" she says softly. "And look at Phil's life—it's a mess! Money can't make things perfect, no matter how they seem. And besides, I think we're doing just fine for ourselves!"

"Yes we are," I say, standing up to give her a quick hug. "But when I have dinner with Grandpa tomorrow night I'll still broach the subject of the money shortage, see if he steps up to the plate. Are you sure you don't want to come along?"

She grimaces theatrically. "Gee, you know, I'd like to, but I have a date with Milo, my new boyfriend. The medical student. *The poor one.*"

He is looking much better and the bruise on his forehead from hitting the steering wheel is almost gone. But my father darkens when I bring up the subject of the expense of school.

"U of O is going to cost roughly twice what Davis would have, even with the scholarship they're giving her," I note. "She'll be spending all her savings, but even so, since I always said I'd help her with law school, this is going to hurt a bit."

I can't bring myself to ask if he might pinch off a leaf of his money tree, so I just leave it there. And there is silence.

"I don't understand why you don't just make her pay for the whole thing herself!" he growls.

"Because, Dad, she can't work and go to law school—at least the first two years. It would just be too much. And I don't want her to take out tens of thousands of dollars in loans that would take her until she's forty to pay back! She's not going to be making a lot of money as a public interest lawyer."

"So you're going to mortgage your own future to make sure she has one that's nice and easy?" He glowers. Barbara is looking increasingly uncomfortable.

"Dad, I've always seen our futures as intertwined," I say, trying to remain even. "We are a team, she and I—it's different from when I was young."

"When you were young we told all you kids that we'd pay for four years of college and not one day longer!" He's starting to steam. "And if you wanted to lollygag around after that it would be on your dime."

Now my buttons are pushed and I'm fuming. "Is *that* what she'd be doing, Dad? *Lollygagging?* I could swear that she was going to bust her butt in law school for three grueling years so she could make things better for herself—and for the world!"

I stop myself before I get more pissed, realizing we come from completely opposite points of view on this. There's no sense in asking for something his brain can't justify. I take a deep breath and change the subject to the Giants' spring training, which is just about to start; as always, baseball is the great equalizer.

I manage to get out the door and into my car before the tears come. I call Rosalind and snifflingly tell her what happened.

"I can't believe it," she says. "I can't believe he wouldn't help you."

"Well, to be honest, I didn't even ask him! I could tell it was a lost cause so I just dropped it. But what I can't bear is how wrong he made *me* feel. I suddenly felt like I was in high school being lectured again about not bringing the car back without a full tank. Just because I want to help my daughter get ahead!"

"So what are you going to do?" she asks sorrowfully.

"I'm looking into refinancing my place," I sigh. "Again. And maybe getting a home equity line of credit. We'll be fine. We always are, even if it's by the skin of our teeth. Erin's going to use her savings for living expenses, but I agreed to send them a fat deposit of several thousand dollars next week, so I need to move quickly."

"Well, don't let it get you down," she says. "You are beloved in this town! And you can't afford to be derailed. You have the big anniversary salon in a couple of weeks and your big birthday in a month! We just need to find you a date."

Dear Rosalind—always trying to patch the potholes in life's road with a bucketful of romance.

"Actually," I say, feeling myself brighten, "Lenny might be coming out here next month to check out a recording studio. But I'm trying not to get my hopes up too high."

"Well, I hope he remembers your birthday, too. Because this is going to be a great dinner party! Not big, but elegant. I've decided Bix is the place!"

It all sounds good, heart-patchingly good—and fortunately, it's also mostly free.

"What's this I hear about you having financial issues?" Phil asks when I drop by his office. I am incredulous.

"Is this the kind of thing that passes for gossip these days? Who told you?"

"Someone who loves and is worried about you," he says.

Rosalind.

"Well, she's a doll, but I'm handling it," I say, slouching into his leather armchair. "But damn it, I am so tired of walking the money tightrope. It's been decades now. I thought that when I turned fifty I'd have more to show for it."

"Well, let's see," he says, holding out one hand and ticking off the fingers. "You have a posse of fantastic friends, a daughter who loves you, a column that's the talk of the town, your health, which was in question just weeks ago . . ."

"I know." I smile. "It's all true. I just keep wondering about karma, and whether I can expect the universe to throw me a bone someday, based on the amount of giving I've done."

He smiles wearily. "I'm sure when the time comes, you'll have an E-ticket to heaven. In the meantime, if your misery loves company, take comfort in knowing I'm getting kicked out of my house. It's going on the market, and she thinks it shows better empty. So I'm looking for a rental. And starting over again myself."

"Starting over in a rental?" I ask, astonished. "That hardly seems fair!"

"I know. But you know what? I don't care. I'm getting my freedom, and I'm getting my life back. And I have you to look to as a role model of fine single living."

He smiles, and I hold out my arms in a welcoming gesture. "Welcome to the club. Just don't take my cues about fiscal responsibility and you'll be fine."

A week later I'm in the bar of the Four Seasons on Market Street, interviewing a famous New York author about her latest book. We are drinking Champagne (she insisted!), getting along like sisters, and gossiping more than interviewing, while I stare at her Jimmy Choos and wonder how much they cost.

Over her shoulder, I see an unexpected sight: Rosalind peeking around the corner, grinning and waving her hand in a frantic little gesture. *Come here!*

I excuse myself to the author and find Rosalind around the corner, beaming like a little girl at an Easter egg hunt. She is clutching an envelope.

"I knew you had to make your deposit this week to Erin's law school, and your friends decided they wanted to make it a little easier for you!"

Almost trembling with excitement she thrusts the envelope at me. Confused, I reach in and pull out a stack of checks, some attached to notes. There must be twenty of them here from friends, including Dan and Dayna, Craig, Po and Michele, Vanessa and Billy, Claudia, Rosalind and Dieter, Stephan—and yes, Phil. My eyes are so full of tears I lose track of the counting. But there are several thousand dollars sitting in the palm of my hand.

"Oh dear God," I gasp. "Rosalind, what have you done? I don't know if I can accept this!"

"Well, you have to, because I'm not about to take it all back!" she grins teasingly. "Vanessa and I collected them. We couldn't think of a more deserving pair than you and Erin."

I swallow my minor sense of embarrassment at being the subject of a charity drive and just let it in: I am loved and supported. I hug Rosalind close, and murmur, "Thank you, thank you, thank you . . ." while trying to collect myself.

"You better get back to your interview!" Rosalind winks, and sidles off quietly.

The author is blown away when I confess what had just happened, in part to explain my smudged eye makeup. "Wow, there must be some pretty great people in San Francisco!" she exclaims, and clinks my Champagne glass with hers.

"Yes." I laugh. "You could say so."

I can barely wait until the interview is over to call Erin at her work desk. She doesn't understand what I'm saying at first, but when she does, she bursts into tears. "Mom, this is all because of what kind of a friend you are." She sniffles. "That's pretty amazing."

"No, honey, it's also because of what kind of human being *you* are," I say. "And that is *also* pretty amazing."

And when I reach Phil, I have to needle him. "Thank you, dear boy, for your part in this! I am stunned. But I thought you said karma was about getting *love* back, not dollars?"

"Well," he says simply, "I didn't want to spoil the surprise. So has the universe thrown you a big enough bone? Still need a man?"

I laugh. "The jury's still out. But at this point, even if a prince does come along, at least he doesn't have to be a rich one."

Of Friends and Fears

"Am I crazy or is Diego flirting with you?" whispers Rosalind after the burly author leaves my side briefly and heads to the bar. We're starting to gather for the third anniversary salon, for which I am dressed to the nines. And he seems to have noticed.

"Yeah, well, we've seen before how long his attentions last—just long enough for the next svelte young babe to come in the door." I smirk. "Although perhaps he's heard what a rich woman I am now, thanks to my friends!"

"Right!" She laughs, waving to the just-arriving Dieter. "Although now that you've sent in Erin's deposit, you're back to square one."

"No, not at all." I smile. "At the risk of sounding cheesy, I feel richer these days than I ever have—regardless of what I actually have in the bank."

"Okay, here comes Diego again," she hisses, as he starts heading in our direction. "Maybe you should flirt with him. Aren't you still needing a date to Bix for your birthday dinner party?"

"Maybe, but not enough to settle for someone who will be looking over my head all evening at the waitresses. Besides, I'm still holding out hope that poo-head Lenny will make it. And if he blows me off," I say, noticing my favorite Internet geek walking in the door, "there's always Craig. . . ."

"Well, I think you might be wrong about that!" says Rosalind, eyebrows raised. "Good God, it looks like Craig has himself a date!"

She's right. He walks in, grinning broadly, with a slightly younger looking woman next to him; this must be the "friend" he asked if he could bring. She's no Julia Roberts but she is lovely and smiling shyly, and I suddenly feel all fuzzy for my pal.

I avoid the returning schmooze-hound Diego and sidle up to Craig. "Where did she come from?" I whisper to him, giggling. "Is this a new girlfriend? Spill!"

"Ah, well, we shall see," he says, blushing. "This is only date number three. But since I've had only first dates for years, a third date is a good sign!"

Craig is not the only one who asked if he could bring a "friend" tonight. Claudia was all atwitter about a new guy she met at the San Francisco Zen Center: a brainy CPA who approached her after meditation this week. "He's an accountant, can you believe it? And might be a little boring," she e-mailed me yesterday. "But he's really sweet and kind and normal. I need you to check him out for me!"

From first glance, across Foreign Cinema's patio, he looks promising—tall as she, slightly gawky, dressed somewhere between Gap and Rolo, with heavy glasses that make him look a little less hip than Elvis Costello. He's completely adorable. And maybe even her age.

"Jane, Tom; Tom, Jane," she says, cutely nervous. "Thanks for letting me bring him! I promise he'll mind his *P*s and *Q*s."

He shakes my hand and stammers, "I've heard so much about you from Claudia. I'll try to be clever and witty since she tells me everyone here is."

"Oh gawd! Don't believe it." I wave my hand. "It's easy to keep up with the banter as long as you drink enough."

"So my dear, are you getting all kinds of grief about your column today?" she teases. "What made you want to poke that hornet's nest?"

I wince. "Yeah, maybe the most hate mail ever. But that whole situation really got my goat—these poor, tender men boycotting stores that sell T-shirts for little girls that say things like 'boys are stupid, throw rocks at them.' They're all worked up about the impact these T-shirts might have on boys. And where I don't think these shirts are great, my point was, where are these men when their daughters are being called bitches and ho's in school because it's how rappers refer to them? And how come no one complains about an entire style of T-shirts that's called the wife-beater?"

"There she goes, on her soapbox again!" booms Phil's voice behind me. I turn around to give him a sheepish hug, grateful that something interrupted my terse political dissertation, which has no place at a salon. "Hey, your column is getting tons of hits on the Web site today. I imagine you're going to get a lot of angry mail on this one."

"What else is new?" I sigh. Phil loves the exchange of invective, but I can only see it as a necessary evil. "Yes, it seems there are a lot of angry men out there."

"Jane has become the spokesperson for all things female and single," Phil says, turning to a shockingly gorgeous and young woman waiting awkwardly behind him.

"This is Chris," he says to me. "My *friend*." He seems to emphasize that word as if to say *Don't ask a lot of questions*. Yet I can tell by the way she watches him, all at once anxious and admiring, that even if he considers her a friend, she considers him more.

"I read Jane every week," says Chris, shaking my hand with long, cool fingers. "You rock."

"Oh, I love her already!" I joke, and excuse myself, giving Phil a raised "wow" eyebrow as I depart.

God, so many "friends" tonight. Maybe that's what I need, that kind of new friend. The kind that looks worshipfully at you and wants to impress you. The kind that might eventually be slavishly devoted to you and marry you. The kind . . .

"Earth to girlfriend: where are you?" Peter is studying my face quizzically. "Do I detect a note of envy? A hint of covetousness? Several new suitors with the usual suspects tonight, I see."

"You see clearly in all respects, my friend," I sigh, embracing him. "It's spring and the suitors are leaping out of the foliage on Mission Street. For everyone but me, it seems! But really, life is good and I don't have cancer and, all things considered, I'm doing just fine. And how about you. Do you know your dates to go to London?"

"Soon after your birthday!" He smiles. "So I can still come to Rosalind's soiree. In fact, are you still thinking of going to Paris? Maybe you could meet me in London?"

"Sorry to say, it ain't gonna happen. That infusion of cash from my friends was a tremendous boost, but it's still awfully expensive to go. The airfare alone . . ."

"Hail to the almost-birthday girl!" says Po boisterously, giving me a snug hug while Michele greets Peter. Since this is the first I've seen them since Rosalind's check drive, I thank them profusely for their part of the gift. "Oh, well, Erin's the best; we hope if our baby is a girl she'll be just like her." Michele smiles.

"Any word on the sex?" I ask them quietly. "And can I announce the offspring-in-the-making tonight?"

Po hesitates. "I think we'd rather wait until Michele is fully three months along," he says. "We've only told a few people so far. And we won't know the sex for a few more weeks."

Michele rolls her eyes. "I personally don't care, but Po's so convinced it's going to be a girl that he's already bought a tiny little Giants dress!"

"So if it's not a girl, perhaps it will be a cross-dressing boy?" I joke.

"And how are you doing, speaking of little girls?" asks Po. "I was sorry to hear Erin has to go out of state. I know how much you've enjoyed having her around these last few years."

"I'll . . . be . . . okaaaay," I say slowly, blinking and realizing I could easily well up. When are those damn HRTs going to kick in?

"But you're right, it's hard. She's my family. When she goes, I'll have only, well, *these people*!" I hold out my arms to the gathered throng—and then laugh at my own ridiculousness. In truth, I have no complaints.

The toasts tonight are effusive and tipsy as usual.

"These last few months, I've become more aware than ever how lucky I am to be in the heart of this group," I say, looking out at twenty-five expectant faces. "Through my health scare, and into my financial scare, you guys were with me all the way. I won't single out those who contributed to Erin's school fund—you know who you are and Erin's thank-you notes are coming—but thanks also from me, from the bottom of my heart."

I raise my glass. "It's because of all of you that my life is so . . . fucking . . . *good*!"

There is a roar of approval loud enough to annoy other patio diners, many here-here's and clinkings of glasses.

"But wait, but wait!" says Po, standing up and calling things back to order. "I want to also toast our Jane, on the eve of her fiftieth birthday in a few weeks! I wish her only the best on this milestone—and congratulate her for a banner romantic year that included several new men and more sex in the backseat of a car!"

Gawd, I groan to myself during the applause and glass-clinkings, *I should never have told him about that little episode.*

But the toasts aren't done yet. Marco stands up, and bangs his glass as well for attention. "I also have something to say, but mine is more of an announcement."

I'm hit by sudden apprehension, as Marco puts his hand on Elsa's shoulder. "I just want to say something about Elsa, who has changed my life, whom I love so much . . ." His voice quavers as he hesitates.

Oh my God, look how in love he is. I know what's coming.

". . . and who has just agreed to be my wife." There are gasps all around, and then a wave of applause. Both Claudia and Rosalind make wide-eyed contact with me, looking slightly aghast, worried about me. But something has clicked, and for the first time all I feel is joy. This is really where he belongs. This is really right.

"Bravo!" I shout, rising to my feet and holding out my glass. "To Marco and Elsa, whom I introduced, and who were clearly meant to be together always! Many decades of happiness to you both!"

Elsa smiles at me, eyes damp with emotion and gratitude. I raise my glass to her and smile back.

As the group begins to disperse, I notice Rosalind and Dieter in heated discussion off on a side patio. Well, mostly Rosalind, as Dieter is hanging his head and mostly listening. She is gesturing wildly with her hands. Then abruptly, she turns on her heel and heads for the door. As she passes me, she bursts into tears.

"Fuck it," she says.

I follow her toward the door and pull her by the arm into the women's room. "Talk to me!" I beg.

"I'm done! I just realized I'm crazy to keep staying with someone who's too afraid of settling down to marry me." She sobs. "I want what I just saw! I want someone who's not afraid of declarations of love—and I mean real love, not just lavish gifts and promises. I want it all. Is that wrong?"

"It's not wrong," I tell her, grabbing some toilet paper to dab her eyes. "But you knew what Dieter was about since you got with him four years ago. I thought maybe you'd come to work with his limitations. I mean, you guys have been house hunting!"

"I know." She sniffles. "But it's not enough. I want it all: the white picket fence, the big wedding, and *babies*. I want them now. So I'm done with this engagement. Done with Dieter. Can I please have a ride home?"

I'll use the time to try to convince her to sleep on it and wake up, sober and with a fresh perspective, to consider her options. He loves her and she loves him; shouldn't that be enough?

When I get home, my joie de vivre tempered by the disturbing ending to the evening, I am further pummeled by hate mail—almost all of which is from men.

"Ms. Ganahl, how do you sleep at night knowing your opinions are nothing more than irresponsible, feminist rantings? How does the *Chronicle* justify paying your salary? How do you justify your *very existence?*"

That's a tough one, validating one's very existence. Because I'm kind to animals and take care of my family and friends? Because I have something to say that women seem to find helpful? I think about responding to him, but kill the e-mail, unsure of what to say.

But even more disheartening is an e-mail from Lenny, who writes at long last with his April dates in San Francisco. "It looks like I'll be there the week of the 15th to check out The Plant studios and talk to producers. It would be great to see you if you're around and if you're free. Maybe you could look into getting us some tickets to whatever shows sound good while I'm there? Lenny."

What the fuck? The week of the fifteenth? The week *after* my birthday? This, after I've told him how many times that my birthday is the eighth? *And* he's asking me to do him a *favor?* Oh dear God, I feel like putting my boot heel into the computer screen.

Instead, I do what I always tell myself not to: answer an e-mail in the heat of the moment.

"Disappointed! Was hoping you'd be in town the week before, as the 8th is my birthday. And I doubt I shall be here the week of the 15th, as my plan is to escape for a little vacation away from craziness at home and recent medical and fiscal crises. Paris was my dream but is too expensive methinks. So, sorry I won't be here and that you'll have to do your own ticket buying. Life is full of little injustices. Jane."

I hit send, realizing I may never hear from him again. But I'm tired of keeping my anger in check when it comes to him . . . to anyone. If he bails, he bails. The thought provokes a rush of sadness but I refuse to entertain the beast.

Why do I keep chasing this bitter-tasting carrot? Because I'm a woman, and women are hardwired to believe the hype: having a man will fix everything and make you blissfully, orgasmically happy.

At least my generation thinks so.

Erin, emissary from the next generation, calls as I'm going to bed that night, and she's also in tears. Is it a full moon?

"I broke up with Milo tonight." She sniffles. I want to wearily point out that this is something like her third or fourth breakup in the last year, but since she rarely weeps when jettisoning some unlucky lad, this one must have hurt somehow.

"What happened?"

"I don't know! I just kind of freaked out. I told him I thought since I was going to law school soon it didn't make sense to keep seeing each other."

"So you didn't like him that well?"

"No, that's the thing!" she says, her voice breaking. "I really think I could have been in love with him."

I sit up in bed. "So, I don't understand. If you thought you were falling in love, why would you cut it off?"

"Because there are more important things to think about, Mom. Like school and what I'm going to be doing in life—and his medical career."

This seems incomprehensible to me, since I would pretty much cut off my right arm for true love. But this is Erin's generation: more centered, sensible, unstuck to the hype.

"Wow, I'm sorry honey. It's just that you haven't been in love very often, so I can't believe you're just letting it go. Don't you want to be married?"

"Sure, someday," she says hesitantly. "Probably."

Probably?

"But not enough," she adds, "to sacrifice all my plans."

"Well, but what happens if your work becomes so important that you miss out on marriage?"

"Then"—she draws a deep breath and stops sniffling—"I'll live my life like a fabulous single woman with a lot of friends and fun things to do and an important job. Just like my mom! And that would be just fine."

"Thanks honey," I sigh, full of emotions, "for just validating my existence."

Kübler-Ross Was Right

How am I supposed to turn fifty in a week with even a shred of dignity and grace when my world is at sixes and sevens? I'm even getting cussed out on the radio.

The craziness with the antiboy T-shirts column reached a crescendo two nights ago when I was asked to go on a local public radio station to talk about it. It was late and the moon was full; it's the only other reason I can think of—other than garden-variety Jane-loathing—why almost a dozen calls were of the crank variety. Well, that and the station didn't have a budget for a call screener. "*Suck my dick*," hissed one before the hostess hung up on him. "*Dyyyyyke*," purred another. Another wanted me to discuss the finer points of blow jobs.

I glanced nervously over my shoulders in the parking lot as I left, and double-checked my locks when I got home.

It reminds me of a quote a female reader sent me once: "When you make your mark in the world, watch out for guys with big erasers."

In print, I've been called all manner of names, from the B word to the C word to the D word: dunderhead. *Dunderhead?* I was itching to write back: "Zounds, methinks thou hast borrowed thy vocabulary from the last century!" But I've already been warned about being too flippant with readers, and even abusive ones can't be told where to stick it.

Besides, it's hard to keep one's sense of humor when one is pierced with enough arrows to bring down a bull elephant. And exhausted from dealing with crises of various sorts: family, health, finance, and friends—especially this breakup between Rosalind and Dieter. And apparently there will be no reconciliation; she called today to say that she'd taken off her ring and he agreed it would be best if they went their separate ways.

What? This does not compute! These are two wonderful people, neither of whom is the Bad Guy, who were so much in love! It's becoming clear that, in the postmillennial world, perhaps love just isn't enough. But if not love, what the hell else is there? Perhaps not even communication: Lenny has not responded to my recent snapping. Did I really expect otherwise?

And this turning fifty bullshit; I never got the heebie-jeebies about aging up, but I sure do now. Nightmarish thoughts abound, pondering this once-perky body sliding farther south every hour, until it's planted in the grave.

I resist telling all these things to Lisa when I make my weekly check-in call. For one thing, she's not doing very well; she's down to a hundred pounds and they think they might have picked up fragments of tumor on her recent MRI. But she insists she's doing just fine, and wants to hear how things are for me. So I tell her: the good, the bad, the oh-so-ugly—including my insecurities about turning fifty.

She chuckles hoarsely. "Well, the only thing worse than getting older is the alternative."

"God, what a putz I am to complain," I groan.

"Not at all. These things are important. Can you get away for a weekend or something? You sound stressed."

"I don't know, maybe. It's just so hard to step back from my fucking life."

"Hey," she says softly, "be thankful for your life, be thankful for the time you have."

"I am. I mean, I shall be. Love you, Lisa. Keep fighting."

I remember having said these words before.

Lisa's idea was a good one: getting the hell out of Dodge. Let those with arrows pointed in my direction play hide-and-seek. So after canceling my commitments, I head north to a much-loved rental cabin on Tomales Bay to ponder the questions weighing on me so heavily, come to terms with Erin's leaving, turn down the noise in my mind, and get away from the havoc the column wreaks. Do a little soul-searching, a lot of reading.

And a lot of crying. It always happens when I go on one of these rare retreats and get up close and personal with my disappointments and losses: youth, time, love, sister, mother, waistline. It's good to throw myself down the rabbit hole so I can come out the other side renewed. Like having been to a therapist for six months, but having done all the work myself. This time, I wonder if it might not be so easy to purge, since these HRTs should be kicking in any week now.

Nope, not a problem. The faucet turns on as soon as I am unpacked and continues for hours, the couch pillows receiving my outpouring of self-indulgent frustration. Eventually, sick of myself and having stayed too long at my own pity party, I emerge from the cabin, red-eyed but ready to rebuild.

Elisabeth Kübler-Ross, whom I read in quantity during the Death Years, was right: after upheaval, crisis, tragedy, comes acceptance. I need a second helping, please.

And this is a perfect place for reconciliation with one's past and present. The silence is disconcerting. There are no phones—my cell barely works—and no TV. Just a radio to check for emergencies in this post-9/11 world, and of course, the first Giants games of the new season. But there is a subtler sort of background music: wind in the pine trees, birds trilling, and the lapping of the water on the bay shore.

When I go on a solo trip, I'm always freaked out for the first day at least: at the lack of company, the absence of stress. But this time feels different. This time, meltdown endured, I settle into it like a foot into a worn slipper. I am shocked at how good it feels to not talk to anyone or read e-mails for hours. To sit outside and drink tea and read. To take a nap and eat cookies if I want to. To revel in not having to consult anyone about one damn thing, or feel pressured to solve one of my friend's problems while avoiding my own.

And anyway, it's not like I've joined an isolated convent; I'll only have two days of extreme solitude because Erin has said she's coming up for my last night here. I'm thrilled, since her time in San Francisco is winding down, and she's so busy with friends and work that I've hardly seen her these last few weeks.

Sitting on the cottage's deck at sunset and drinking a gin and tonic, I watch the shore birds stick their beaks in the sand looking for dinner. *Maybe I had all my chances at love and blew them,* I think. *I had more men than most (fifty or fifty-five, anyway), and more chances than most. Was I too dismissive? More in search of a good lay—and a good story—to recognize a man I could get old with? I don't think so.*

But . . . what if I'm too dysfunctional to know?

The thought makes me laugh out loud, sending the birds into a panicked dash from the beach.

Something in my gut tells me I'm not done with men, that there will be more to love—and maybe even one to settle down with. But even if there's not, and I get old alone, would that be so bad? I'd have Erin, because even if she moves to a mountaintop in Kathmandu, I'll be there with her. I'd have my writing, maybe I'll even write a book. I'd have my friends or make some new ones. Maybe even grandchildren! I'd better start learning to bake at some point. I'd also take classes in yoga, like my mom did, and art.

Yes! I'd become a painter!

One thing for sure is I have to stop looking for Leo. I'm not entirely sure a soul mate like him exists. Maybe he's a complete figment of my imagination, my wishful thinking. The tears threaten again when I reflect on a lifetime of selling myself short, of falling in love with men who don't value me. The very thing I've written about, lectured Erin and my girlfriends against, I have turned into a career.

The good news is: it's never too late to pull one's head out of one's arse.

Suddenly filled with the urge to write, I flip to a fresh page of the notepad.

I think we're seeing the birth of a new demographic entity: the career single woman.

No, I don't mean the single career woman—plucky dames epitomized on TV by Mary Richards, played by Mary Tyler Moore, who consider a good job a major life goal, but one that can easily be jettisoned when Mr. Right comes along.

I'm talking about career single women, who choose never to marry or never marry again after getting divorced. Women for whom being single becomes a career unto itself. Women like me. (Maybe.)

It's a priority for every career single woman to figure out what she wants and hone her philosophy, since this is a new road we're paving. To come to love the unmitigated freedom of not being married. To accept the notion that we need not be half a couple to be fully realized humans.

That's the hardest part. Talk about an engrained belief system—starting with Bridal Barbie and ending with your grandmother asking if you're a lesbian because you're not married yet at forty, which happened to my friend Claudia. The world wants to marry us off, but is that better for us? Is it the best thing in all cases?

I look up from my notepad and out at the bay. No, it's not. As I was reminded in Oregon, I sensed as long ago as college that marriage might not be for me, but somewhere along the line I bought into thinking it should be. And I learned, through two difficult unions, that marriage is neither a lifesaver nor a godsend. At best, it can be a loving, acutely wonderful coming together of souls; but more often than not, it's a trade-off: your space and peace of mind for the commodity of belonging. For the thrill that you fit in.

I feel suddenly incensed at myself.

Grow up, girlfriend. You've *chosen* to stick out like a purple sore thumb; no one held a gun to your head and told you to live this way. You chose it. Not only are you not married, you shine a flashlight on the dark path to someplace else for all those women just like you. You take stands and you sometimes get excoriated for them. And you're also rightly well loved, even if it's not by the man you think should love you. So snap out of it!

My tears dry without tissue, and I go to sleep that night feeling a strange combination of high and sober. That song from *The Music Man*, "The Sadder but Wiser Girl," keeps floating through my head like a mantra: I may be sad, but maybe I'm wising up at last.

When Erin arrives at the end of day two, she finds me on the cabin's deck, reading. "Honey!" I sing out, with a smile that seems permanently affixed to my mug. "Welcome to bliss central!"

She is impressed.

"Did a lot of drugs up here, did you?"

"Did a lot of thinking, which is sometimes better than drugs," I say, pouring her a lemonade. "When I get back to real life, I plan to make a little more time for quiet contemplation."

"Ha! I'll believe that when I see it. So, what did you contemplate? Other than your navel?"

"Well, for one thing, as far as this whole money issue goes, I realize I need to get over feeling hurt by Grandpa's point of view. When I get home I'll tell him I'm sorry for not respecting it and letting it get in the way of our great relationship. And anyway, I'm a total hypocrite for wanting him to rescue me after a life of standing on my own two feet."

She chuckles. "Ironic, considering as soon as you make a statement like that, your friends ride in on their white horses."

"Right, we do have a Prince Charming, but it's a group!"

Seeking Erin's feedback, I ask if I can read my column snippets out loud to her. Afterward, she seems downcast. "It just seems like you're giving up on love, and I really want you to have that," she says.

"No, don't you see? I'm not giving up on love; I'm giving up my outmoded pictures of love—my romantic notions. Maybe my romantic future will be more like a here-and-there thing, as it's been lately, and not a full-time marriage or even co-habitation. Besides, with all the chaos in relationships around me, being single is seeming pretty sweet these days."

Erin thinks a moment. "The more I think about marriage, the more ambivalent I feel. I mean, I *think* I want that, but the idea of being with someone twenty-four/seven makes me a little claustrophobic, you know?"

"Erin, I can't imagine you wanting to be with anyone longer than a month or two!" I laugh. And why should she? She has her life ahead of her, and she has many men to meet and fancy and break up with. And maybe even love.

"But if that day comes, and I suspect it might," I add, "I'll be right there to help you pick out some butt-ugly china pattern, just like I did at your age."

"*My age?*" she echoes. "What a crazy, scary thought! Thank God times have changed."

Yes, thank God. She has choices today that I didn't allow myself at her age. You got married out of college, you made babies. You put your life on hold for everyone around you. You died of suffocation.

That night, rather than cook on the cabin's Spartan stove, I take us to dinner at Manka's, an acclaimed restaurant nearby. The tables are squeezed in tightly, and next to us is seated an elderly couple. She is wearing a corsage, he's in a suit. They are beaming. The waitress congratulates them for being newlyweds.

"We just got married today," he tells nearby tables proudly. "We're both seventy-nine but feel like we're twenty-one."

One can only guess the ramifications of that statement on the wedding night ahead. We are living in the Viagra Age, after all.

She tells Erin and me that they were each other's dates for the senior prom in high school. They lost track of each other in their twenties but met again recently after their respective spouses had died. It was, they said, magic.

"I was afraid to get old," she says, smiling, "but now I look forward to it." They squeeze each other's hands.

Erin gives me the big eyes, as she does when she is moved to the point of tears. "That is about the sweetest thing I've ever heard in my life," she whispers.

I admit to a slight swelling in my own throat. Wow, that would be nice to have. Wouldn't it? To get old holding someone's hand? To be loved despite the onset of wrinkles and incontinence?

Shake it off, shake it off. You're a career single woman now, remember? You're going to take painting classes and write novels in a seaside cottage and wear purple. Not wait on an old geezer who needs assistance with his God-knows-what bodily functions.

As we leave, we bid the newlyweds good luck, to which they both respond: "We've already had it!"

Erin gives me another dose of the big eyes.

That night, as we're both reading in the big feather bed in the loft, I watch Erin start to fall asleep, her *Harry Potter* volume sinking to her chest as her eyes drift off. In this dim light I can imagine her five years old again, snuggling up in my bed for her nightly affirmation.

Mommy, am I your best friend? Will we always be together?

Yes, angel, always my best friend. And we will never part.

She casts starlight on my life; it will still reach me from Oregon.

"Almost forgot," she murmurs, rousing herself and putting her book on the nightstand. "My lease is almost up and I don't want to renew it for just two months. Can I just . . . come and move in with you until I go to Oregon?"

I want to leap out of bed and dance a tango of joy. "Of course, you don't have to ask."

She rolls over again. "Okay, and I promise that if—I mean, when—you get a new man, I'll give you lots of space."

She smiles and falls asleep. My little girl, my best friend.

Edified and at relative peace, I head for home. I know I'll have three days' worth of e-mails—hate and otherwise—to slog through. Most of it's routine, but I'm taken off guard by number two hundred or so.

"Jane, I'm a schmuck," writes Lenny. "I forgot when your birthday was—I thought it was a week later. I'm going to try to change my dates to be there for the big day . . ."

What? What did he say?

". . . unless you already have a date, in which case I am happy to be relegated to backup. You are more than patient. And if Paris would make you happy, I can help you with that. Lenny."

Help me? Help me with what? My heart's beating and my head's rushing with wonder. *Is he inviting me to Paris?*

I get up from the computer and start dancing like a fool around the house, singing "I'm going to Paris! I'm going to Paris!" and incurring the scorn of the cats, who are already pissed at me for leaving them for three days.

"You're right," I say to Noodge, my ancient scowling male, bending down and stroking his grizzled face. "I ought not get excited. I've been down this road too many times already. Besides, I am fine on my own, right?"

I finish the column that I started on Tomales Bay with a smile and a sigh.

> *It's also important to realize that it's OK to be a fickle female and to flip-flop. To be utterly committed to a life of dating, freedom—perhaps solitude—one minute, and then yearn to bond intimately and forever with someone the next. It doesn't mean we're insane (necessarily).*
>
> *It's just an arm-wrestling match between the old world and the new.*

Leo Would Be the First to Sing

"Happy birthday to you, happy birthday to you!" Erin bursts through my bedroom double doors, singing and carrying a tray. "Happy birthday dear Mommy . . . and she's a geezer, too!"

Dear Lord, the day is finally here! And how nice to wake up happily, being served breakfast in bed, with the cats lounging nearby. I pull up into the sitting position and plop a pillow on my lap, on which Erin precariously balances a tray that offers strawberries and milk, an homage to our coastal home, and grits and eggs, an homage to our white trash Southern roots.

"I'm a what?" I yawn, rubbing my eyes and chuckling.

"Geezer, you know?" she says, leaning over to kiss me on the cheek. "A raisin? A blue-hair? Fifty years old today!"

"Thanks, honey, really appreciate the support. You are *so* cut off. No law school money for you!"

She laughs. "That's okay, between the scholarship and student loans and Rosalind's charity drive, my first year will be almost covered."

I look at the clock. "God, honey, it's only eight a.m.! Did you really get yourself out of bed to do this? I'm astonished."

"See, I can do it if it's important! Or . . . if you're not going to do it for me. Besides, I need to get up to the city to bring another load down from the apartment."

Erin's already moved half her stuff in and it's making chaos of my home. She puts glasses down everywhere but in the dishwasher, her music drives me insane, and she spoils the cats by feeding them human food. And I'm treasuring every last moment, knowing that soon her laugh will echo only through phone lines.

"Oh, I forgot to tell you," I say, munching my berries, "Grandpa and I talked yesterday. We both apologized for our spat, and he said if we needed money, he'd be happy to help."

"You're kidding! What did you say?"

"I told him thank you, and I thought we'd be okay, and that I prided myself on maintaining my financial independence."

"But . . . ?" she says, doing the gimme gesture with her hands.

I grin. "But I also told him I'd let him know for sure. I may be proud, but I'm not stupid."

She laughs. "Grandpa, so predictable. And is he really going on another walkabout next week? I guess he was able to get over his fear. . . ."

"Well, he's only going as far as Tahoe, but I fully support him in doing it. We can't live in fear of what *might* happen in life. And besides"—I wink—"age is just a number, right?"

She rolls her eyes, picking a piece of egg off my T-shirt that had dropped there. "Okay, what have you done with my mother? The one who was freaking out about turning fifty?"

"I think it's like when I turned forty—I worried for the longest time how it would be, and then when I got to that date, I realized it was just another day. Besides, I feel pretty good about things." I smile at her. "That always helps make aging a lot less scary."

"Plus," I add, "I talked to Lisa yesterday and she is doing great—the doctors are amazed at how she's responding to treatment. So yeah, I'm turning fifty, but I have all my organs and no major complaints. "

"And what about Lenny?" she asks, flopping down beside me and turning on Saturday-morning cartoons. "Is he really coming tonight? And is he still saying he's giving you Paris for your birthday?"

I've spoken with Lenny twice this week; each time he was harried and rushed, neither time did he mention the fact that it's my birthday nor his offer to "help me with Paris." I finally asked him what he meant by it, and he responded cheerfully, "Look, I'll talk to you about Paris when I get there, but I have the miles and the time to make it happen."

"I've been chewing on those words all week," I tell Erin. "He has the miles and the time to make it happen? I mean, God, could it be true that we're really going to go to Paris? These kinds of things happen to Rosalind, not to me!"

I flop back on my stack of pillows, reveling like a movie star.

"Well," she responds, brows furrowed, "don't forget what a bad communicator he is, and how he's let you down before. Several times."

"You know"—I smile—"it's possible. But right now I'm just elated that I have the date I've wanted with the man I've wanted for my fiftieth party. The rest is gravy."

My mood refuses to be undone, even when I check my e-mail and find that the hate mail is now raining down from all over the country. Apparently the column was posted on a national hooray-for-downtrodden-men Web site, and the response has spiraled from that. Feeling impatient, I flick all of them into the trash folder. It's all become a bit silly. Here I've written in this year about single women's political power, the implicit sexism of cosmetic surgery, the dangers of dating married men, even the rise of single culture in foreign countries. But the thing that has gotten the country's goat is this stupid thing about T-shirts. Sigh.

Here's one from Phil. "Happy birthday—see you tonight, yes? And is it okay if I bring Chris?"

"Hmmm." I tease him. "This would be your 'friend' Chris, who seems to be omnipresent lately? The one responsible for your brand-new grin?"

"The very same," he answers. I have a good feeling about this.

The next e-mail, with the subject line "You ignorant slut," is too intriguing not to open. "Dear Feminazi and man hater, do you and the world a favor, go home, clean the house, cook dinner and don't breed! The world is better off without anymore little feminazis like you."

This time I can't resist answering.

"Too late!" I respond, glancing up at Erin as she walks by with another box marked OREGON. "I already had one and she's going to be a lawyer."

"Happy birthday, birthday girl!" says Rosalind in her anticipated morning call, her usual ebullient tone muted in recent weeks by the crash-and-burn of her engagement. "We're all set for tonight at eight p.m. at Bix! Just us, Po and Michele, Peter and Claudia—and Lenny, if you're sure he's going to make it."

She doesn't know that *I* know this is actually a big party: that when I get there, around twenty of my friends will have commandeered the upstairs of my favorite bistro. They'll yell *surprise*! *Woo-hoo!* And I'll act like it is. Why spoil her fun by telling her the word got out because Phil can't keep his massive social calendar straight? "Hey, what are we supposed to wear to your big shindig?" he asked the other day in his office. Oops!

"You're so sweet to do all this," I tell her. "When things have been so tough for you lately. And yes, I confirmed with Lenny when he got to town last night. But with him, you never know until we're walking in the door."

"Well, if he bails," she says, "I know a certain art curator who always asks about you! I have him on stand-by; he said he'd come if you wanted a date."

Oh lordie, she's referring to Fudd, whom I've seen now and then in recent months at various functions. But he never hits on me, which I suspect is because he's never quite gotten over the utter shallowness of my art knowledge. I think this hookup is Rosalind's fantasy, not his.

"Well, I don't think he's particularly interested, but if I get stood up, I suppose it's better than going to a dinner party alone, *n'est-ce pas*?"

I cringe, realizing Rosalind is doing just that—and it's a party she's hosting. "Oh, I'm sorry, honey. Are you sure you're okay?"

"No, not really." She sounds distant. "But I don't feel bad about choosing myself in this situation. If I'd stayed with Dieter I'd have felt worse and worse about myself, the longer we went without marrying. I miss him, I still love him, but sometimes you just have to draw the line."

"Yes, I've gotten better this last year at doing just that. But then you pay for your standards in solitude—although I must say, solitude is getting sweeter all the time!"

Who said that? Was it really me?

"So what are you wearing?" she asks. "I need to change the subject to something far more important!"

Well, that was tough. It's the perennial problem of wanting something new but not flashy, hip but not teenage, sexy but not slutty.

To that end, I did the spring sale at Bloomie's and got a shortish skirt (what the hell, I still got the legs), with which I'll be wearing flats (I ain't got the circulation in the legs) and a sequin top left over from the holidays that scoops low in front (exposing what, exactly?). But this will all go over well with Lenny, who at least used to love it when I sexy it up a bit. The night is an intriguingly blank slate.

"Happy birthday, sweetie!" Peter says on the phone. "How are you feeling?"

"Good! Surprisingly good. Not only am I turning fifty with almost zero tears, I hit a new career high this week: I got ridiculed on the air by Rush Limbaugh!"

"Shut up! How is this possible?" Peter, the lifelong radical, sounds like he's smacking his lips with glee. "You'll have to share the story tonight!"

"Yes, there will be a lot of wonderful toasts, everyone's doing so great. Your possible movie deal, of course, and Erin's new journey. Po told me yesterday that he and Michele are having a girl, Claudia is way into her very first 'normal' guy—her CPA, who brings her flowers at every date. And I think Phil has found someone wonderful, too."

"And if I know you, nothing makes you happier on this day of days than the contentment of the people you love," he says sweetly. "But what about you? On the love front, I mean? Is this man really going to Paris with you, after barely being present for you this year?"

"I'm not sure," I admit. "Perhaps he wants to make up to me now for his year of only sporadic attentiveness? To be honest, I've been too preoccupied in the last few months with my health, the column, and Erin to worry about Lenny too much. I guess he is what he is, and clearly at this point he's not going to magically change."

There is silence on the other end; I know Peter takes a dim view of Lenny. "Well, girlfriend, if he's what you want, I want you to have him. I'm just not sure *he* deserves *you*. Just don't fall into a Rosalind-Dieter situation; make sure he's giving you himself and not just his material goods. He can afford both. And you're more than worthy."

"Thanks, dear heart," I say quietly. "I'll try to remember that. And I'll see you tonight."

My car can't drive fast enough to The City, knowing what pleasures wait for me there.

Lenny is staying at the Hyatt Regency this time—every trip, it's gotten a little fancier. But this is great, I think as I exit the freeway: it's just a quick drive, or a slightly longer walk, to Bix from here—in case alcohol takes a toll, as it almost certainly will.

And what a beautiful night the heavens have arranged for my fly-up to AARP age! The fog-free sky is turquoise over the Bay, and the lights of the Bay Bridge, strung up like glowing pearls from San Francisco to Treasure Island, will soon be reflecting in the waters beneath.

I arrive at the designated time of six p.m.—I'd suggested we have a couple hours to "hang out" (read: get caught up and hopefully have sex) before he has to face the double onslaught of going to my party and meeting my friends. I call up to his room from the desk and he's sounding jangled and grouchy. Come up, he says, there's a key for you at reception. I know this routine by now. I try not to act like I feel like a call girl; they hand me a card key without trying to act like they think I'm a call girl. But I still feel a little like one, in my short skirt ascending the glass elevator, worried that anyone standing down below will get a shot of my naughty bits.

I decide to play it out.

"Call girl!" I yell when I knock on his door. He opens it and gestures with one hand to come in while he holds his cell phone in the other. He is clearly in the middle of something, putting one arm straight out to give me a half-hug. But he is not smiling.

"I don't give a fuck!" he bellows at some unknown agent-or-other.

"Tell Columbia that was not our agreement!" Hearing him thus makes me feel a bit deflated. I mean, I wasn't expecting him to be the first person to sing "Happy Birthday" to me, but how lovely that would have been! The door opens, he's there to greet me, there is Champagne and cake, and he has his guitar at the ready. *Happy birthday to you, happy birthday to you, happy birthday dear woman of my dreams . . .*

"Fine! Fuck it! We can play it that way."

Not only is his suite devoid of visible signs of birthday cheer, it's littered with clothes and newspapers. His laptop is open, lights are fully on. It does not put me in the mood for romance. I would have lit some candles or put on some music. But that's never been his style.

He hangs up at last, and walks over to where I'm sitting in an armchair, feet propped on an ottoman. "How you doing?" he asks, giving me a kiss on the forehead and then pulling a cigarette out of the pack. I guess his smoking-cessation hypnotist sessions have failed him. "You look swell. What's the occasion?"

I resist the urge to throttle him. "The *party*, Lenny . . . ?"

He chuckles deeply. "I know. I was only yanking your chain."

Exhaling a plume of smoke, he goes into his suitcase, pulls out an envelope, and tosses it on the ottoman in front of me. "Open it!"

It's an American Airlines certificate with my name on top. "I'm not sure how to read this?" I hesitate, flushed with excitement.

"It's enough miles to cover a trip to Paris," he says, sitting down next to me. "See, I have over a million now. After the health scare and everything, I'd say you deserve a break!"

This sends me sideways a little. No mention of my birthday in any of this. Or of him going with me.

"That's wonderful, thank you! But . . . weren't you thinking of coming along?"

He pulls back and looks at me with incredulity. "No way! After the

Grammy nomination, my label wants me to get this new album done right away! In fact, we were just arguing over the budget. Can you believe those assholes were wanting me to do it on the cheap?"

He stands up and walks off, fuming, to stub out his cigarette. The Paris certificate is sitting in my hands like a lifeless bird.

I put it down and stand up to say something, although I'm not sure what. But he turns around, quickly and unexpectedly, and embraces me.

"Now, what was that about a call girl?" he says, grinning, and starts kissing me and pulling off my clothes. His touch is too irresistible, even in my crestfallen state, for me to want to stop him. And in a flash we're on the bed, lights on, semiclad, having sex with the heat and rhythm that has been our strongest suit for all these years now. But if my heart is happy, hearing him say my name over and over again as he does, my head is elsewhere, refusing to let my body free to enjoy this.

"That was great babe," he pants, exhausted. He rolls off, kisses my cheek, and grumbles: "Wake me up in an hour, and I'll go to that party with you. What's it for again?"

And then he konks out, as has been his weakest suit. Mouth open, pants around his ankles, collapsed to one side like the Hindenburg, he begins to snore. I watch him for a little while, and it starts to feel like staring down a tunnel with no light at the other end. Eventually I get up and straighten my clothes.

"The party is for *me*," I say quietly to his snoring figure. "Because it's my birthday, because I'm fifty . . . and because I'm doing just great."

I collect my jacket and purse—and the mileage certificate in my name. I may be proud, but I'm not stupid. When I get to the door, I turn around to look at Lenny one last time, and can't resist smiling despite the dull ache in my chest.

At last! A new image of you to replace the old one.

I turn out the light, and I'm gone.

I'll need to call Rosalind and tell her I'm coming alone. No need to try and get a date for me, I'm okay without one. After all, Erin and my friends will be there! In the meantime, I have one delicious hour all to myself. I'll walk along the Embarcadero, watching the turquoise sky behind the bridge turning to sapphire, and plan my very first solo adventure in Paris.

I just know that the lights on San Francisco Bay will be gorgeous.

Acknowledgments

When writing a novelized memoir, one must stitch together a heap of stories—most the God's truth, some closer to fiction—to make one coherent whole. You might wonder, what was true? First and foremost: every male "misadventure"! Which is one reason all my romantic partners' names and identities have been smudged; some are even composites of two guys, and shall remain forever anonymous.

Some scenes were fictionalized to suit my purposes, others scrupulously true-to-life, still others a combination of places and things I really did with things I wish I'd done. Almost every conversation was had, whether in that setting or another.

Some of my friends' names are *not* changed because it's kind of pointless to try to smudge them. They know who they are and you probably do, too. Thanks to those who let me use our friendship as grist for the mill: Phil, Po, Michele, Peter, Dayna, Dan, and Craig.

Thanks also to the rest of the salonistas: without you my life would be so dull! Drinks on me! Special thanks to Julian, Martin, Cynthia, Michael, Maya, Wendy, Kelly, Belle, Gayle, and Vanessa.

Thanks to the devoted readers of "Single-Minded"; it was a fantastic four-year run. Join me on my new adventures at janeganahl.com! Thanks also to the *Chronicle* for allowing me to use snippets of my columns. Special thanks to David Wiegand: *Chronicle* editor, island of sanity, dear friend.

More thanks:

- To Jack and the Litquake gang: books and booze, babies!
- To Ali Bothwell Mancini: a kinder, gentler editor no one could hope for! Thanks for making this fun.
- To Ellen Levine: agent extraordinaire, source of endless great advice, who really got it.
- To Jonathan: the first one I thought worthy. Take care of our treasure.
- To Lisa G.: I'm sorry you didn't make it to see the book! I tried to use the title you suggested, but that didn't get very far. Thanks for the lesson in going with grace. And to the rest of my college friends—Connie, Melissa, and Lynn: thanks for reminding me where I started.

And most importantly: to my family.

To my darling nephews Rob, Skyler, and Theo: do as I say, not as I do! To Rob and Julie: your union reminds me that marriage can be beautiful. To Barbara: you're a joyful addition to the family. To Anne: dear sister and friend, I forgot my wallet; can you get lunch this time? To Terry: I know Lisa is smiling.

To sister Lisa: I miss you every day, but you would be proud: I think I finally got it. And to Mom: you're my inspiration, pure and simple.

To Dad/Captain Bob—still going strong at eighty-five: may the road always rise up to meet you. Love you, Dad.

And to Erin: you're the reason for all this. Thanks for your patience and your unconditional love and the galaxy of laughs. Here's to more adventures down the road.